C000083217

A Man of One Book?

John Wesley's Interpretation and Use of the Bible

STUDIES IN EVANGELICAL HISTORY AND THOUGHT

A full listing of all titles in this series appears at the end of this book.

STUDIES IN EVANGELICAL HISTORY AND THOUGHT

A Man of One Book?

John Wesley's Interpretation and Use of the Bible

Donald A. Bullen

Foreword by Kenneth G.C. Newport

Paternoster: thinking faith

MILTON KEYNES · COLORADO SPRINGS · HYDERABAD

Copyright © Donald A. Bullen 2007

First published 2007 by Paternoster
Paternoster is an imprint of Authentic Media
9 Holdom Avenue, Bletchley, Milton Keynes, Bucks, MK1 1QR
1820 Jet Stream Drive, Colorado Springs, CO 80921, USA
OM Authentic Media, Medchal Road, Jeedimetla Village,
Secunderabad 500 055, A.P., India
www.authenticmedia.co.uk
Authentic Media is a division of IBS-STL UK, a company limited by guarantee
(registered charity no. 270162)

13 12 11 10 09 08 07   7 6 5 4 3 2 1

The right of Donald A. Bullen to be identified as the Author of this
Work has been asserted by him in accordance with the Copyright,
Designs and Patents Act 1988

All rights reserved. No part of this publication may be reproduced,
stored in a retrieval system, or transmitted in any form or by any
means, electric, mechanical, photocopying, recording or otherwise,
without the prior permission of the publisher or a licence permitting
restricted copying. In the UK such licences are issued by the
Copyright Licencing Agency, 90 Tottenham Court Road, London
W1P 9HE.

British Library Cataloguing in Publication Data
A catalogue record for this book is available from the British Library.

ISBN 978-1-84227-513-9

Typeset by the Author.
Printed and bound in Great Britain
by Nottingham Alphagraphics.

STUDIES IN EVANGELICAL HISTORY AND THOUGHT

Series Preface

The Evangelical movement has been marked by its union of four emphases: on the Bible, on the cross of Christ, on conversion as the entry to the Christian life and on the responsibility of the believer to be active. The present series is designed to publish scholarly studies of any aspect of this movement in Britain or overseas. Its volumes include social analysis as well as exploration of Evangelical ideas. The books in the series consider aspects of the movement shaped by the Evangelical Revival of the eighteenth century, when the impetus to mission began to turn the popular Protestantism of the British Isles and North America into a global phenomenon. The series aims to reap some of the rich harvest of academic research about those who, over the centuries, have believed that they had a gospel to tell to the nations.

Series Editors

David Bebbington, Professor of History, University of Stirling, Stirling, Scotland, UK

John H.Y. Briggs, Senior Research Fellow in Ecclesiastical History and Director of the Centre for Baptist History and Heritage, Regent's Park College, Oxford, UK

Timothy Larsen, Professor of Theology, Wheaton College, Illinois, USA

Mark A. Noll, McAnaney Professor of History, University of Notre Dame, Notre Dame, Indiana, USA

Ian M. Randall, Senior Research Fellow, International Baptist Theological Seminary, Prague, Czech Republic

*To Joyce who has given support over many years
and made this book possible*

Contents

FOREWORD

Working across disciplines is always something of a challenge. It is also something of risk. As Jesus himself is reported once to have said 'no one can serve two masters', and this is true in an academic context no less than any other. Having divided loyalties can be problematic. The stark reality is that there is a constant danger that while seeking to keep up with developments in one area, one will be overtaken by those in another. Working at the intersection of two areas of human enquiry can hence be an uncomfortable place to be. It is also exciting.

In this book the fruits of one such enquiry will be seen. It is a study that brings together some of the insights of late twentieth and early twenty-first century biblical scholarship with contemporary Wesley studies. The results are helpful to both. To biblical studies this book is a reminder that theories of interpretation are important, for the way in which the Bible is read can make a difference. Sometimes, quite often in fact, those who read the Bible and interpret it are doing so for reasons that go far beyond any purely intellectual enquiry. For Wesley the Bible contained the very words of God – to be lived, not dissected; to be imbibed not analysed. The air which early Methodism breathed was saturated with 'aroma of Christ' – the preaching and receiving of the Word. That interaction of text and reader, preacher and receiver, had consequences: it gave a sense of divine purpose and a sense of authority. Wesley was nothing if not a Bible-centred person and Methodism was nothing if not a Bible-centred movement. If Elie Halévy is to be believed, Methodism saved England from a revolution, but even if one does not subscribe to such a view, there can be no doubt that Methodism has been a powerful force in society. The cocktail that was Wesley's interpretation of scripture has hence been important. Lives (if not nations) have been changed by what Wesley read in his text. Biblical interpretation makes a difference.

To Wesley scholars the importance of this book is equally significant. Wesley is held in high regard in such circles and rightly so. He was a man of immense spiritual insight, religious energy and theological aptitude. However, such a high regard for Wesley can lead to unrealistic interpretations of his work. This is particularly noticeable in the nineteenth century, but it has persisted into the twentieth and twenty-first. One such unrealistic interpretation is to take the view that 'Wesley believed the Bible'. No doubt he believed he did and no doubt that belief was sincere. But if biblical studies have demonstrated nothing else in recent times, they have surely underscored the point that readers of the Bible read the text in the light of their own experience. Wesley read the Bible as a high-church Arminian Anglican and what he found within its covers was, unsurprisingly, high-church Arminian Anglican Christianity. It is this dynamic that Dr Bullen here explores.

It is some time now since Dr Bullen first approached me with a view to conducting research. His first degree at Liverpool Hope University, an MPhil, was a study of the work of E.P. Sanders and his contribution to New Testament studies. I was delighted when the degree was awarded. I am used to shaking the hands of students at graduations and never seeing them again. Such, thankfully, was not the case with Dr Bullen, who within a few weeks, literally, was back at my University with a proposal for a PhD. Dr Bullen, who is an ordained Methodist minister, has a very detailed understanding of his own tradition and it was this together with his study of contemporary biblical scholarship that made him the ideal candidate to carry out the kind of research that is presented here. I believe that this is an important contribution to two disciplines. It is certainly a good read and a detailed piece of research and I am delighted now to see it published and available to a wider audience.

Kenneth G.C. Newport
Assistant Vice-Chancellor and Professor of Christian Thought
Liverpool Hope University
October 2006

PREFACE

This book is based on the thesis I submitted for my PhD at Liverpool Hope University College (now Liverpool Hope University), validated by Liverpool University in 2004. That was not the thesis that I had set out to prepare. Following the successful completion of research for an MPhil in the work of E. P. Sanders on the Pauline Epistles, my original intention was to work on another New Testament theme. There were a number of changes before eventually it became a study in John Wesley as a reader of the Bible. My New Testament studies combined with a lifelong but sometimes less than simply scholarly interest in Wesley led to a realisation that his claim to be 'a man of one book' (the book being the Bible) was open to question. Although it was possible to understand Wesley's assertion, it was of some considerable surprise to find that more recent scholarship had not picked up this point and challenged it. The veneration in which Wesley was held by many obscured the reality of the man and his teaching. The insights of the more modern biblical Reader-Response criticism have not been applied to research into Wesley's interpretation of the Bible although they do offer a new way to understand better the man, his teaching and his work.

My gratitude is due in particular to Revd Professor Kenneth G.C. Newport of Liverpool Hope University whose New Testament scholarship and expertise in Wesley studies have helped me to avoid the more glaring errors. He has encouraged a good style and sound content in the presentation. Ursula Leahy, also of Liverpool Hope, meticulously read earlier drafts of the thesis and made invaluable comments on style and content for which I am grateful. These comments have been of considerable help in the preparation of the book.

My research required time being spent in five libraries, Liverpool Hope, Liverpool University, John Rylands Library, Manchester, St Deiniol's, Hawarden, and the Wesley Historical Society Library at Oxford Brookes University. In all places I have received considerable help and the staff in all those places offered me the utmost courtesy and assistance.

In addition, these days the resources of the Internet make information available at home that otherwise would not be so readily obtained elsewhere.

It would be very remiss of me not to give public expression to my gratitude to Paternoster and its officers and staff who have given me considerable assistance in the preparation of this work for print. In particular I am grateful to Dr Anthony R. Cross for his meticulous guidance through the process of getting the book into print.

A further and very considerable debt is to my wife Joyce who is a careful proof-reader and critic of style. She has accepted that John Wesley has moved into our home over the last few years (often with his brother Charles!) and occupied a prominent place in many a conversation. The final stages of the production of the thesis and subsequently this book owe much to her unstinted care and assistance.

Having said all that, the responsibility for what is written must rest with me and the remaining imperfections are all mine. The work is original. Its arguments and conclusions are those to which my research has led me.

Where there is reference to scripture in the body of the work the lower case 's' does not imply any view of the inspiration (or lack of inspiration) of the Bible. It is merely an attempt to be consistent with modern usage, although the practice of other authors is followed in the quotations from their works.

By the nature of this research, there are many quotations from the works of John Wesley and Wesley scholars. The convention followed here is that all references to books are in the present tense. References to authors now deceased are in the past tense and for the purpose of this book this is roughly taken as down to the work of Albert C. Outler. References to later and living scholars are in the present tense. Quotations, where given, are in the words and style of the authors concerned.

ABBREVIATIONS

BE (with Volume number)	*The Bicentennial Edition of the Works of John Wesley*
Vol. 1	*Sermons I,* 1-33, edited by Albert C. Outler, Abingdon Press, 1984
Vol. 2	*Sermons II*, 34-70, edited by Albert C. Outler, Abingdon Press, 1985
Vol. 3	*Sermons III*, 71-114, edited by Albert C. Outler, Abingdon Press, 1985
Vol. 4	*Sermons IV*, 115-151, edited by Albert C. Outler, Abingdon Press, 1987
Vol. 9	*The Methodist Societies, History, Nature, and Design*, edited by Rupert E. Davies, 1989
Vol. 11	*The Appeals to Men of Reason and Religion and Certain Related Open Letters*, edited by Gerald R. Cragg, Abingdon Press, 1975
Vol. 18	*Journals and Diaries 1 (1735-1738)*, edited by W. Reginald Ward and Richard P. Heitzenrater, Abingdon Press, 1988
Vol. 19	*Journals and Diaries 2 (1738-1743)*, edited by W. Reginald Ward and Richard P. Heitzenrater, Abingdon Press, 1990
Vol. 20	*Journals and Diaries 3 (1743-1754)*, edited by W. Reginald Ward, Abingdon Press, 1991
Vol. 21	*Journals and Diaries 4 (1755-1765)*, edited by W. Reginald Ward, Abingdon Press, 1992
Vol. 22	*Journals and Diaries 5 (1765-1775)*, edited by W. Reginald Ward, Abingdon Press, 1993
Vol. 25	*Letters I (1721-1739)*, edited by Frank Baker, Oxford University Press, 1980
Vol. 26	*Letters II (1740-1755)*, edited by Frank Baker, Oxford University Press, 1982

CPD   *The Constitutional Practice and Discipline of the Methodist Church*, Vol. 2, Methodist Publishing House (revised annually)

UMC   The United Methodist Church (in America)

John Wesley - The Man of One Book?

Rupert Davies was an acknowledged British Wesley scholar of the twentieth century and he wrote that:

> Wesley is quite clear in his own mind as to the source of his doctrine of salvation [...]. He claims to derive it immediately from Scripture, and from nowhere else at all. [...] This claim is repeated time and time again in all Wesley's writings and it is not unjustified.[1]

This statement appears in Volume 1 of a four volume work authorized by the British Methodist Conference and therefore has considerable weight within Wesley scholarship. It represents a view widely held within Wesley scholarship. Further examples of the way in which Wesley scholars have accepted this as fact are given in more detail in Chapter 1. However, the quotation itself probably tells the reader more about the views of Davies than it does about the theological methodology of Wesley. Davies is not alone in his statement for he inherited and accepted almost without question the received wisdom of those who had written about Wesley from 1791 onwards, this being the year of Wesley's death. All these writers repeated nearly at face value all that Wesley was believed to have said about his reliance on scripture. It is this commonly accepted view that is questioned in this book.

Wesley did indeed describe himself as *homo unius libri*,[2] and claimed that, for him and for Methodists, scripture was to be seen as authoritative in matters of both faith and practice. Other authorities, e.g. tradition, reason and experience could, perhaps, supplement the Bible, but not contradict it.

---

1 Rupert Davies, 'The People Called Methodists "Our Doctrines"' in *A History of the Methodist Church in Great Britain,* Vol. 1, eds. Rupert Davies and Gordon Rupp, Epworth Press, 1965, p. 148.

2 See, for example, the Preface to the 1746 edition of *Sermons on Several Occasions*, *BE* Vol. 1, p. 105 and the sermon 'On God's Vineyard,' §1.1, *BE* Vol. 3, p. 504. Scott J. Jones in *John Wesley's Conception and Use of Scripture*, Kingswood Books, 1995, p. 31, points out that these two references were dated 1746 and 1787 respectively and indicate a view held both early and late in Wesley's post-Aldersgate life.

This point is considered in more detail in Chapter 2. It may be noted that in 1746 Wesley wrote an article, 'Thoughts upon Methodism',[3] in which he wrote concerning Methodists 'The Bible is the whole and sole rule both of Christian faith and practice.'[4] This was not the only time he made such a statement. For example, Wesley's *A Plain Account of Christian Perfection* dates from 1767. In it he wrote that 'In the year 1729 I began not only to read but to study the Bible, as the one, the only standard of truth, and the only model of pure religion.' (paragraph 5.) Thus Wesley maintained that, for him, the authority of the Bible was established as a major item of belief by 1729 and had not changed over the years.

Scott Jones, a leading American Wesley scholar, gives the usual understanding of Wesley on this point. According to him:

> Wesley's understanding of revelation, inspiration, and the infallibility of Scripture leads to the conclusion that Scripture is the written word of God and as such is authoritative for Christian faith and practice. He frequently insists that it is Scripture alone that carries such weight and that no other authorities are necessary to prove a point.[5]

Scott Jones is right. Wesley did make such claims. However, it is contended here that Wesley himself did not fully understand the way in which he had come to his own interpretation of the Bible. That is neither to condemn nor praise him; it is a simple statement of fact. This is a weakness that most modern Wesley scholarship has done little to correct.

Before giving more critical consideration to Wesley's claim to be a man of one book, there are three disparate points to which reference must be made. The first is the relevance of Reader-Response in modern biblical scholarship to this study. The second is the need to detail the primary sources being used. The third is a clear statement of the main contentions being made, together with a summary of the arguments of this book.

The Role of the Reader

Recent biblical scholarship has drawn increasing attention to the role of the reader in the interpretation of the Bible and it will be seen that this is relevant to the study of Wesley as a person whose work is apparently so strongly Bible based. The argument of such scholars is that without a reader the text has no effect. Thus it is now often argued, in the interplay between the author, the text and the reader, the dominant partner is the reader.

---

3   *BE* Vol. 9, pp. 527-30. This appeared much later in the *Arminian* Magazine, 1787.
4   *BE* Vol. 9, p. 527.
5   Scott J. Jones, *John Wesley's Concept and Use of Scripture*, Kingswood Books, 1995, p. 35.

Reader-Response criticism did not originate with biblical scholarship. Many extensive studies have taken place in recent years on readers and the reading process. For example, Jane P. Tomkins has brought together a series of articles by a variety of scholars involved in determining the meaning of non-biblical literary texts.[6] They all have an interest in the way readers engage with a text and interpret it but they do not represent a unified system. In their diversity, they have one point in common: they have moved from the study of authorship and text to a study of the encounter between the reader and the text.

In more recent times reader-centred approaches to texts have come increasingly to dominate the biblical-interpretation agenda. For example, Mark Allan Powell has a section on 'Reader-Oriented Approaches' in his work *The Bible and Modern Literary Criticism.*[7] Here Powell notes that the Reader-Response approach contains within itself a number of references to ways in which readers make sense of texts. Among these is the highly influential work of Stanley Fish. Powell makes the comment:

> For reader-oriented critics, who have rejected such standards as authorial intent and structural analysis as determinative for meaning, Fish says, agreement on interpretation can occur among those who share the same basic reading strategy. Accordingly, Fish dubs his own model for "affective stylistics" to be but one such strategy that a community might use.[8]

Referring to Reader-Response criticism and the work of Fish, Powell makes a further comment:

> Although any single reading of a given text is never the "right" one, agreement in interpretation does occur among those who share the same reading strategy. Within an interpretive community, then, readings may be recognised as being in or out of accord with the accepted strategy.[9]

Thus, for the present purpose, it may be noted that the 'interpretive community' of Wesley was not that of George Whitefield or Count Zinzendorf. All three understood the meaning of the biblical text in accordance with the doctrinal position within the traditions with which they were comfortable. Powell also comments that:

---

6   Jane P. Tomkins, *Reader-Response Criticism From Formalism to Post-Structuralism*, The John Hopkins University Press, 1980.
7   Mark Allan Powell, with the assistance of Cecile G. Gray and Melissa C. Curtis, *The Bible and Modern Literary Criticism: A Critical Assessment and Annotated Biography*, Greenwood Press, 1992, pp. 11-12.
8   Powell, *The Bible and Modern Literary Criticism*, p.12.
9   Mark Allan Powell, *What is Narrative Criticism? A New Approach to the Bible*, SPCK, 1993, p. 17.

In Biblical studies, the science of hermeneutics focuses on issues concerning the authority and inspiration of Scripture. Virtually all Christian communities are quick to identify the Bible as "the Word of God," even if there are different ideas as to how such an identification should be construed.[10]

In the Introduction to the influential volume *The Cambridge Companion to Biblical Interpretation*, John Barton similarly comments 'It takes two for meaning to be perceived.'[11] This again reflects the fact that there has been a major shift in interest within biblical studies in recent years. Increasingly emphasis has been placed upon the completed works and their interpretation by the readers. Thus W.R.F. Browning, in an article on 'Reader-Response Criticism,' makes the point that:

Biblical scholars, especially in America, have argued that in addition to the rigorous examination of the text to discuss the theological ideas in the writings and the accuracy of the history and the identity of the authors, the part played by readers of the books is also important; for, as with a sermon, the words are lifeless until the person reading or hearing begins to ask questions.[12]

Reader-Response criticism is therefore far removed from the historical-critical method of study, although Barton, in common with a number of other biblical scholars, argues that there is still place for that.

Robert Morgan, in a chapter on 'The Bible and Christian Theology,'[13] makes what some would consider a very controversial point but one which is clearly relevant to the argument here. According to him 'The Bible itself has never of itself given birth to theology.'[14] Morgan then goes on to argue that part of the process of theologising is the interpretation of scripture by the reader. He admits that 'Protestant theology was bound into a new dependence on Scripture by its repudiation of the Catholic magisterium.'[15] However, he also makes the point that 'Scripture was still read within a traditional Christian doctrinal framework.' The implication of this for the study of Wesley's theology is clear. The point being made in this book is that Wesley came to scripture with a theology already formed in his mind. It may have received some modification but basically his interpretation of scripture was based on what he brought to the study from all the varied influences that helped formulate his own theological position.

---

10   Powell, *What is Narrative Criticism?*, p. 98.
11   *The Cambridge Companion to Biblical Interpretation*, ed. John Barton, Cambridge University Press, 1998, p. 1.
12   W.R.F. Browning, *Oxford Dictionary of the Bible*, Oxford University Press, 1995, p. 315.
13   Robert Morgan, 'The Bible and Christian Theology', *The Cambridge Companion to Biblical Interpretation*, pp. 114-128.
14   Morgan, 'The Bible and Christian Theology', p. 114.
15   Morgan, 'The Bible and Christian Theology', p. 121.

Applying the principles of Reader-Response criticism to the study of Wesley's use of scripture, it is not only possible it is highly likely that, in interpreting the Bible, Wesley understood the text to mean things which, at least sometimes, the original writer may not have intended. Therefore this is a study of the way in which Wesley read the Bible, presenting a view that, rather surprisingly, is not found in mainstream Wesley scholarship. In a twenty-first century context, however, it is appropriate, and indeed necessary, to note the work on Reader-Response criticism and to ask whether this throws any light on the way Wesley read and interpreted scripture. As will be seen, the rather odd view that Wesley simply read the Bible and believed what it said may well be a serious misconception long overdue for correction.

Reader-Response criticism is not to be confused with what Heikki Räisänen described as the 'effective history' of the New Testament.[16] He poses the question "What effect has the Bible had?" and points out that much of modern scholarship devotes its energies to examining the biblical texts, setting them in their original context and is thereby concerned with Christian beginnings. Much less effort is devoted to researching the influence that the texts have had on later generations. This is a reader-centred approach but it concerns itself mainly with the text of the Bible itself and how the text causes the readers to interpret the scriptures in the way in which they do in their own generations.

All that is written above about Reader-Response criticism and modern biblical scholarship is material familiar to the average twenty-first century theological undergraduate. Furthermore, Methodism has produced many biblical scholars of international repute. Names that could be mentioned include C.K. Barrett, Morna Hooker, James Dunn and John Ziesler whose New Testament work has been based in Great Britain. Norman Snaith and John Snaith are father and son Old Testament Scholars. In America E.P. Sanders has a Methodist connection. Many are specialists in the field of historical criticism but are, no doubt, familiar with the increasing emphasis on the role of the reader in biblical interpretation. Therefore, a student who has researched biblical subjects and who turns to Wesley studies may be forgiven if s/he is perplexed that the insights of these outstanding Methodist biblical scholars are not used in the research into questions relating to Wesley's biblical interpretation. It is almost as though there are two guilds and the one has little to do with the other.

It may also be noted that Methodist ministerial and theological training in Great Britain, often set in an ecumenical context, takes full cognisance of

---

16   See Heikki Räisänen, 'The Effective 'History' of the Bible: A Challenge to Biblical Scholarship' in *Scottish Journal of Theology,* 45 (1992), pp.303-324. Räisänen develops some of the themes from this article in *Beyond New Testament Theology,* SCM Press, 2nd ed., 2000.

modern biblical scholarship. Methodist local (lay) preachers have prescribed studies that reflect such scholarship. For many years local preachers in training preparing for their examinations were expected to read W. David Stacey, *Groundwork of Biblical Studies*,[17] which raises all the usual historical critical questions, although it does not take note of Reader-Response criticism. All Methodist presbyteral ministers must have first become local preachers. It is both surprising and disturbing that Wesley scholars have not appropriated the insights and skills of both the findings and the methods of modern biblical scholarship in interpreting Wesley.

The Primary Sources and their Use

The place to begin research into the influences that fashioned the life of Wesley and his interpretation of the Bible is in his written works, especially the *Journal*, his letters, and the sermons. The use of primary sources is essential. The publication, even now not yet complete, of the Bicentennial Edition of Wesley's works has made a considerable addition to the resources available for scholarly research.[18] The work was initiated by Albert Outler and many Wesley scholars have participated in this work, including the late Frank Baker. The recovery of much of the original Wesley text is due to Baker's meticulous work. Where possible these volumes have been used as a primary source. However, there is still a substantial gap in the number of those available, up to fifty per cent still not yet completed and published. Even at this late date, these works still show no sign of appearing. This is regrettable as they would make the work of researchers into Wesley studies easier and, more importantly, more accurate. Therefore earlier versions of Wesley's works, where necessary, have been used to supply the gap.

Richard Green provided a bibliography of Wesley's works in chronological order with brief notes.[19] Most Wesley scholars of the mid and late twentieth century have used these works as primary sources for Wesley studies and it is necessary to be aware of this in any study relating to John Wesley.

---

17   W. David Stacey, *Groundwork of Biblical Studies*, Epworth Press, 1979.
18   Although popularly known as the Bicentennial Edition of the Works of John Wesley, the title of the various books is simply *The Works of John Wesley* followed by a volume number and some indication of the contents of the volume. Fuller details of the volumes to which reference is made will be found in the List of Abbreviations and the Bibliography.
19   Richard Green, *The Works of John and Charles Wesley - a Bibliography*, C.H. Kelly, 1896. This was revised and enlarged in 1902.

Reference is also made to the invaluable work of Charles Wallace Junior on the letters of Susanna Wesley.[20] This contains the fullest collection of her letters currently available.

The list of the works of Wesleyan scholars and others relating to Wesley from 1791 to 1900 in the bibliography is not exhaustive but includes all the major works to which reference is made in this book. The important point to note is that they are primary documents in the sense that they illustrate the way in which Wesley's successors have presented the man to their readers. A study of their contents supports the contention that the aim of these writers was not simply to give an objective account of the life of Wesley because they frequently contain a hidden agenda influenced by the issues confronting the Wesleyan Church of the authors' own generation.

It might be assumed that a simple and straightforward reading of Wesley's correspondence and *Journal* would provide insights into the reasons that led him to his interpretation of the Bible and his understanding of the Christian faith. Indeed, it is clear that there is a considerable amount of material available to the student but three cautionary points need to be added concerning the use of these sources. First, as Christopher Idle has commented in publishing an abridgement of the *Journal*,[21] 'We see here what John Wesley wanted us to see.'[22] Idle relied on Curnock's eight-volume *Standard Edition* of the *Journal*. He quotes from the Preface to the first printed extract, 1739, 'It was in pursuance of an advice given by Bishop Taylor, in his *Rules for Holy Living and Dying*, that about fifteen years ago I began to take a more exact account of the manner wherein I spent my time, writing down how I had employed every hour.'[23] However, it is to be noted that Wesley subsequently used that material selectively to establish those points that he thought to be important. The *Journal* was not a private document but was itself edited and published in sections. It is possible that the purpose in publishing may not have been simply to record past events, but rather to make a point in relation to what was happening at the later time. For example, Wesley's account of the years from 1738 to 1740 were published some time after his decisive break with the Moravians in the summer of 1740 and may well be coloured by what happened in that year and later as the controversy continued. This particular point will be taken up in Chapter 4.

W. Reginald Ward was editor or co-editor of some of the volumes of *Wesley's Works* in the Bicentennial Edition. He makes a valid point:

---

20   Charles Wallace Jr., *Susanna Wesley*, Oxford University Press, 1997.
21   Christopher Idle, *The Journal of John Wesley (Abridged)*, Lion Paperback, 1986. (A new, but largely unchanged, edition was published in 2003).
22   Idle, *Abridgement*, p. 9.
23   Idle, *Abridgement*, p. 17. See also *BE* Vol. 18, p. 121.

The reader may now well ask why, since every published part was described as
An Extract of the Rev. Mr. John Wesley's Journal, the textual prehistory of the
publication may not simply be elucidated by reference to the manuscript *Journal*
from which the *Extracts* came. The answer to this question is that no such journal
exists, and that it is in the last degree unlikely that it ever did.[24]

Consequently the diaries, often in a shorthand which has only more recently
been decoded through the work of Heitzenrater, may give greater insight
into the thoughts of Wesley at the time they were written. Even here it is
necessary to ask critical questions about whether these diaries express
Wesley's innermost thoughts and views or even whether he was fully aware
of those influences that fashioned his fundamental beliefs. This is not to
criticise Wesley as a person but to attempt to get to the heart of what was
authoritative for him.

The second point relates more specifically to the use of the
correspondence. The letters were preserved and, in many cases, edited by
Wesley, and then some were included in published works or *The Journal.*
BE Volume 25 contains a number of letters addressed to or written by
Wesley in the years 1721-39, including a considerable number from Samuel
and Susanna to him. Many deal with the normal issues of family life, of
finance and, sometimes, of strained relationships, usually resolved by the
good offices of members within the family. Nevertheless this
correspondence does give some indication of the influences that were, at
that time, fashioning the mind of the young Wesley but the fact that he
selectively edited even those letters addressed to him before their
publication must be borne in mind. They too presented to the reader of the
published works the points that Wesley wanted the reader to hear and
understand.

The third point relates to the sermons. These were written and published
works, not necessarily the same as those actually preached to the Methodist
societies or wider public. They were designated by Wesley and by the later
Wesleyan body as part of the doctrinal standard to which preachers should
subscribe. They are thus of considerable importance in establishing what
beliefs were required of Wesley's assistants. Earlier biographers who were
also preachers in the Wesleyan tradition were steeped in them, regarding
them as a source for Wesley's thought. While this assumption is basically
sound, they need to be examined critically and with care.

In examining Wesley's editing of other people's works his exceedingly
cavalier attitude to the editing of the originals may be noted from the
preface to the fifty volumes in the *Christian Library* that he produced for
his preachers to study.[25] He wrote 'Who will be at the pains to extract the

---

24   *BE* Vol. 18, p. 85.
25   John Wesley, *A Christian Library.* Vol. 1 was published in 1748 in Bristol.

Gold out of the base mixtures?'[26] On the following page he commented 'I have been obliged, not only to omit the far greater part of several eminent authors, but also to add what was needful, either to clear their sense, or to correct their mistakes. And in a design of this nature, I apprehend myself to be at full liberty to do so.' Wesley clearly felt it was his responsibility, and also well within his authority, to determine what his preachers should read.

The conclusion is that there are abundant primary sources available to the researcher, but that they must be used with critical care, not least because both Wesley and his biographers have created a smokescreen that obscures at least some of the truth about the man and his work. Whether this was done deliberately or not by either Wesley or his biographers is a question to be asked at various stages in the work.

A Note on the Calendar

The Gregorian calendar, reforming the older Julian calendar, was not adopted in Great Britain until 1752. At that time, New Year's Day in England was moved from March 25 to January 1. Thus there may be slight confusion in John Wesley's earlier life over the year intended in references to dates in the period from the beginning of January until March 24. For the sake of clarity here dates are normally given as though the New Year had begun on January 1. In fact, as early as 1736, in the *Journal*, Wesley was referring to January 1 as the beginning of the New Year.

A Summary of the Arguments in this Study

This book notes that the received wisdom of Wesley scholarship has within it a considerable veneration of the person of Wesley, depicting him as simply a man of one book. The scholars gave inadequate attention to the complex influences that were at work in Wesley as he read the sacred text. The earlier biographers of Wesley in particular, so it is argued here, sometimes quite deliberately obscured the evident influence of the High-Church Anglicanism. Subsequently Wesley scholarship in both Great Britain and America has suffered considerably from failing to recognise this since the result has been altogether too simplistic a view of Wesley's complex interaction with the biblical text.

An exploration is made of the evidence, especially the primary evidence, available to demonstrate that Wesley came to his method of biblical interpretation in his earlier years through a diversity of routes, many of which originated in the family life and religious practices in the rectory at Epworth. Further influences included those encountered in his reading in his Oxford days, the contacts with the Moravians leading up to

---

26 *Christian Library*, Vol. 1, p. iv of his introduction to the whole series.

the Aldersgate experience in 1738, and the controversies that followed. However, the principal contention is that the main influence on Wesley throughout was that of eighteenth-century High-Church Arminian Anglicanism and that it was this that led him to read the Bible in the way he did. It will be noted that, on occasions, Wesley claimed the main doctrines he embraced and their biblical roots were such that, in his own judgement, he deviated from them only in marginal ways during his later life. However, it will also be noted in later chapters that some modern scholars rightly question Wesley's judgement on this point. Nevertheless, whatever be the case with regard to his doctrinal position and whether he did develop or change his views or not, it is contended throughout this study that the main sources of influence on his interpretation of the Bible changed but little throughout his life.

Chapter 1 begins with a critical review of the Wesley literature available on the subject of Wesley and the Bible, including the biographies dating from the nineteenth century, as well as its influence on some more modern works. It is clearly shown that many of the earlier biographies are primary sources for establishing the views of their authors rather than giving an objective account of the life and work of Wesley. It is strongly argued here that Wesleyan scholarship recognised the Arminian theology of Wesley and affirmed the biblical basis of his work but failed to see his interpretation of scripture in its eighteenth-century High-Church context.

In Chapter 2 reference is made to more recent Wesley scholarship, especially that in America in the second half of the twentieth century. Here the idea of the Wesley Quadrilateral, the authority of Bible, tradition, reason and experience, is critically assessed. It is strongly argued that the debate over the Quadrilateral in fact related far more to the theological needs of the twentieth-century American United Methodist Church than to the study of Wesley's biblical interpretation. However, the concept of the fourfold basis of authority does offer some considerable insight into Wesley's theological methodology and biblical interpretation. It is a useful tool but does not fully explain in itself how Wesley read the Bible. A brief review of works published in 2002-2003, marking the tercentenary of Wesley's birth, is given. This has been slightly extended to show that works subsequently published still echo the traditional understanding of Wesley and the way in which he read the Bible. This brings the context of the present work up to date and marks the literary terminus of this part of the study.

Following the survey that shows the gaps in earlier scholarship, the remainder of the book offers an analysis of the way Wesley interpreted the Bible as he did. Here it is shown that far from being a man of one book, he was influenced by many authors and many books and that, while he would have argued otherwise, the Bible was more a mirror for his beliefs than the source of them. Consequently Chapter 3 examines the influences on

Wesley's reading of the Bible in his early years at Epworth, followed by an assessment of his Oxford years and other experiences that helped fashion his biblical interpretation. Chapter 4 moves on to an examination of the relevance of the events in Wesley's life in America leading up to the crucial Aldersgate experience back in England in the summer of 1738. This includes the influence of the Moravians on him and the importance of experience in the interpretation of the biblical text.

Chapter 5 contains a critical investigation into Wesley's claim to be a Church of England man to his dying day. It is in this context that attention is given to the influence of tradition and reason on his interpretation of the Bible, also noting his contacts with the Roman Catholic Church and some major Catholic authors. Chapter 6 explores the story of Wesley's disputes with the Calvinists in as much as they illustrate the use of authority and influences at work on Wesley's understanding of the interpretation of scripture. The difference between Arminians and Calvinists within the Church of England sheds considerable light on the way the protagonists came to their respective conclusions. Chapter 7 explores in greater depth the nature of the authority and interpretation of scripture for Wesley with special reference to his own writings on the subject.

The concluding chapter draws together the main points to emerge from this study and gives some indication of where further work needs to be undertaken on the questions raised throughout this book.

Therefore this is an examination of the way in which John Wesley read the Bible. It is not a simple biography or a general study in the life of Wesley. It is not just a consideration of the influences that fashioned his thinking although these are, at times, central to the discussion. For this study, the primary documents are the works of Wesley. However, as has already been explained, it is also contended that many of his biographers have misunderstood or misrepresented the manner in which he came to the Bible. Therefore late eighteenth-century, nineteenth-century and some twentieth-century authors have been quoted as primary texts in themselves. These are examined not so much as sources for the discovery of Wesley's biblical interpretation as illustrations of the way in which later writers interpreted Wesley's life and doctrines. It is argued that Wesley, in presenting his interpretation of Scripture, carried to its pages many of the ideas that he claimed were derived from a study of those texts. In particular Wesley came early to an eighteenth-century Anglican High-Church Arminian position which influenced the way he understood scripture and its interpretation.

In the light of the points made in this Introduction it is therefore appropriate now to turn to Chapter 1 and to begin a study of the mass of literature on Wesley that emerged in the years following the death of John Wesley.

Chapter 1

A Critical Overview of the Literature on John Wesley from 1791-1900 and its Effect on Twentieth-Century Works

Wesley Scholarship 1791-1900

In this chapter three points will be established about Wesley scholarship from 1791-1900 and its influence on subsequent authors. First it was, with certain noteworthy exceptions, narrowly confined within the Wesleyan community, and consciously tried to remain so. Second it showed such excessive veneration for Wesley that it may well be described as hagiography. Third, and most important for the present study, it depicted Wesley as a Bible-based person, a man of one book, without asking what led him to such a belief in the Bible or questioning deeply why he believed the scriptures to have the authority he claimed they had or why he interpreted them the way he did. Reflecting a growing awareness of these points, Randy Maddox, an acknowledged American Wesley scholar, writes:

> From the time of his death through the nineteenth century the vast majority of publications dealing with Wesley fit into the category of biography. Far from being detached scholarly accounts, these biographies were typically triumphalist panegyrics and/or defences of Wesley. [...] In short they were hagiography. This is not to say these biographies were devoid of conviction about Wesley as theologian. Quite the contrary! They generally operated with distinctive assumptions about this topic just below the narrative surface (where their particular model of Wesley could exercise powerful influence, without having to be defended).[1]

It would, of course, be inappropriate to criticise earlier biographers because they did not engage in historical research simply in order to understand the truth about Wesley. There are perhaps degrees of objectivity in biographical

---

1   Randy L. Maddox, 'Reclaiming an Inheritance: Wesley as Theologian in the History of Methodist Theology' in *Rethinking Wesley's Theology for Contemporary Methodism*, ed. Randy L. Maddox, Kingswood Books, Abingdon Press, 1998, p. 214.

material in the work of any age. However, it will be shown, these authors frequently presented their work in such a way that they misrepresented the work of Wesley as an interpreter of the Bible. Maddox shows an awareness of the problem, but it is necessary to examine this in more detail to grasp the hidden agenda of the nineteenth-century authors and the reality about the way Wesley came to his understanding of the meaning of scripture. His thought had become, in part, obscured or suppressed. Many nineteenth century authors depicted Wesley as coming from a study of the Bible to an interpretation that led to the emergence of Methodism.

The argument here is that a study of the eighteenth-century material shows that Wesley came from, and carried with him, his Anglican convictions into his reading of the Bible and it was from this that Methodism emerged. Thus the major contention of this chapter is that, although some early works on Wesley acknowledged that he was an eighteenth-century High-Church Arminian Anglican, the mainstream[2] nineteenth- and twentieth-century Wesley biographers largely ignored or played down this influence on his biblical interpretation. That is not to deny the point made by Rupert Davies that 'Throughout the first half of the nineteenth century there were many Methodists, notably among the leading ministers, who wished for the breach with the Church of England to be healed.'[3] What is being argued here is that the influence of the Church of England on Wesley, particularly in his interpretation of the Bible, is understated in the earliest biographies and increasingly suppressed in later works. Biographies were written in such a way that they distorted and diminished the record of this influence on Wesley, although it was never denied that he was an Arminian.

Note is also made of the fact that Wesleyan scholarship was very defensive. There was a concern by many to present Wesley in the most favourable light. Therefore many of these early works have to be read with considerable care if they are to be used in the search to find those influences that shaped the life and beliefs of Wesley. Non-Wesleyan authors, usually Anglican, often presented another view and there was conflict between the two schools of thought. Both sides assumed, often without direct statement, that Wesley's teaching was Bible-based but differed strongly in the way they saw this working out in his life. The influence of the earlier nineteenth-

---

2   The term 'mainstream' is used in this chapter to describe writers who were in the
      continuing Wesleyan body and to distinguish them from Anglican authors on the
      one hand and those who went into branches of the Methodist Church other than the
      Wesleyan tradition. 'Church Methodists' is a term frequently used to describe those
      within the Methodist movement who consciously tried to remain within the Church
      of England and from whom the mainstream wished to be clearly distinct.
3   Rupert Davies, *Methodism*, Epworth Press, second ed. 1965, p. 126

century Wesleyan scholarship strongly influenced all later interpretations of Wesley and his thought.

In the years immediately following Wesley's death the Wesleyan preachers faced the priority of establishing the Wesleyan body, defining the relationship that they had with the Church of England and dealing with early divisions within their number. Although there was call for a definitive and authoritative biography of their founder, some of the first works to appear were from authors outside mainstream Wesleyanism. There were then responses from within the main body of his successors. This pattern of works being written by those not in the mainstream Wesleyan body being countered by what were regarded as more definitive works was repeated for a considerable period of time. It is fitting therefore that attention is now given to those who, in the earlier years following Wesley's death, wrote from an Anglican or a Church Methodist point of view before making a critical assessment of those who came to be regarded, within the Wesleyan tradition, as being the acceptable standard biographies.

Early Works that Set Wesley in the Context of the Church of England

It is to be expected that publications immediately following the death of Wesley in 1791 should reflect a high degree of veneration for the man to whom the writers owed so much. An example is to be found in Liverpool where on Sunday March 27th, less than a month after Wesley's death on March 2nd, W. Hobrow preached a memorial sermon.[4] Hobrow was not listed among Wesley's preachers and it is a reasonable deduction from a reading of his sermon that he was from within the Anglican tradition. The veneration shown towards Wesley is partly explained by the fact that the author owed his own spiritual awakening nearly 30 years earlier to him. His move to Liverpool was largely due to a letter from John Wesley written to him in 1786, a letter that apparently has not survived, although Hobrow made direct reference to it in his sermon.

Hobrow's account of Wesley's life and experience up to May 24th 1738 followed closely the account in Wesley's Journal. The highly detailed and emotional account of the death must have been obtained by Hobrow from eyewitnesses. It is of note that Hobrow saw the essence of Wesley's theology as the doctrine of perfect love, writing 'We frequently use as St.

---

4   W. Hobrow, minister of the gospel, *Sermon on the Death of Rev J Wesley A. M. Chaplain to the Countess Dowager of Bucan Delivered at the New Chapel Liverpool in Edmund Street Liverpool Sunday March 27th 1791*. On April 19th he completed the preface of a printed version for publication. No publisher is given so it was probably privately circulated but printed by H. Hodgson of Castle Street, Liverpool. A copy is in the Liverpool University Library.

John, the phraise, PERFECT LOVE, instead of the word PERFECTION.'[5]
He also quoted 1 John 3:9 'Whosoever is born of God doth not sin, because
he is born of God.'[6] He asserted that the doctrines which Wesley taught
were no other than the doctrines of the Church of England, and that his
teaching was that of the Prayer Book, the Articles, and the Homilies.[7]
Hobrow was strongly opposed to Calvinism and Antinomianism. In the
unquestioned appeal to scripture he was a forerunner of later Wesley
biographers who accepted uncritically Wesley's use of the Bible as the
apparent source and authority for his teaching. The sermon shows the high
regard in which Wesley was held and it is an example of those writings that
understand his teaching to be biblically based Arminianism. It also is
evidence for the existence of at least some at that time who believed that
Wesley's work should properly be continued within the Church of England.

Similar views to those of Hobrow are to be found in the earliest
published biography of Wesley, that by John Hampson junior.[8] Hampson
had been one of Wesley's itinerant preachers who had become a priest in
the Church of England. He had respect for Wesley but the Memoirs were
intended to justify the separation of John Hampson and his father, another
of Wesley's itinerant preachers, from Methodism.

Referring to the task of writing a life of Wesley, he made the comment:

> Someone would be certain to undertake it: and considering the colour of his most
> intimate connections, and the unlimited deference, with which, in this circle, it has
> been the fashion to regard him, a danger was apprehended, lest the public should
> be misinformed, either by the suppression of some important facts, or by a partial
> and inaccurate relation.[9]

Those words were prophetic, as will be seen when the work of mainstream
Wesleyan writers is examined below. In the preface Hampson claims to
have consulted Wesley's works including the Journals, although the last
extracts had not then been published, and to have had access to
correspondence dating from 1724-39. Authors within the Wesleyan
community would have been unhappy with statements such as 'Whoever is
acquainted with the subject, must have perceived in the progress of
Methodism, the operation of a principle which, in every stage, has debased
and degraded it; that is, a frequent tendency to enthusiasm and
extravagance.'[10]

---

5   Hobrow, *Sermon on the Death of Rev J Wesley A. M.*, p. 13
6   Hobrow, *Sermon on the Death of Rev J Wesley A. M.*, p. 20.
7   Hobrow, *Sermon on the Death of Rev J Wesley A. M.*, p. 22.
8   John Hampson junior, *Memoirs of the Late John Wesley, A. M., with a Review of
     his Life and Writings, and a History of Methodism*, 3 Vols., Sunderland, 1791.
9   Hampson, *Memoirs*, Vol. 1, p. i-ii.
10   Hampson, *Memoirs*, Vol. 2, p. 130.

Volume 2 ends with a chapter entitled 'The Consecration of Bishops and Ordination of Priests for America, by Imposition of the hands of Mr Wesley.'[11] Hampson was extremely critical of the step that Wesley had taken and opposed it with considerable logic.

Volume 3 begins, inside the front cover, with an advertisement:

> The Executors of Mr Wesley having taken much pains, by notice and advertisements, to prevent the circulation of these Memoirs, or any other account of Mr Wesley, than that which they are now preparing, and which is signed by their names.

Hampson was thus explaining why he ignored the steps taken by official Wesleyanism, especially asserting the right he had to use the correspondence that had come to his attention.

The same volume contains a chapter on 'A review of His [Wesley's] Character.'[12] This is better balanced than some of the contemporary assessments of Wesley the man. In it Hampson made some critical statements, for example 'We now come to the last feature in Mr Wesley's character; his love of power. He has been often charged with this propensity; and the charge is not yet refuted. We will say more. We challenge any man to refute it.' Such words led to the continuing Wesleyan movement closing ranks against him.

Hampson acknowledged that he differed from Wesley on certain points, but made reference to the Bible as the source of doctrine for both Wesley and himself in the words 'Those doctrines of Methodism, which are peculiar, are either not true or dubious, or indifferent; while those, which are confessedly scriptural and just, are such as they hold, not alone, but in common with Christians of other denominations.'[13] The implication is that Hampson regarded the Bible as the supreme authority for doctrine, that he also understood this to be the authority accepted by Wesley, but that, at certain points, they interpreted it differently. This illustrates the point made in Reader-Response criticism that people do claim biblical authority for doctrines but come to different conclusions as to the meaning of scripture.

Hampson presented a critical, although generally appreciative, assessment of Wesley and his work, regarding much of his teaching as biblically based but arguing strongly that the proper development of the Methodist movement should have been continued within the context of the Church of England.

Hampson's work was followed by that of John Whitehead, a former Methodist itinerant who had attended Wesley as his physician and preached

---

11   Hampson, *Memoirs*, Vol. 2, pp. 171-216.
12   Hampson, *Memoirs*, Vol. 3, pp. 165-209.
13   Hampson, *Memoirs*, Vol. 3, p. 121.

the sermon at Wesley's funeral service. Whitehead also strongly opposed any break with the Church of England. His two-volume work appeared in 1793-6.[14] He noted the delay in the publication of the Life, and stated that the first reason was 'the cruel and persevering opposition of some of the Methodist preachers, against the execution of the work.'[15]

As W. Reginald Ward in the Bicentennial Edition of Wesley's Works points out, Whitehead devoted so much of his space in getting Wesley to the evangelical experience of 1738 that he had to pass over the later years of mission and travel in summary fashion.[16] Whitehead, like Charles Wesley and John Hampson, was very critical of Wesley's ordinations and strongly opposed to any separation from the Church of England but this was dealt with more briefly in the later part of the work. Furthermore, Whitehead did not endear himself to Wesleyan Methodist leadership with the words 'The present system of government among the Methodists requires such arts of human policy and chicanery to carry it on, as, in my opinion, are totally inconsistent with the openness of gospel simplicity.'[17]

His comment on the Deed of Declaration of 1784, setting up the authority of Conference and the legal hundred, was equally trenchant:

> So far was he from forming any design of a Deed of this kind, that, I have good evidence to assert, it was some time before he could be prevailed upon to comply with the proposal: and, as in most other cases where he followed the same guide, he soon found reason to repent.[18]

On the question of Wesley's ordinations, he quoted, with approval, an old preacher's description of them as 'a hodge-podge of inconsistencies.'[19] It is perhaps not surprising that Whitehead was strongly criticised within the continuing Wesleyan body.

Whitehead did not give much consideration to questions relating to the influences that fashioned Wesley's life and thought. However, there is the underlying assumption that Wesley was a Bible-based person but there is also a hint that Wesley sometimes came to conclusions without fully assessing the evidence.[20] Whitehead did not discuss how Wesley came to a

---

14   John Whitehead, *The Life of the Rev. John Wesley, M.A.*, 2 Vols., Stephen Couchman, 1793-6.

15   Quotation from the Preface, page not numbered.

16   See BE Vol. 18, pp. 95-6.

17   Whitehead, *Life*, Vol. 2, p. 477.

18   Whitehead, *Life*, Vol. 2, p. 412.

19   Whitehead, *Life*, Vol. 2, p. 420.

20   See, for example, Henry D. Rack, *Reasonable Enthusiast, John Wesley and the Rise of Methodism*, Abingdon Press, second ed. 1993 p. 351, quoting Whitehead, p. 486 and pp. 491ff.

biblical basis for his teaching but, nevertheless, he did emphasise the need for his work to be continued within the Church of England.

Robert Southey was an Anglican writer who was also Poet Laureate. He had been strongly influenced by eighteenth-century rationalism but had moved to a more traditional Anglican position before writing his *Life of Wesley*.[21] His work was published in 1820 and was the first biographer not to claim direct personal knowledge of Wesley. He was very critical of what he saw as the enthusiasm of Methodism. Southey did not claim to have researched any further primary material but relied upon the published works on or by Wesley available at that time. His respect for Wesley was clear, but he was not writing from within the Wesleyan community. However, he did make critical comments such as his account of the events of May 1738, no doubt displeasing to Methodist writers, in which he said 'Here was a contradiction in terms - an assurance which had not assured him [Wesley].'[22]

Of note for the argument of this work is Southey's comment:

> Wesley never departed willingly or knowingly from the doctrines of the Church of England, in which he had been trained up, and with which he was conscientiously satisfied after full and free enquiry ... Upon points which have not been revealed, but are within the scope of reason, he formed for himself opinions which were generally clear, consistent with the Christian religion, and creditable, for the most part, both to his feelings and judgement. But he laid no stress on them and never proposed them for more than they were.[23]

These words are taken from the beginning of Chapter XX on 'Wesley's Doctrines and Opinions.' The whole chapter gives a summary of Wesley's doctrines as based on the Bible and experience. A typical example relates to the fall of man:

> The fall of man is the very foundation of revealed religion. [...] It is a scriptural doctrine: many plain texts directly teach it. It is a rational doctrine, thoroughly consistent with sound reason, though there may be some circumstances relating to it which human reason cannot fathom. [...] It is an experimental doctrine. The sincere Christian carries the proof of it in his own bosom.[24]

It should be noted that Southey understood Wesley's teaching to be Bible-based, although the scriptural teaching was understood in the light of the Formularies of the Church of England and of tradition, confirmed by

---

21 Robert Southey, *The Life of Wesley*, 'New Edition', Bell and Dalby, 1864. First published in 1820, there were subsequent editions. The quotations given here are largely unaltered in the different editions
22 Southey, *The Life of Wesley*, p. 99.
23 Southey, *The Life of Wesley*, pp. 348-9.
24 Southey, *The Life of Wesley*, p. 353.

experience and undergirded by reason. The reaction of mainstream Wesleyan scholarship against Southey was undoubtedly in part due to the fact that Southey's assessment of Wesley was regarded as being over influenced by philosophy and under-influenced by scripture. In Chapter 2 attention will be given to the way in which American Wesley scholarship has emphasised the primacy of the authority of the Bible for Wesley but has placed alongside that authority the influence of tradition, especially that of the Church of England, reason and experience. The quotation from Southey shows that the idea was not entirely new when put forward in the twentieth century.

A link of note with Wesley's contemporaries is evident in that Southey asked Alexander Knox for further information about Wesley and also for a comment on his [Southey's] work. Alexander Knox (1757-1831) was born in Londonderry of parents who became Methodists. He was a member of Wesley's society for a short time but withdrew before he was twenty years old. In later life he became something of a recluse and lived in Dublin. He was a close friend of Wesley in Wesley's later years and Wesley often stayed with him when in Ireland.[25] Knox possessed 40 or 50 letters exchanged between Wesley and certain, mainly female, correspondents. The quotations from Knox are from that volume unless otherwise stated. Knox's notes on Wesley were dated 1825 and the comment on Southey's work was written in 1827.

Knox appears at first sight to be another who contributed to the developing veneration of the saintly Wesley. Knox wrote 'It would be far too little to say, that it was impossible to suspect him of any moral taint, for it was obvious that every movement bespoke as perfect a contrariety to all that was earthly or animal as could be imagined in a mortal being.'[26] Knox continued that this was particularly true of Wesley's last twenty years and that 'the period, therefore, of my acquaintance with him was that also of his improved views.' However, this rather idealistic view of Wesley's character did not lead Knox to the conclusions of the mainstream Wesleyan authors. Knox argued that Wesley was a lifelong Anglican who wanted his people to remain within that church. Knox, in his comments included in later editions of Southey's work, referred back to his earlier *Considerations on a Separation of the Methodists from the Established Church*, (1794), in which he had written:

> You know, and the world knows, that amongst innumerable other declarations of his sentiments on the subject, Mr. Wesley, so late as 1790, published the following expressions:- I never had any design of separating from the Church. I

---

25   See the note in the 1925 edition of Southey's work, Vol. 2, p. 419.
26   Southey, *The Life of Wesley*, pp. 343-4

have no such design now. I do not believe the Methodists in general design it, when I am no more seen.[27]

This work was published prior to the decision of the Conference that led to separation of the Methodist societies from the Church of England. The quotation continued by noting that Wesley went on to admit that many would leave the Church of England but then continued 'I live and die a member of the Church of England, and that none who regard my judgement of advice will ever separate from it.'

The reasons Knox was not quoted by the mainstream nineteenth-century biographers of Wesley, and one of the reasons that the later editions of Southey's work were not highly regarded, are clear. Knox did not denigrate the character of Wesley, but he did present a different interpretation of the intentions of Wesley with regard to relationships with the Church of England for the Methodist societies than what actually happened under the leadership of the Wesleyan body that emerged.

Southey's work, with its literary merit, although critical of Wesley and his teaching, still had considerable respect for him but did not examine in depth the influences that led him to his beliefs and actions, nor did it give any detailed account of the way in which Wesley read the Bible. The work of Southey and the additional comments by Knox again emphasised the High-Church Anglican Wesley and were not readily accepted by Wesleyan scholarship.

It is of note that the 1864 edition of Southey's work contains footnotes with extracts from Richard Watson's criticisms of Southey, without further comment.[28] Watson had been charged by the Wesleyan Conference with the task of rebutting Southey's work. In the second edition of Watson's work, 1821, pp. 9-24, there is a section on 'Mr Southey's Theological Qualifications,' which relates to Wesley's conversion, 1738, and Watson's assertion that Southey was unable to understand it.

Thus there were late eighteenth- and early nineteenth-century non-Wesleyan authors writing from an Anglican perspective who were close to the sources then available and who saw clearly both the strengths and weaknesses of Wesley. They recognised that the Bible was his main source for doctrine and central to his thinking but they also highlighted the fact that the doctrines and practice of the Church of England were fundamental to his understanding of the meaning of scripture for his, and their, day. Hampson had received Anglican orders, Whitehead saw the future of Methodism in relation to the Church of England and Southey wrote from an Anglican position with a degree of objectivity.

---

27   Alexander Knox, *Considerations on a Separation of the Methodists from the Church of England*, Bristol, printed by Bulgin and Rosser 1794, p.19.
28   Richard Watson, *Observations on Southey's "Life of Wesley"*, T. Blanchard, 1820.

Mainstream authors, aware of the great interest in the life of Wesley, felt compelled to present the story of his life and work in a way that was a contrast to those who emphasised the Anglican influences on him and his continuing allegiance to the Church of England. It is noteworthy that this was the work of Wesleyan preachers/ministers and not the lay members of the societies. It is to their works, asserting the primacy of the Bible for Wesley but playing down the Anglican influence upon his scriptural interpretation, that it is necessary now to turn.

The Formation of the Mainstream Tradition of Wesley's Life and Work

Only a year after Wesley's death, Thomas Coke and Henry Moore published their life of Wesley.[29] Coke was an Anglican priest who was a central figure in the events surrounding Wesley's ordinations of those intended for the American work. He continued to be a leading figure within Methodism when he was in Great Britain. Moore was an itinerant who was highly influential in the closing years of Wesley's life and onwards into the early nineteenth century. The authors claimed that their work was based on Wesley's Journals and other papers which had been made available to them and also on private conversations that they had had with him in the years immediately prior to his death. They heard of the earlier events of Wesley's life from the ageing Wesley. This work was hurriedly produced partly to present, from within the continuing Wesleyan body, an answer to the work of Hampson. The antipathy of Moore to Hampson in Moore's later work[30] was thus evident at this earlier stage and the need for writers within the continuing Methodist body to claim Wesley as their own Bible-based founder can easily be seen.

Coke and Moore throughout described Wesley in the highest terms. One example of the way that they refused to see any fault was in the account of his marriage, which, they had to admit, was not a happy one. They stated that in every point Wesley was virtuous and that his wife was severely at fault.[31] The work assumes that Wesley was a biblically-based person. In the dedication the authors wrote 'You know his [Wesley's] resolute and patient adherence to the plain, yet powerful, religion of the Bible,'[32] and commented that 'His controversial pieces he wrote as need required. First,

29   Thomas Coke and Henry Moore, *The Life of the Rev John Wesley, A.M., Including an Account of the Great Revival of Religion, in Europe and America of which He was the Chief Instrument.* The dedication is dated March 1, 1792 in London.
30   See below where comment is made upon the two volume biography produced in 1824-5.
31   See Coke and Moore, *The Life of the Rev John Wesley*, p.305.
32   Coke and Moore, *The Life of the Rev John Wesley*, pp. iii-iv.

to preserve those who were in danger of being seduced from the plain religion of the Bible: and, secondly, if possible, to recover those who had fallen into the snare.'[33] The claim is that Wesley's teaching was based on the Bible but it assumes, in eighteenth- and nineteenth-century style, that biblical truth is self-evident.

Coke and Moore laid the foundation for a respect for Wesley as a person of the highest character and as a man of the Bible which, though no doubt merited, was not a healthily critical one. In an attempt to justify the emergence of a continuing Wesleyan Methodist body distinct from the Church of England, they exalted the esteem in which Wesley was held and played down his Anglican allegiance, stressing his direct dependence on the Bible.

In 1824/5, the ageing Henry Moore produced a work which did not go much beyond the story recounted in the earlier volume that had been jointly produced with Coke.[34] It contained extensive, if selective, quotations from the published works of Wesley. Moore was clearly writing to keep the biographical work on Wesley rooted within the Wesleyan community. The book contains criticisms of works by those who had been Wesley's assistants but had separated from Methodism, or who, as in the case of Southey, had had no direct connection with the founder of Methodism.

The Preface gives an outline, from Moore's perspective, of the history of the publication of the lives of Wesley.[35] He made the point that the Hampsons, father and son, were not named members of the Methodist Conference, the legal hundred, when Wesley established Conference as a legal entity through the Deed of Declaration in 1784. The Hampsons were out, in, and then out again of the itinerancy and the younger man became an Anglican priest, later Rector of Sunderland. Thus, Moore claimed, Hampson was writing to vindicate his position and disagreed with Wesley's later actions. Moore thought that Hampson wrote from self-interest.

Moore then noted that Whitehead was one of the trustees of Wesley's papers and that he was commissioned, and paid, by the Conference to write his Life of the Rev John Wesley in order to counter the work of Hampson. He claimed that Whitehead eventually wrote an independent *Life* for greater financial advantage. He accepted that parts of the work were good but he took exception to much of Whitehead's attitude and comments. He also claimed that the surviving Wesley papers rightly belonged now to him (Moore) wherever they were. Moore also claimed that the work he prepared jointly with Coke was in response to the work of Whitehead, but without

---

33 Coke and Moore, *The Life of the Rev John Wesley*, p.482.
34 Henry Moore, *The Life of the Rev John Wesley, A.M., Fellow of Lincoln College, Oxford*, John Kershaw, 2 Vols., 1824-5. On the title page it was noted that Moore was the only surviving trustee of the Wesley manuscripts.
35 Moore, *Life*, Vol. 1, pp. i-xiv.

financial gain to the authors. As this earlier work was in fact produced ahead of Whitehead's, which was still in course of being written, it appears more logical to assume that it was written in response to Hampson and in anticipation of the work of Whitehead. In this later work Moore was critical of Whitehead's comments about the 1784 Deed writing 'What Dr. Whitehead has asserted, respecting Mr. Wesley having repented of this transaction is totally unfounded.'[36]

Moore was also scathing about Southey, commenting that 'It has been generally acknowledged by competent judges of religious biography, that the names of WESLEY and SOUTHEY were never destined to be joined together in the same sentence.'[37] His later work was intended, in part, to answer Southey.

Moore saw Wesley as a Bible-based person, quoting Wesley's own words with approval: 'In the year 1729, I began not only to read, but to study the Bible, as the one, the only standard of truth, and the only model of pure religion.'[38]

Moore also commented that:

[Wesley] began his religious course, as all sincere persons do, who are convinced of sin with placing the Holy Law of God before him and striving to bend his Spirit to its sacred preaching, resolved even to risk 'the destruction of the flesh, that the spirit might be saved in the day of the Lord Jesus.'[39]

The significance of the Bible for Moore, and for Moore's understanding of Wesley, is further illustrated in a comment about Methodist work in Scotland:

Dr Chalmers, and other pious ministers, seem to have adopted in good measure, Mr. Wesley's views, and their success has been so great, that multitudes have been roused from their self-righteous delusion, so that the simple and powerful religion of the Bible bids fair to become again the religion of Scotland.[40]

Clearly the early biographers had their own perspective on Wesley. It is also clear that, through Moore, mainstream Wesleyanism was trying to suppress views which it did not approve, while making the claim that Wesleyan theology was Bible-based. There was lacking any of the emphasis on the Church of England found in the non-Wesleyan authors. Works about Wesley were being used to justify the existence of Methodism as a Bible-based body independent of the Church of England

---

36   Moore, *Life*, Vol. 2, p. 299.
37   Moore, *Life*, Vol. 1, p. xi.
38   Moore, *Life*, Vol. 1, p. 101.
39   Moore, *Life*, Vol. 2, p. 401.
40   Moore, *Life*, Vol. 2, p. 254.

Richard Watson also prepared his work *The Life of the Rev. John Wesley, A.M.*, in part as an answer to Southey.[41] Watson referred to Southey's work about which he was clearly unhappy and suggested that he would have been better advised to turn away from his philosophical explanations and consult either St Paul or the Formularies of the Church of England. Southey was, for Watson, not respectful enough of Wesley's person and teaching. It is also of note that, writing from within the Wesleyan community, Watson placed great emphasis on Wesley as a person whose life, work and teaching was based on his understanding of scripture. Watson quoted Whitehead and Southey, sometimes critically, but, it should be noted, sometimes as authorities on Wesley. In another work his main criticism was that 'The Wesley of Mr. Southey is not, in several of his most important characteristics, Mr. Wesley himself; and the picture of Methodism which he has drawn is not exact, either in tone or composition.'[42]

It is not necessary to pursue Watson's criticisms in detail, but many related to what Southey perceived to be Wesley's 'enthusiasm.' Thus Watson wrote 'Mr. Southey's more specific charges of enthusiasm are founded on the doctrine of assurance, taught by Mr Wesley, and on certain irregularities in persons strongly affected under his preaching in the early period of his ministry.'[43]

Watson wrote about John and Charles Wesley coming to experience justification by faith in 1738 and used biblical references to describe it. Referring to what he termed the conversion of the Wesleys, he commented 'Everything in the account of the change wrought in the two brothers, and several of their friends about the same time, answers therefore to the New Testament.'[44]

Watson also commented 'No man more honestly sought truth than Mr. Wesley, and none more rigidly tried all the systems by the law and the testimony. As to authority he was "a man of one book."'[45] Watson frequently used the phrase 'authority of Scripture.'[46] He contrasted Southey's philosophic approach with what he saw as the biblically-based theology of Wesley. As Thomas Langford, an American Wesley scholar,

---

41 Richard Watson, *The Life of the Rev John Wesley A.M.*, John Mason, fourth ed. 1835, first ed. 1831.

42 Richard Watson, *Observations on Southey's "Life of Wesley"*, T. Blanchard, 1820, p. 2.

43 Watson, *Observations*, p. 52.

44 Watson, *The Life of the Rev. John Wesley, A. M.*, p. 63.

45 Watson, *The Life of the Rev. John Wesley, A. M.*, p. 199.

46 See, for example, Watson, *Observations*, p. 55.

comments '[Richard Watson] particularly stressed the deductive use of Scripture and vigorously defended a high doctrine of scriptural inerrancy.'[47]

Thomas Langford also comments '[Watson] insisted that all his arguments were based on experience; the only saving knowledge we have of God and the world.'[48] However, Langford makes it clear that experience is the method by which Watson came to understand the Bible, which was his supreme authority, and that he saw this in Wesley's works.

Watson did refer to the influence of their family on the Wesley boys in the words

> The advantage of such a parentage to the Wesleys was great. From their earliest years they had an example, in their father, of all that could render a clergyman respectable and influential, and in the mother, there was a sanctified wisdom, a masculine understanding, and an acquired knowledge, which they regarded with just deference after they became men and scholars.[49]

Altogether apart from what, today, would be seen as arrogant sexism in the comment, it is clear that Watson carried the hagiography to include the whole family. Referring to Wesley's intention in 1725 to take deacon's orders, Watson wrote 'His mother's admirable letters were among the principal means, under God, of producing that still more decided change in his views which soon afterwards began to display itself.'[50] Watson saw the influence of family and the authority of scripture, but did not indicate how Wesley came to the particular interpretation of scripture that was so important to him.

Watson's disregard of Wesley's Anglican allegiance is evident in his reference to the Conferences of 1744, 1745, 1746 and 1747 and the setting apart of Wesley's preachers with the words 'Here he [Wesley] took his stand, and he proceeded to call forth Preachers, and set them apart or ordained them to the sacred office.'[51] This is evidence that Watson did not present the Anglican John Wesley in the way that certain other, non-Wesleyan, authors had done. No loyal Anglican would have regarded the actions as ordination. However, in a footnote he recognised that this predated the later ordinations and that some would object to the use of the term at this time. Wesley would certainly not have used that language.

---

47 Thomas A. Langford, *Practical Divinity: Theology in the Wesleyan Tradition,* Abingdon Press, 1984, p. 60.
48 Langford, *Practical Divinity*, p. 62.
49 Watson, *The Life of the Rev. John Wesley, A. M.*, p. 3.
50 Watson, *The Life of the Rev. John Wesley, A. M.*, p. 6.
51 Watson, *The Life of the Rev. John Wesley, A. M.*, p. 159.

A work of rather different character was that of the Methodist scholar Adam Clarke, three times President of the Wesleyan Conference.[52] His book created the impression of a very holy, devout and honourable family, giving birth to children of great virtue. It was not a critical work, although it showed evidence of considerable scholarship. In Clarke, hagiography extended to the whole Wesley family 'Such a family I have never heard of, or known; nor since the days of Abraham and Sarah, and Joseph and Mary of Nazareth, has there ever been a family to which the human race has been more indebted.'[53] He does not define what he means by scriptural, but, by this time, it was assumed that Wesley was Bible-based with a correct understanding of scripture. This is not the language of critical scholarship.

Referring to the revival of religion in which Wesley was involved, Clarke used the phrase 'Rev. John Wesley and that great revival of Scriptural Christianity which it has pleased the world to call Methodism, and the subjects of which it terms Methodists.'[54] Langford notes that Clarke was a biblical scholar and comments 'He [Clarke] assumed that the scriptures provide a complete interpretation of the nature and work of God.'[55] Clarke, no doubt, saw his own reliance on the authority of the Bible as reflecting what he understood of Wesley.

Clearly by the late eighteen-twenties a picture was prevalent of John Wesley as a saintly biblically-based Arminian and this picture, sometimes deliberately, obscured other elements such as the human frailties of Wesley and the context of the High-Church Anglicanism which influenced his interpretation of the Bible. Those not directly concerned with Methodism as an independent Church were, at times, more critical of Wesley and, not surprisingly, saw Anglicanism as a major influence on his scriptural interpretation. The needs of Methodism as it struggled to its feet were such that it should have a Bible-based founder not dependant on the influence of any other church. Its authors so depicted Wesley.

Late Nineteenth Century Works

In 1850 Rev. Orlando Thomas Dobbin, Irish clergyman and author wrote *Wesley the Worthy and Wesley the Catholic*, in which he gave fulsome praise but wrote '[Wesley] never contemplated the formation of a sect,

---

52 Adam Clarke, *Memoirs of the Wesley Family*, R.J. Kershaw, 1823, commissioned by the Conference of 1821. Clarke produced a work which gave biographical details of many of Wesley's ancestors on both his father's and mother's side, with notes on his uncle Matthew, his parents, his brothers and sisters.
53 Clarke, *Memoirs of the Wesley Family*, p. 543.
54 Clarke, *Memoirs of the Wesley Family*, p. x.
55 Langford, *Practical Divinity*, p. 55.

much less of an enemy or rival to the Church of England.'[56] The second part of the work, written by Charles Adams, of the Methodist Episcopal Church, contains the sentence 'He loved the Church of England much, but he loved the Holy Catholic Church more.'[57]

Isaac Taylor, not in the mainstream Wesleyan tradition,[58] laid stress on the importance of experience in the words 'As the FIRST element of that revival which Methodism so extensively effected, we have thus alleged to be an awakening of the dormant religious consciousness, or innate sense of our relationship to God, the righteous Judge.'[59] As a non-Wesleyan he made little reference to Wesley as a biblically-based person. He did describe Methodist preachers as 'men so imperfectly educated, and so slenderly furnished with biblical knowledge as most of his preachers were.'[60] Again some veneration for the founder of Methodism is obvious in this work, although Taylor writes from the viewpoint of a later generation with less theological argument than some of the earlier biographers. He is of note here for the fact that he provoked a very defensive reply from within mainstream Wesleyan Methodism.

This response came from George Smith in 1857.[61] Smith's work was also critical of Southey. Arguing against Taylor that Aldersgate did represent Wesley's conversion experience he wrote

> Wesley, from a prayerful and diligent study of the scriptures, regarded himself as being in a state of spiritual darkness and bondage; and held that he was then "born again," "renewed in the spirit of his mind," and brought into "the glorious liberty of the children of God." And fifty years of subsequent godly experience confirmed him in that judgement.[62]

In continuing the veneration for Wesley and arguing against the work of Taylor, it is of note that Smith made reference to the scriptures. His references to the subsequent fifty years of Wesley's life do not take account of Wesley's own later reassessment of the Aldersgate experience to which more attention will be given in Chapter 4. Earlier, in Smith's account of events leading up to Aldersgate, he made the point 'He [Wesley] knows that he is not prepared for heaven. Is this statement compatible with the

---

56   Orlando Thomas Dobbin, *Wesley the Worthy and Wesley the Catholic* Ward & Co., 1850, p. 77.
57   Dobbin, *Wesley the Worthy and Wesley the Catholic*, p. 101.
58   Isaac Taylor, *Wesley and Methodism*, Brown, Green and Longmans, 1851.
59   Taylor, *Wesley and Methodism*, p. 155.
60   Taylor, *Wesley and Methodism*, p. 238.
61   George Smith, *History of Methodism*, Vol. 1, Wesley and his Times, Longman Green, Longman and Roberts, fourth ed. 1863, Preface to first ed. dated 1857.
62   Smith, *Wesley and his Times*, p. 590.

doctrines of the New Testament? Or is it a fit subject for ridicule and sarcasm?'[63] Smith thought that he, unlike Taylor, knew the answers.

Smith stated that he was prepared to acknowledge, although he did not give examples, that Wesley did have faults but he objected to Taylor's reference to Wesley's great defect in the words 'He was, we are told, "not so gifted with the reflective facilities, that a comprehensive grasp of human nature could have been possible to him."'[64] Smith would not accept this criticism, writing dismissively of Taylor. This is a good illustration of the way in which the mainstream Wesleyan writers were very defensive against any non-Wesleyan author's attempt to comment critically about Wesley. The influence of the Church of England on Wesley was disregarded even as the influence of Aldersgate was strongly argued. The influence of Bible and experience were emphasised and the independence of Methodism from the established Church was stressed.

Six years after Smith's work appeared, Abel Stevens published his major work *The History of the Religious Movement of the Eighteenth Century Called Methodism Considered in its Different Denominational Forms, and in its General Relation to Protestantism.*[65] The preface to the 1878 edition makes it clear that Stevens wrote from within the Wesleyan tradition and that he did not approve of what he saw as the bias of Southey's work. A later version of this work by Stevens was *The Illustrated History of Methodism, Being an Account of the Wesleys, their Contemporaries and their Times.*[66] In this he wrote 'Methodism came forth from the gates of Oxford [...] to recall the masses to their bibles.'[67] Although, Stevens noted 'He [Wesley] professed to adhere faithfully to the fundamentals of the Church of England,'[68] Stevens continued relating the story of Wesley in the way largely laid down by his Wesleyan predecessors.

In 1865 Robert Brown, a Methodist minister, gave a lecture "on behalf of the funds of a new Wesleyan Chapel."[69] Having referred to the parental discipline in Epworth, he continued:

---

63   Smith, *Wesley and his Times*, p. 129.
64   Smith, *Wesley and his Times*, p. 604, quoting *Wesley and Methodism*, p. 81. The place where Smith allows that Wesley may have had (limited) failings is on page 606.
65   Abel Stevens, *The History of the Religious Movement of the Eighteenth Century Called Methodism Considered in its Different Denominational Forms, and in its General Relation to Protestantism*, John Willey and Co., 3 Vols. 1863-5, also published by Conference Office, 1878.
66   The copy in the Manchester John Rylands Library is undated, but takes the story to 1839. The publisher was James Sangster and Co. This work contains the bulk of the earlier book and is clearly a further edition of it with a new title.
67   Stevens, *The Illuminated History of Methodism*, Vol. 1, pp. 14-5.
68   Stevens, *The Illuminated History of Methodism*, Vol. 2, p. 147.
69   Robert Brown, *John Wesley's Theology*, Jackson, Walford and Hodder, 1865.

> Accordingly, when Wesley was brought to the study of God's book, he received it
> not as a theory of speculative doctrine, but as life-inspiring; and the life thus
> inspired threw itself back, in a sublime reaction, upon the study of the book.[70]

In a footnote he assured the reader that this did not exclude moderate
Calvinism. This was in response to his comment, referring to Susanna
Wesley 'Do not startle at the discovery that this mother in Israel presumed
to make use of the thoughts of her own conscience, in the critical
examination of God's holy word.' Thus Brown allowed some space for
reason, but his main interest was in what he termed conscience, writing 'It
is a Divine inspiration, the voice of God within us, the law written upon the
heart.'[71] Brown continued the tradition of describing Wesley as a Bible-
based man, but allowing place for reason and experience.

Unfortunately Brown did not discuss the influences on Wesley's
interpretation of the Bible but simply assumed that there was only one right
interpretation and that Wesley understood it.

Julia Wedgwood, daughter of Josiah Wedgwood and sister of the mother
of Charles Darwin, was not herself in the Wesleyan tradition. She relied on
earlier authorities and wrote the influential *John Wesley and the
Evangelical Reaction of the Eighteenth Century* in 1870.[72] She made
comment that 'Wesley's attachment to the Church [of England] did not
wear out.'[73] This is of note inasmuch as there was considerable debate on
the relationship between the Wesleyan Methodist Church and the Church of
England at this time, set in the context of the Anglo-Catholic revival. The
Wesleyan Conference Office later published a response to Wedgwood
written by a Mrs Coslett.[74]

R. Denny Urlin of the Middle Temple, Barrister, writing from an
Anglican perspective in *John Wesley's Place in Church History*,[75]
acknowledged the value of the works of Whitehead, Southey and Watson,
although he had some reservations about the accuracy of Watson,
particularly in his account of the break with the Church of England. The
Appendix Note C refers to Wesley's phrase 'homo unius libri' and argues
that it is impossible to be a man of one book. He referred specifically to
Wesley's use of the Church fathers and his interest in the scientific

---

70   Brown, *John Wesley's Theology*, p. 9.
71   Brown, *John Wesley's Theology*, p. 7.
72   Julia Wedgwood, *John Wesley and the Evangelical Reaction of the Eighteenth
      Century*, Macmillan and Co., 1870.
73   Wedgwood, *John Wesley and the Evangelical Reaction of the Eighteenth Century*,
      p. 382.
74   Mrs Coslett (Edith Waddy), *The Father of Methodism - A Sketch of the Life and
      Labours of the Rev John Wesley, M.A.*, Wesleyan Conference Office, second ed.
      1879.
75   R. Denny Urlin, *John Wesley's Place in Church History*, Rivington, 1870.

knowledge of his day. He also commented that Henry Moore's remaining trustee did not allow access to Moore's papers including the Wesley material.

Urlin also wrote a biography of Wesley.[76] It is written from a sympathetic Anglican point of view. It is of note because he has appendices on 'The Wesley Manuscripts,' and 'Wesley's Journals.' He stressed the need for access to the primary sources and traced their history subsequent to 1791, regretting his inability to gain access to them. This is further evidence of Wesleyan suppression of primary materials.

Luke Tyerman's three-volume *The Life and Times of John Wesley*[77] became a recognised and standard work from 1871 onwards. Tyerman was a prominent and influential minister and scholar in the Wesleyan Methodist Church. On the last page he concluded:

> His [Wesley's] physique, his genius, his wit, his penetration, his judgement, his memory, his diligence, his religion, his conversation, his courteousness, his manners, and his dress - made him as perfect as we ever expect man to be on this side of heaven.[78]

Typical of Tyerman's comments was that on Wesley's claim to be a man of one book in the preface to the 1746 edition of *Sermons for Several Occasions*:

> Wesley went to the only point of pure knowledge existing, and deduced his creed, not from Böhler's notions, but from the Book of God. His belief was thus founded upon a rock, and he felt it so. He declares, that his mind is open to conviction; but, at the same time, he was conscious that he had, not only human, but divine authority for what he taught.[79]

It is clear that for Tyerman Wesley was Bible-based. Experience arose from his understanding of scripture. At the same time the assumption was that scripture's meaning was clear and Wesley's interpretation correct. What was not discussed was how Wesley came to believe that the Bible taught the things that he understood it to teach.

Tyerman gave prominence to the Aldersgate experience with the comment:

> For ten years he [Wesley] had believed in Christ, but never believed as he did now. He had been intensely pious; but now he possessed power over himself and

---

76   R. Denny Urlin, *The Churchman's Life of Wesley*, SPCK, New Edition Revised and Corrected, undated but published circa 1885.

77   L. Tyerman *The Life and Times of John Wesley*, Hodder and Stoughton, sixth ed. 1890. The first edition was published in 1871.

78   Tyerman. *The Life and Times of John Wesley*, Vol. 3, p. 660.

79   Tyerman, *The Life and Times of John Wesley*, Vol. 1, p. 532.

sin which he had not possessed before. He had practised religion; but now he experienced its bliss [...] There was sunshine in his soul which lit up his face, and which turned the severe ascetic, for a season at least, into a joyful saint.[80]

Despite the undoubted value of Tyerman's work, the sometimes uncritical emphasis on the biblical and evangelical Wesley is plain for all to see.

It is reasonable to surmise that the growth of the influence of the Anglo-Catholic movement in the Church of England led to a reaction against the Established Church within Methodism. Many Wesleyan scholars, rejecting the nineteenth-century High-Churchmanship, may have wrongly assumed that eighteenth-century High-Church Anglicanism was similar and wished to distance their founder from it. Thus James H. Rigg (1821-1909), a leading Wesleyan and one-time principal of Westminster College, was strongly opposed to Anglo-Catholicism. In his work *The Churchmanship of John Wesley, and the Relations of Wesleyan Methodism to the Church of England*,[81] he acknowledged the work of Wedgwood as being outside Methodism but sympathetic towards it.[82] However, his main concern was to separate Wesley and Methodism from High-Church Anglicanism. He wrote of Wesley's Aldersgate experience 'Here ended really his High Church stage of life.'[83] His view is clearly expressed in the words 'I have no hesitation [...] in saying that there is not the remotest possibility of the Wesleyan Methodist Church ever being absorbed in the Church of England.'[84]

Rigg appreciated some aspects of prayer-book Anglicanism and was Bible-based in his theology, wanting to see this reflected in the life of Wesley.

H.W. Houldon had been engaged in a controversy with Rigg in the correspondence columns of the Guardian Newspaper in 1868-9. It has been surmised that he was the author of the anonymous 'An Old Methodist,' *John Wesley in Company with High Church Men*.[85] He commented 'John Wesley was, and ever remained - his own Words being witness - a High Churchman.'[86] That the dispute over the relationship between Wesleyanism and the Church of England was not over is also evidenced by Frederick Hockin of St John's College Cambridge writing as an Anglican. *John*

80 Tyerman, *The Life and Times of John Wesley*, Vol. 1, p. 180.
81 James H. Rigg, *The Churchmanship of John Wesley, and the Relations of Wesleyan Methodism to the Church of England*, Wesleyan Conference Office, 1878.
82 Rigg, *The Churchmanship of John Wesley*, p. 33.
83 Rigg, *The Churchmanship of John Wesley*, p. 38.
84 Rigg, *The Churchmanship of John Wesley*, p. 7.
85 Anon., *John Wesley in Company with High Church Men*, Church Press Company, 1870.
86 Anon., *John Wesley in Company with High Church Men*, p. vi.

Wesley and Modern Methodism,[87] was published to dispute the work of Rigg.

By the latter part of the century the aura surrounding the name of Wesley within Methodism was considerable but it is clear that outside the Wesleyan Methodist Church there was awareness that the popular image of him had been presented uncritically.

John Telford was a leading Wesleyan of his day and his biography of Wesley was published in 1886.[88] It may be taken as typical of the popular scholarly approach to Wesley's life at that time. Telford, son-in-law of James Rigg, accepted the traditional view of the scriptural basis of Wesley's thinking supplemented by the influence of experience. Telford drew upon the standard biographies available to him and was aware of Wesley's Journal, letters and other works. However, it is a triumphalist work in which Wesley is depicted in the most glowing terms. He related the story of the conversations with Peter Böhler in 1738 as illustrative of this.[89] The reader is prepared for this even in the Introduction where he wrote 'Suggestions and criticisms have been carefully weighed, and no pains spared to render the portrait of England's chief evangelist as lifelike as possible. Every day adds to the reputation of John Wesley.'[90]

He also referred to the four volumes of sermons published by Wesley as the doctrinal standards for his preachers and in particular to the preface where he claimed to be homo unius libri.[91] This claim Telford accepted without question.[92] By the end of the nineteenth century, within Wesleyan scholarship, the biblical basis of Wesley's teaching was unquestioned. Telford in almost every instance depicted Wesley as being in the right but without examining the point critically. Typical is the reference to the Moravian controversy and the disturbances in the Fetter Lane society 'The Wesleys were closely associated with it until the excesses of the Moravian teachers compelled them to withdraw.'[93]

The assumption was that Wesley was right and, if there were disputes, particularly in biblical interpretation, those who differed must have been wrong. Telford's work has to be used with some caution, which is of added significance when it is remembered that Telford's eight volume edition of

---

87 Frederick Hockin, *John Wesley and Modern Methodism*, Rivington, 1887.

88 John Telford, *John Wesley Into all the World*, Ambassador, 1999, Ambassador Classic Biographies, a reproduction of the 1902 edition of Telford's biography of John Wesley. The first edition was dated 1886.

89 Telford, *John Wesley*, p. 98.

90 Telford, Introduction to *John Wesley* - page not numbered.

91 Telford, *John Wesley*, p. 325.

92 See Telford, *John Wesley*, pp. 324-6, where he quotes extensively from Wesley's Preface to the Sermons with approval.

93 Telford, *John Wesley*, p. 99.

Wesley's letters became the standard reference work during the earlier part of the twentieth century.

A hundred years after Wesley's death, J.H. Overton's *John Wesley* was published.[94] Overton, an Anglican priest, was appreciative of Wesley's life and work but gave a somewhat different account from that of the mainstream Wesleyan authors. However, he continued in the tradition that saw a biblical basis to Wesley's thought with the comment:

> By this standard of holy scripture as interpreted by his own branch of the Church, he was not only prepared to abide in general terms but was quite ready to submit every one of his tenets to be tried by this touch stone.[95]

Overton recognised that Wesley's biblical interpretation was that of an Anglican.[96] However, Overton had difficulty in reconciling the ordinations of certain of Wesley's preachers in later life, and suggested that Wesley did so reluctantly and under great pressure. He also shrewdly commented 'He [Wesley] carried Epworth about with him to the end of his life.'[97]

This is a convenient point at which to conclude the summary of nineteenth century literature on Wesley. John C. Bowmer makes a valid comment:

> The nineteenth century presentation of Wesley, which is notably different in emphasis from that of Dr Whitehead and Henry Moore, both of whom were personal friends and biographers of Wesley, is no doubt due to the fact that Methodism of the mid and late nineteenth century was reacting to the Oxford movement in such a way that it both failed to appreciate the quickness of movement which was about in the Anglican Church and also minimised the Eucharistic worship of its own.[98]

However, it is to be noted that the continuing influence within the Wesleyan tradition was that of Telford rather than Overton.

Some Examples of Twentieth-Century Wesley Scholarship

By early in the twentieth century modern critical approaches to the Bible were becoming accepted by many Methodist biblical scholars. However, it is clear that the influence of the earlier biographical works on Wesley continued to dominate Methodist scholarship which repeated without

---

94   J.H. Overton, *John Wesley*, Methuen and Co., 1891.
95   Overton, *John Wesley*, p. 71.
96   See Overton, *John Wesley*, pp. 196-206.
97   Overton, *John Wesley*, p. 179.
98   John C. Bowmer, *The Sacrament of the Lord's Supper in Early Methodism*, Dacre Press, 1951, p. ix.

question much of the work of earlier mainstream Wesleyan writers. Illustrative of the influence of traditional Wesley scholarship is the reaction that greeted the publication of Sir Arthur Quiller-Couch's novel, *Hetty Wesley*.[99] The 1928 edition contains a preface to the 1908 edition which makes the point:

> Now the trouble with my Wesleyan critics is not that they consent to dismiss my book as "caricaturing" the Wesley family, and the elder Samuel in particular, but the language in which they condemn it proves that they have never so much looked the facts in the face. Worse, it raises a suspicion that they do not face the facts because they do not dare.[100]

The book was based on considerable research telling the story of a very human family which contrasted with the earlier hagiography. Quiller-Couch captured the atmosphere of an Anglican family with the strong Anglican influences on John Wesley.

It will perhaps be helpful to note and discuss some further examples of the continuing influence of earlier scholarship, beginning with Richard Green. In 1905, he quoted approvingly Wesley's words on Easter Day 1789 in Ireland, writing 'With this in view I have uniformly gone on for fifty years, never varying from the doctrine of the Church at all; nor from her discipline, not of choice, but of necessity.'[101] Green was indebted to Whitehead, Coke, Moore and Tyerman.

W.H. Fitchett was an Australian Methodist minister who wrote works on Methodism and also on the British Empire. Writing a year later than Green he echoed the traditional Wesleyan view on Wesley and the Bible in the words 'Now Methodism is committed to no special theory as to the inspiration of Scripture; but it accepts the Bible as the one source of divine knowledge and the supreme test of theology.'[102] Referring to the controversy over Wesley's Anglican allegiance, Fitchett wrote

> Who studies, in a word, this the most keenly criticised aspect of Wesley's work, finds in it the picture of a man who with an obstinate High Church bias drawing him in one direction, a bias due to birth and training and temperament; whilst, step by step led by Providence and compelled by facts, he moves on a path which leads to quite another goal, a goal undesired but not wholly unseen.[103]

Fitchett also stressed the Moravian influence on Wesley.

---

99   Sir Arthur Quiller-Couch, *Hetty Wesley*, J. M. Dent & Co., first ed. 1903.
100 Quiller-Couch, *Hetty Wesley*, p. viii.
101 Richard Green, *John Wesley Evangelist*, Religious Tract Society, 1905, p. 520.
102 W.H. Fitchett, *Wesley and His Century: A Study in Spiritual Forces*, Smith, Elder and Co., 1906, p. 433.
103 Fitchett, *Wesley and his Century*, p. 469.

John S. Simon's scholarly five-volume work refers to the primary sources, but is still more strongly influenced by the nineteenth-century biographies.[104] His work was triumphalist, depicting Wesley planning for the future. Thus he wrote 'In this volume I watch him [John Wesley] as he lays the foundations of the Methodist Church. They were so carefully and securely laid that, up to the present time, they have determined the character of the building erected on them.[105]

Simon acknowledged Wesley's Anglicanism, arguing:

> We see that he [John Wesley] was a firm believer in the doctrines of the Church of England which related to the salvation of the individual. Those doctrines were ignored by the clergy and their congregations. They were embedded in the articles and homilies, but Wesley awoke them from their slumber, and, in the religious societies and in the open-air assemblies, they once more made their great appeals to the conscience of Englishmen.[106]

However, Simon then commented 'If we compare the Wesley of the Holy Club and the Wesley of Georgia with the Wesley of 1739 we are almost startled at the contrast. The punctilious High Churchman can scarcely be recognised.' Simon may have judged eighteenth-century high-churchmanship in the light of nineteenth-century high-churchmanship. Certainly, under the influence of earlier Wesley scholarship, he was not prepared to accept that Wesley was anything other than an evangelical low churchman.

Furthermore, referring to Wesley's relationship with Clayton, the non-juror and former member of the Holy Club, Simon comments 'If Wesley had placed himself under the control of the Manchester High Churchmen the Methodist revival would have been impossible.'[107] For Simon, Aldersgate 1738 was noteworthy as the time of Wesley's conversion, but also something more, writing 'The dawn of a great reformation was touching the skies.'[108]

A little later Maldwyn Edwards wrote *John Wesley and the Eighteenth Century*.[109] He repeated without detailed argument the traditional view of Wesley with the words 'He was [...] a High Churchman, but his Toryism

---

104 John S. Simon, *John Wesley and the Religious Societies*, 1921, *John Wesley and the Methodist Societies*, 1923, *John Wesley and the Advance of Methodism*, 1925, *John Wesley The Master Builder*, 1927, *John Wesley the Last Phase*, 1934, all published by Epworth Press.
105 Simon, *John Wesley and the Methodist Societies*, Preface, without a page number.
106 Simon, *John Wesley and the Religious Societies*, p. 333.
107 Simon, *John Wesley and the Religious Societies*, p. 189.
108 Simon, *John Wesley and the Religious Societies*, p. 193.
109 Maldwyn Edwards, *John Wesley and the Eighteenth Century*. Epworth Press, 1933, revised ed. 1955.

remained unchanged, and his Churchmanship was greatly modified in the course of his life.'[110] On this and the following page Edwards argued that Wesley's life's work modified his churchmanship but that socially and politically he remained in the same position throughout his days. Edwards appeared quite happy to criticise Wesley's political and social views, but less happy to criticise his theological and ecclesiastical stance.

The effusive attitude is also apparent in C.E. Vulliamy's work. This is well illustrated in the comment:

> No purely formal analysis can bring to a reader's mind the true picture of John Wesley. His bright serenity, his godliness and courage are easily perceived. The glowing faith, which gave such peculiar charm to his face in old age, can be described in simple terms as the sign of Christian love and Christian practice. But no simple terms can reveal the deeper things of the spirit, or disclose the source of that abounding piety which makes a man at once so truly human and so truly divine. Wesley, above all, was a man of God, striving to reach nothing short of perfection, yet humble and always perceiving clearly the distance between desire and attainment.'[111]

The influence of earlier writers is still evident 'The men who knew him and wrote about him in his later life - Coke, Moore, Whitehead, Hampson and Clarke - were not men with literary skill, and they were chiefly concerned with a purely objective account of Methodism.'[112] It is of note that he includes Whitehead and Hampson in this list. This work, however, is not of great help in tracing the influences that fashioned the life and beliefs of Wesley.

In 1964 V.H.H. Green[113] presented a more human Wesley than some earlier works, especially with reference to his relationships with his female friends such as Sophy Hopkey, Grace Murray and Molly Vazeille who became Wesley's wife. Additionally Green makes the comment:

> The confluence of heredity, the educational religious training to which he [Wesley] was submitted, the particular influences to which he was subjected at Oxford, contributed to fashion a young man who was to be very much out of the ordinary.[114]

This represents some slight move in the direction of a consideration of the sources which were an influence on Wesley's life. Green also made the observation that:

---

110 Maldwyn Edwards, *John Wesley and the Eighteenth Century*, p. 15.
111 C.E. Vulliamy, *John Wesley*, Epworth Press, 1931, p. 349.
112 Vulliamy, *John Wesley*, p. 350.
113 V.H.H. Green, *John Wesley*, Thomas Nelson & Co., 1964.
114 Green, *John Wesley*, p. 9.

[Wesley] remained a faithful member of the church in which he had been brought up and ordained, and such changes as he envisaged were inspired by his understanding of the primitive church of apostolic times. [...] Personally credulous and indeed superstitious, his approach to the scriptures and the problems that they were beginning to represent in more acute fashion than in earlier periods was cautious and conservative. He was basically as suspicious of innovation in religion as he was in everything else.[115]

The image of the Bible-based person is maintained but some recognition is given of the other influences that helped develop Wesley's thought.

The older views are also reflected in the words of A. Skevington Wood, a popular Methodist preacher and writer of his time, 'Wesley was a Biblical preacher par excellence. [...] Wesley's message was taken from the authoritative record of salvation-history to be found in the pages of holy writ.'[116] For Wood, critical examination of Wesley's works was limited, in the sense that the utmost respect had to be shown to the man and his teaching, which was understood to be Bible-based.

In 1965 Rupert Davies wrote

In a larger historical perspective we can of course say that Wesley repeats with modifications the Protestant interpretation of Scripture, and that this, even if we ourselves believe it to be in principle the right one, is in the last resort only one of several possible interpretations.[117]

This, however, is only stated by Davies in order to accept the fact that Wesley was influenced by Luther, Calvin and others. It falls far short of a full analysis of the complex influences that led him to read the Bible as he did.

Conclusions Concerning the Influence of Earlier Wesley Biographies

In this chapter it has been argued that the question of the authorities accepted by John Wesley has often been treated quite superficially. There is a fundamental difference between, on the one hand, the source and cause of belief in a doctrine, and, on the other hand, that which confirms, supports or develops that belief. Here it is being contended that many Wesley scholars have dealt with the second alternative but then have used their conclusions as though they were the answer to the questions raised by the first. It may be noted, for example, that Henry Rack makes reference to the influence of Lord Peter King and Bishop Stillingfleet on Wesley's thinking about the

---

115 Green, *John Wesley*, pp. 154-5.
116 A. Skevington Wood, *The Burning Heart*, The Paternoster Press, 1967, p. 209.
117 Rupert Davies, 'The People Called Methodist: I. "Our Doctrines,"' in *A History of the Methodist Church in Great Britain*, Vol. 1, 1965, p. 148.

primitive church and the possibility that presbyters and bishops were in essence of the same order.

Rack makes a pertinent comment:

> But it is also very common for him [Wesley] to use respectable 'authorities' to fortify or justify positions he wished to hold for other reasons; or simply as apologies for actions he had been forced to take by other circumstances. He always read his authorities very selectively to support what he wished to do or thought ought to be done.' [118]

The major contention in this study is that Wesley's interpretation of the Bible was influenced throughout his life by his High-Church Arminian Anglican roots and that this has not received the notice that it should in most earlier, and many later, works on his life.

A further point implicit in most of the biographies of Wesley in the mainstream Wesleyan tradition, which is not emphasised by the authors, is that a major controversial period of Wesley's life was in the earlier years following his Aldersgate experience in 1738, and that many of his helpers, assistants and colleagues of those years either parted company with him or predeceased him. In his later years Wesley became a national and more popularly venerated figure, surrounded by younger assistants of his own selection and it was these later followers of Wesley who interpreted Wesley's works, repeating what they knew of the person who was to them both hero and saint.

Thus there was a tradition built up that saw no fault in Wesley and which certainly did not explore at any great depth the influences that made him the person that he was or that led him to the beliefs which he propounded in his sermons, Journals, and correspondence. It is therefore clear that in various ways writers from the early nineteenth century onwards have repeated views which regard Wesley's major authority as being in scripture, although they do not explore precisely what it means to make such a statement. There can be no doubt that was the impression given through Wesley's works, but that does not necessarily indicate the way in which Wesley came to his views and it remains to be seen what were the sources of the beliefs he held. What made him think as he did?

The next chapter will explore some newer approaches to the way in which Wesley's interpretation and use of the Bible is to be understood. Note will also be taken of what American Wesley scholars have come to describe as the Wesleyan Quadrilateral. A brief review will also be given of

---

118 Rack, *Reasonable Enthusiast, John Wesley and the Rise of Methodism*, p. 292.

the Wesley works published in 2002 and 2003 to commemorate the tercentenary of Wesley's birth and subsequently.

CHAPTER 2

Wesley Scholarship in the Late Twentieth and Early Twenty-First Centuries

Modern Wesley Scholarship

In 1988 Richard P. Heitzenrater lamented the lack of scholarly works on both John and Charles Wesley,[1] noting that even then the recent works on the Wesleys showed little evidence of full critical and historical research because of their veneration for the founder of Methodism. Heitzenrater is one of the leading Wesley scholars whose works have appeared in the late twentieth century.[2]

Illustrations of the earlier disregard for scholarly criticism in the biographies of Wesley were given in Chapter 1 but evidence that it still continued is found in, for example, the almost uncritical veneration of Wesley in the chapter 'John Wesley' by Maldwyn Edwards in *A History of the Methodist Church in Great Britain*, volume 1.[3] This is the more noteworthy because the work was authorised by the Methodist Conference in Great Britain.

The argument here is that some newer approaches became evident from the mid-twentieth century onwards. It was only from that time onwards that there was a serious attempt to get behind both the hagiography evident in the nineteenth century and Wesley's own public image. However, little, if any, research has taken place into Wesley as a reader of the Bible. Only more recently has there been some acknowledgement of work still to be done in this area. This scholarship is briefly examined here.

Note is also taken of the work of American Wesley scholars on what they term the Wesley Quadrilateral. This offers some help in understanding

---

1   See Chapter 11, 'John Wesley and the Historian's Task', Richard P. Heitzenrater in *Mirror and Memory, Reflections on Early Methodism*, Kingswood Books, Abingdon Press, 1989.

2   See, for example, Richard P. Heitzenrater, *Wesley and the People Called Methodist, Abingdon Press*, 1995. An earlier work of Heitzenrater was *The Elusive Mr Wesley*, Vols. 1 and 2, Abingdon Press, 1984.

3   Maldwyn Edwards, *A History of the Methodist Church in Great Britain*, volume 1, ed. Rupert Davies and Gordon Rupp, 1965.

the influences behind Wesley's biblical interpretation and the place of scripture as his primary theological authority, but it is open to further critical comment, as will be illustrated. It is contended that even now Wesley scholarship shows only limited appreciation of the fact that Wesley read the Bible as an eighteenth-century High-Church Arminian Anglican. The recent insights of Reader-Response criticism have only rarely been used. Note is also made of works published in 2002-3 and subsequently in order to mark the tercentenary of Wesley's birth.

A New Approach to the Subject in Works about Wesley

In 1946 William R. Cannon, Dean of the Chandler School of Theology at Emory University, made special reference to the doctrine of justification,[4] writing, '[Wesley] was possessed of one central truth, that man is justified by faith and perfected in love.'[5] Cannon saw Wesley's work as Bible-based: 'The Wesleyan Revival ignored the rationalistic controversy about religion; its leaders felt little could be accomplished through argument; they preferred the plain preaching of the Bible.'[6] This leaves unanswered the question of what the plain meaning of the Bible may be. However, Cannon looked deeper for the sources of Wesley's beliefs, partly into Wesley's own words, writing:

> In truth, a man is a part of all that he has met, and, if at the close of the year 1789 John Wesley was constrained to write, "From a child I was taught to love and reverence the Scriptures ... to esteem the primitive Fathers ... and next after the primitive church to esteem our own the Church of England, as that most scriptural church in the world," is it not reasonable for us to expect to find some influence emerging from Wesley's home and from his church also leaving their traces on his doctrine of justification?[7]

Here at last within the Methodist tradition is recognition of some of the complex influences that fashioned the person and beliefs of Wesley and led him to read the Bible in the way he did.

Cannon also made the point that '[Wesley] was given a taste of the Prayer Book and the Scriptures, but after he had tasted them he was forced to take and retain just as large portions of them as his memory could bear.'[8] Although, understandably enough at that time, there was no reference to Reader-Response criticism, there was acknowledgement that Wesley

---

4   William R. Cannon, *The Theology of John Wesley*, Abingdon Press, 1946
5   Cannon, *The Theology of John Wesley*, p. 7.
6   Cannon, *The Theology of John Wesley*, p. 21.
7   Cannon, *The Theology of John Wesley*, p. 30. The reference is to Wesley's *Farther Thoughts on Separation from the Church of England.*
8   Cannon, *The Theology of John Wesley*, p. 50.

interpreted the Bible through non-biblical sources. Cannon also examined the influence on Wesley of Jeremy Taylor and Thomas à Kempis in 1725 and, two years later, of William Law.[9] He commented, concerning the Aldersgate experience of 1738, 'There he learned for the first time the true meaning of justification by faith.'[10]

Cannon acknowledged the Anglican influence on Wesley's biblical interpretation more than some other Wesley scholars. Cannon also made the point that 'Religion is built on the Bible, and reason is that which enables man to understand the Bible, to grasp its statement of the truths concerning God and his relation to the universe, "and to comprehend his method of dealing with the children of men."'[11] Cannon has not generally been recognised as opening up the way for the debate on the Wesleyan Quadrilateral that was to follow some years later. All the credit has normally be given to Albert Outler.

Note must be taken of the influential work of Henry Rack in his major work, *Reasonable Enthusiast*. This is both scholarly and free from the earlier hagiographic approach.

He comments, for example,

> The problem with John Wesley is not the lack of evidence or even of research on many aspects of his career. It is rather the need to penetrate the Wesley legend created by his followers and biographers and the smoke-screen which Wesley himself, consciously or unconsciously, created by his Journals and other portrayals of himself and his movement. But it is also partly the problem of the tendency of writers on Wesley to concentrate too exclusively on his personal history, on Methodism to the exclusion of the larger religious movement of which he was a part, and on both of these without sufficient attention to the changing society within which their fate was worked out.[12]

Rack's work does consider the political, social and religious influences on Wesley and the movement he established. First published in 1989, it is an outstanding work within British Wesley scholarship based on many years of detailed research. Rack is a historian and not a biblical scholar. He is the first British Wesley biographer to achieve a proper distance from his subject and freedom from the earlier hagiographic approach. His work represents a watershed in British Wesley scholarship and the extent to which it is quoted in the later chapters of this book is some acknowledgement of that fact. The title *Reasonable Enthusiast* indicates that Rack acknowledged that Wesley used reason and experience in his biblical interpretation and that he was not just a man of the Bible.

---

9   Cannon, *The Theology of John Wesley*, pp. 54-60.
10 Cannon, *The Theology of John Wesley*, p. 68.
11 Cannon, *The Theology of John Wesley*, p. 159, quoting Wesley's sermon LXX.
12 Rack, *Reasonable Enthusiast*, p. x.

It should be noted that Stanley Ayling has also presented a much more human Wesley in contrast to the earlier hagiography. Ayling is not a biblical scholar but he is more aware of the Anglican roots of Wesley than some other writers. Thus he comments on Wesley's visit to Herrnhut in 1738 'Wesley's devotion to the forms and doctrines of the English Church did not seriously falter; nor would it do so in the future.'[13] This book is a useful study in the life of Wesley.

Among recent popular biographies of Wesley is that of John Pollock.[14] In the Preface, Pollock comments that the definitive life of Wesley has yet to be written. Pollock, not himself a Methodist, has researched Wesley's Journals and other earlier works on Wesley, and taken note of the *Bicentennial Edition of The Works of John Wesley*. The work is a good popular biography of Wesley but it does not explore the sources of his beliefs, nor, in any depth, the influences that led Wesley to those conclusions. It may be noted that, referring to the events of June 1740 and the conflict with the Moravians, he writes 'he set forth the differences between the new doctrines [...] and the plain teaching of Scripture.[15] Pollock argues that Wesley based his belief solely on the Bible and makes the assumption that his interpretation was correct.

In addition, describing the conflicts over predestination, Pollock stresses the way that Wesley and Whitefield tried to retain good personal relationships and suggests that their disagreement was partly the result of misunderstanding and the result of the influence of others in the situation.[16] Pollock had previously published a biography of Whitefield and it may be that he overstates the way in which both Wesley and Whitefield tried to retain a good relationship. He does not explore the way in which Wesley and Whitefield claimed to base their teaching on the same authority and yet came to different conclusions. Pollock, although attempting to write a biography based on full research still falls into many of the errors of earlier works on Wesley. He still emphasises the biblical basis of Wesley's thought and teaching but he is more aware than some earlier writers of the need to set a human picture of Wesley properly in its eighteenth-century context.

Peter Barber, writing in 1988 from within the Methodist Church's Division of Ministries with the responsibility for local (lay) preachers' training, made a valid point about Wesley and biblical preaching, writing:

> My proposition is that while many say with one breath that the context of the text
> sets the parameters for the interpretation and application of a text of Scripture,
> with another breath they use the text as the pretext for the exploration of a theme

---

13   Stanley Ayling, *John Wesley*, Collins, 1979, p. 97.
14   John Pollock, *Wesley the Preacher*, Kingsway Publications, 2000.
15   Pollock, *Wesley the Preacher*, p. 141.
16   Pollock, *Wesley the Preacher*, pp. 142-4.

or idea, or what in the media is termed a 'sound bite', which acts like a refrain throughout the sermon or as a convenient launch pad. Let us begin with Wesley. An analysis of his forty-four sermons, in terms of how much note they take of the context of the text, reveals: i) when there is an exposition of the biblical text and its context, it is almost inevitably within the introduction to the sermon only; ii) once he is in the body of the sermon his doctrine takes over; iii) he liberally sprinkles his sermons with diverse texts and does not necessarily return to his original text.[17]

Although Barber is not a recognised Wesley scholar and is more concerned with the work of the preacher and the use of the Bible, this quotation is relevant to the theme of this study. It would have been helpful if his remarks had been taken up in British Methodist scholarship. Note will, however, be taken of more recent work of British scholars later in the chapter, but it is timely to turn now to the Wesley Quadrilateral and the work of American Methodist scholars over the past forty years.

The Wesleyan Quadrilateral:
The United Methodist Church and John Wesley

The term 'The Wesleyan Quadrilateral' describes the framework of Wesley's theology as being based on scripture, tradition, reason and experience. It is necessary to examine the historical background to the way in which this term came into vogue and to make critical comment about the reasons why it happened. The point that is being made is that it was developed primarily for the benefit of United Methodist Church in its theological debate, particularly in its ecumenical context, and at a certain period in its history. Admittedly reference to this term is also found in the work of scholars from other Churches in the Wesleyan/Methodist tradition but it will be shown that the reference to the Quadrilateral had its origins in the United Methodist Church. It was not at first intended to be used as a method for understanding the sources of authority for Wesley but a number of scholars have used it in that way, seeing the concept of the Quadrilateral as a useful tool for investigating Wesley's method of biblical interpretation.

In fact the Quadrilateral, as applied to Wesley by American scholars, describes the way that he presented his theological arguments, not the method by which he arrived at them. Although the ideas behind the use of the term the Quadrilateral helps in the understanding of the way Wesley read and used the Bible, American Wesley scholarship, like its British counterpart, still largely, with certain exceptions, gives insufficient

---

17   Peter Barber, 'Text or Pretext: An Historical Perspective on the Preacher's Use of Scripture' in *Beyond the Boundaries, Preaching in the Wesleyan Tradition*, Wesley Westminster Series, No. 8, ed. Richard Sykes, Applied Theology Press, 1998, p. 41.

attention to modern biblical scholarship and to the influence of the Church of England on Wesley. The review here is not exhaustive, but does include reference to most of the recognised American scholars from 1960 onward.

In this context it is helpful to keep in mind certain dates. The 1968 General Conference of the United Methodist Church saw the union of the Evangelical United Brethren and the Methodist Church in America. The 1972 General Conference, as part of its *Code of Discipline*, adopted "Doctrinal Guidelines in The United Methodist Church". The 1988 General Conference adopted the document "Doctrinal Standards and our Theological Task" which it included in Part II of the 1988 *Book of Discipline*.[18]

It should also be noted that recent research in American Wesley scholarship has been of a different order from that of much of the earlier, mainly British, works, with greater attention to the primary sources. Even before the formation of the United Methodist Church in 1968 there were indications of renewed interest in Wesley which would lead to a new understanding of the basis of his beliefs.

Ted Campbell argues 'The notion of the "Wesleyan Quadrilateral" was foreshadowed in Colin W. Williams's consideration of "Authority and Experience" in his influential textbook, *John Wesley's Theology Today*.'[19] Williams was an Australian, living and working in America. He had been a student at Drew and, at the time of writing *John Wesley's Theology Today*, was executive vice-president of Aspen Institute which had been founded in 1950 in Aspen, Colorado. It should be noted that Williams did not use the phrase "Wesleyan Quadrilateral."

A study of Williams's book confirms Campbell's comments that the major thrust of his work was to interpret Wesley's teaching and its significance in the wider ecclesiastical context. Williams described Wesley as being in the "Classical Protestant" tradition where 'it is the living word of God as recorded in the Scriptures that is the final authority.'[20] Williams quoted Wesley to support this and used his phrase 'homo unius libri.' He examined the way in which Wesley used the Bible before going on to explore Wesley's use of tradition, reason, and experience. His argument was that, for Wesley, these authorities were subordinate to scripture and helped the reader to understand better the content of the Biblical texts.

Williams makes the statement:

---

18   These dates are taken from Ted A. Campbell, 'The "Wesleyan Quadrilateral": The Story of a Modern Methodist Myth' in *Doctrine and Theology in the United Methodist Church*, ed. Thomas A. Langford, Kingswood Books, 1991, pp. 154-61.

19   'The "Wesleyan Quadrilateral": The Story of a Modern Methodist Myth,' p. 155. The reference is to chapter 2 in Colin W. Williams, *John Wesley's Theology Today*, Abingdon Press, 1960.

20   Williams, *John Wesley's Theology Today*, p. 23.

In summary, we may say that Wesley takes his stand with the Classical Protestant view of authority in exalting the Scriptures as the final authority in matters of faith and practice. He is at one with Luther and Calvin in relating the authority of Scripture to experience by the living witness of the Holy Spirit, who brings the truth of the gospel to the heart of the believer through the record of Scripture. It is also true that Wesley shares a good deal of the Catholic view in the vital place he gives to tradition - particularly the tradition of the early undivided Church and the historic forms of church order and worship. It is true again, that, without allowing it to rise to a position of primacy in matters of doctrine, he shared in the Free Church instance on experience.[21]

This affirms the claim that Wesley's teaching was based on the Bible, his supreme authority. However, it also suggested that tradition, reason, and experience had their place in interpreting scripture, although the precise manner in which Wesley interpreted the Bible needed, in Williams's view, further consideration. Therefore Williams may be seen as preparing the way for the debate that was to follow. The ideas contained within the term 'the Quadrilateral' predated the work of Albert Outler and others who were coming to similar conclusions.

In 1983 the UMC held a consultation on Emory University campus with the title 'Bicentennial Consultation, "Wesleyan Theology in the Next Century: United Methodism Reviews its Theological Task."' The papers were later published.[22] Section IV of the papers was on 'Methodism and Biblical Authority' and subsection 1, by William J. Abraham, was entitled 'The Wesleyan Quadrilateral.' Abraham is a native of Northern Ireland, obtained his doctorate at Oxford but has worked in America for many years, currently being at Perkins School of Theology in Southern Methodist University, Dallas.

Abraham makes a point of some significance for this study:

Historical purists among us will no doubt hope that the current interest in the Quadrilateral is an expression of the renewed desire to expound Wesley's theology simply for its own sake. Their concern is entirely legitimate; indeed it is crucial if a fully accurate account of the Wesleyan Quadrilateral is to become available to us. However, it would be entirely naïve to think that this alone explains the present interest. My own guess is that that interest is related to the wider crisis which confronts Methodism as a theological tradition.[23]

---

21   Williams, *John Wesley's Theology Today*, p. 37.

22   Theodore Runyon, ed., *Wesleyan Theology Today*, Kingswood Books, 1985. This is to be distinguished from Runyon's later work *The New Creation: John Wesley's Theology Today*, Abingdon, 1998.

23   William J. Abraham, 'The Wesleyan Quadrilateral' in *Wesleyan Theology Today*, p. 119.

Abraham makes the further point that the Quadrilateral was important in the pluralism of contemporary American Methodist theology but it remained largely unknown in British Methodism.

Donald A.D. Thorsen is another who makes it clear that the arguments about the Quadrilateral related more directly to the contemporary UMC theological debate than to purely Wesley studies.[24] He points out that this phrase emerged in the late 1960s in the work of Outler while serving on the commission on doctrine and doctrinal standards of the United Methodist Church in America.

Note may well be taken of Abraham's words: 'Wesley is simply a good Anglican therefore in his appeal to the triad of Scripture, tradition and reason. What is distinctive in Wesley is the additional appeal to experience.'[25] Nevertheless, Abraham adds 'Scripture is the primary canon.' Thus he understands Wesley to believe that tradition, especially the Church Fathers and the documents of the Church of England, helps interpret scripture. Reason helps a person to know that God exists, and is useful in daily living and in matters relating to art and science. In relation to scripture reason is a help in interpretation. Referring to Wesley's empiricism and to his emphasis on experience, Abraham sees Wesley's view of biblical inspiration as being linked to the experience of those who wrote the scriptures. According to Abraham the authority of the Bible was understood by Wesley to be linked to the experience of the authors in its writing, as well as to the eighteenth-century readers' experience which confirmed biblical truth.

Abraham therefore recognises that the concept of the Quadrilateral emerged in the ecumenical and doctrinal debate within the UMC, but that it does offer insight into the way that Wesley read and understood the Bible. Abraham is also clear in his acknowledgement that Wesley was strongly influenced by the Church of England's interpretation of scripture. He writes 'Scripture has a special place precisely because the writers have access in experience to the things of God. Thus scripture embodies special divine revelation given in the past to the people of God.'[26] Scripture was still regarded by UMC scholars as the supreme authority. Abraham, however, notes that there was, for Wesley, a difference of degree between the experience of the biblical writers and that of believers in the eighteenth century. Abraham's work is a pointer to the manner in which Wesley interpreted scripture. One way in which it could be taken further would be by the use of some of the insights of modern biblical scholarship regarding Reader-Response.

---

24   Donald A.D. Thorsen, *The Wesleyan Quadrilateral*, Light and Life, Communications, 1990, p. 21.

25   Abraham, 'The Wesleyan Quadrilateral,' p. 120.

26   Abraham, 'The Wesleyan Quadrilateral,' p. 124.

It was at the same consultation that Bruce C. Birch commented that 'In the so-called Wesleyan quadrilateral, which has come to be identified with theology in the Wesleyan tradition, Scripture has a distinct and pre-eminent place alongside tradition, experience, and reason.'[27] Again the reference is to the Wesleyan tradition rather than to Wesley himself.

It is clear from the consultation that the concept of the Quadrilateral was part of the UMC's response to the theological issues of that time, but that some scholars were attempting to read the ideas contained within the term back into the life, work and teaching of Wesley. The emphasis on the supremacy of the Bible may be seen as satisfying the more theologically conservative members of the debate and the precise relationship of tradition, reason and experience to the authority of the Bible was part of the twentieth-century debate as well as a reflection on Wesley's own position.

The Work of Albert Outler

Reference has already been made to Albert Outler who was the most outstanding American Wesley scholar of his generation and was regarded by many as the father of modern Wesley scholarship. As early as 1964 he was paying attention to the sources for the study of Wesley's life, writing:

> In the notes more attention is paid to Wesley's "sources" and contemporaries than to his disciples. This follows from the conviction that he is more fruitfully understood in terms of his own background and context than in the light of the evolution of the Methodist movement after his death.[28]

Outler quoted Wesley's phrase 'homo unius libri' in two places.[29] Although noting that Wesley traced his acceptance of biblical authority back to the days in the Holy Club, Outler did not give attention to the way in which Wesley became a man of one book. Nevertheless, he made the point 'The elements of his [Wesley's] theology were adopted from many sources. [...] Wesley's theology is self-consciously Anglican, but its exact counterpart is not to be found anywhere else in that tradition.'[30] In a chapter entitled 'Tensions within the Church of England,' he quoted from Wesley's *An Earnest Appeal to Men of Reason and Religion*, and pointed out that

---

27   Bruce C. Birch, 'Biblical Theology: Issues in Authority and Hermeneutics' in *Wesleyan Theology Today*, p. 127.
28   Albert C. Outler, *John Wesley*, Oxford University Press, 1964, p. vii.
29   These are to be found in *John Wesley*, p. 89 (cf. CE Vol. 1, p. 105) from the Preface to *Sermons on Several Occasions, 1745-6*. See also p. 106 from Sermon on God's Vineyard, 1787/8, cf. *BE* Vol. 3, p. 504.
30   Outler, *John Wesley*, p. 119.

Wesley vehemently denied that Methodists left the ordinances, doctrines and practices of the Anglican Church.[31]

A clue to the way in which Outler rediscovered the Wesley behind the hagiography of intervening generations is the statement that he came into Wesley studies by 'the discovery of how tightly Wesley had been cocooned by the Methodists and how easily ignored by others.'[32]

He also wrote:

> What I had found in Wesley was a theologian who looked better without his halo - who was, on principle, in dialogue with Christians in many different traditions in his own day precisely because he had been in such fruitful dialogue with so much of the Christian tradition before him.[33]

In 1985 Outler published an article with the title 'The Wesleyan Quadrilateral in John Wesley.'[34] This related the term to the contemporary theological debate, although Outler felt it necessary to root the idea in the work of Wesley. The Lambeth Quadrilateral agreed by the General Convention of the Protestant Episcopal Church in Chicago in 1886 referred to scripture, the Apostles' and Nicene creeds, the sacraments, and the historic episcopate. Outler described a Wesleyan Quadrilateral by way of an analogy to this Anglican statement. This article was reprinted as Chapter 6 in Doctrine and Theology in the Methodist Church, where the Quadrilateral was seen as being part of the ongoing theological debate between the statements of 1972 and 1988 and therefore related to the theological discussions within the UMC.

Thus it was not in origin related to Wesley's biblical interpretation. Outler commented 'The term "quadrilateral" does not occur in the Wesley corpus - and more than once, I have regretted having coined it for contemporary use, since it has been so widely misconstrued.'[35] However, Outler made it clear that he used the phrase to describe Wesley's theological methodology.

> Thus, we can see in Wesley a distinctive theological method, with Scripture as its pre-eminent norm but interfaced with tradition, reason and Christian experience as dynamic and interactive aids in the interpretation of the Word of God in Scripture.

---

31   See Outler, *John Wesley*, p. 417.

32   Albert Outler, 'A New Future for Wesley Studies: An Agenda for Phase III' in *The Future of the Methodist Theological Traditions*, ed. M. Douglas Meeks, Abingdon Press, 1985, p. 42. This is taken from a record of Outler's contribution to the Seventh Oxford Institute of Methodist Theological Studies held in 1982.

33   Outler, 'A New Future,' p. 44.

34   Albert C Outler, 'The Wesleyan Quadrilateral in John Wesley' in *Wesleyan Theological Journal 20*, no. 1 (1985), pp. 7-18.

35   Outler, 'The Wesleyan Quadrilateral in John Wesley', p. 16.

Such a method takes it for granted that faith is human re-action to an antecedent action of the Holy Spirit's prevenience, aimed at convicting our consciousness and opening our eyes and ears to God's address to us in Scripture.[36]

According to Outler, Wesley used scripture, together with tradition, reason and experience to support his teaching but the beliefs and the recognition of the authorities he used came to him, it would be argued by Wesley, through the action of the Holy Spirit.

It is of note here that there is evidence that the term Quadrilateral was not adequate to describe the interrelation between the four elements without stressing also the primacy of scripture. Having referred to the Anglican use of scripture, tradition and reason, Outler continued 'It was Wesley's special genius that he conceived of adding "experience" to the traditional Anglican triad, and thereby adding vitality without altering the substance.'[37] Outler argued that Wesley's theology was strongly biblical. Scripture remained supreme, but it was scripture interpreted within the inter-relationship of tradition, reason and experience.

The point that Outler, perhaps, did not sufficiently emphasise is that Wesley thought that he came to his beliefs through what he felt was already given through the spiritual sense. Included within this sense was the idea of the supremacy of the Bible and the interpretation of scripture as understood through tradition, reason and experience. Outler made a further comment:

Methodists and other Christians have still much to learn about the possible role and function in Christian theologizing of what we have called "the Wesleyan Quadrilateral" - his four-fold guidelines of Scripture as primal font of Christian revelation, of tradition (Christian antiquity) as the sum of the collective Christian wisdom in response to the truth revealed in Scripture; of reason as the God-given discipline of ordering our conceptions as cogently as ever we can; of experience as the assurance of God's reconciling love in Christ, received as a special assurance of God's unmerited favor.'[38]

Outler was undoubtedly on stronger ground when he argued that the Quadrilateral illustrated Wesley's theological methodology than when he saw it as describing the source of his theological beliefs. Outler did not give a clear understanding of why Wesley interpreted the Bible as he did. The Working Group that considered Outler's paper produced 12 points for a 'Provisional Agenda' and point 7 reads 'Wesley professed himself *homo unius libri*. [...] This flaunting of the flag of *sola scriptura* ("scripture

---

36 Outler, 'The Wesleyan Quadrilateral in John Wesley', p. 9.
37 Outler, 'The Wesleyan Quadrilateral in John Wesley', p. 10.
38 Outler, 'A New Future,' p.50.

alone") poses a cluster of crucial and unresolved questions about Wesley's principles for the interpretation of scripture.'[39]

Outler acknowledged the need for research into the influences that brought Wesley to his theological conclusions in the Preface to the first volume of the *BE*, writing 'It is obvious, however, that this edition has a second concern [...] a methodological redefinition of 'Wesley Studies', with special emphasis on Wesley's sources and his special way of using them.'[40] Outler thus introduced the sermons with an acknowledgement that the origins of Wesley's thoughts were deep and complex. Outler also noted, concerning Wesley's roots in the Erasmian tradition 'By Wesley's time, however, it had evolved into a gospel of moral rectitude, but still with its three professed guidelines: Scripture, reason, and Christian antiquity. To this, Wesley added a strong element of mystical piety.'[41] On the following page, Outler commented '[Wesley] had grown up with Scripture as a second language; even in his early sermons one sees the beginnings of his lifelong habit of interweaving Scripture with his own speech in a graceful texture.' Also in the Introduction to Volume 1, Outler noted that Wesley's philosophical method was influenced by Empiricism and the work of John Locke.[42]

In the references to the Wesley Quadrilateral Outler did not offer any extensive comment on Wesley's indebtedness to the Anglican Church within the context of his formative years and his allegiance to that Church in later days. This is perhaps surprising in that Outler's use of the term was influenced by the parallel but somewhat different Anglican reference to a fourfold authority. Thus the exploration of Outler's work in this field shows conclusively that the term Quadrilateral had been developed to serve the UMC of the late twentieth century and that Outler, as a Wesley scholar, was attempting to set this in the context of the works of Wesley. It is therefore now helpful to note the way later American Wesley scholarship used the term, or alternatively failed to refer to it.

American Wesley Scholarship in the Years Subsequent to the First Use of the Term 'The Quadrilateral'

The idea of the Quadrilateral continued to influence American Wesley scholarship but not all authors make direct reference to it. For example, Thomas Langford's *Practical Divinity - Theology in the Wesleyan Tradition* published in 1984, does not even mention the issue. He comments

39   'The Future of the Methodist Traditions' in *The Future of the Methodist Theological Traditions*, ed. M. Douglas Meeks, Abingdon Press, 1985, p. 62.
40   *BE* Vol. 1, p. xi.
41   *BE* Vol. 1, p. 56.
42   *BE* Vol. 1, pp. 58-9.

'[Wesley] was rooted in Scripture as the primary witness to the creatorship of God, the lordship of Jesus, and the sustaining presence of the Holy Spirit.'[43] Langford then goes on to refer to Wesley's Christian Library and the wide range of writings it contained. He acknowledges the many influences from tradition evident in Wesley including those from the Early Church, Eastern writers and Roman Catholics.[44] Referring to the Aldersgate experience, 1738, Langford comments 'Wesley studied the doctrine of justification by grace through faith. This doctrine, he became convinced, was a faithful explication of scriptural teaching and was, as a matter of fact, being realized in the lives of others.'[45] Langford implies that Wesley became convinced of biblical truth partly through the evidence of the experience of others.

Furthermore, according to Langford,

> Wesley intended to be a biblical theologian, Scripture was the fundamental source of his theological expression, every doctrine must be measured against the standard presented in Scripture. What is said about God, about the world, about human beings must be said because the Scripture speaks. [...] The scriptures are the prime source of Wesley's theology, but the Scriptures become God's word only by the lively power of the Holy Spirit.[46]

Thus Langford argues that the Bible was pre-eminent for Wesley but tradition and experience were important for establishing the meaning of the Bible.[47] Therefore he does give some insight into the ways in which Wesley came to believe that the Bible teaching was that expressed in his works. However, he does not deal with the Anglican influence on Wesley. Langford is held in high regard in American Wesley scholarship but he did not add greatly to the understanding of the complexity of ways in which Wesley was influenced in his interpretation of scripture.

Somewhat surprisingly there is no direct reference to the Quadrilateral in W. Stephen Gunter's work, *The Limits of 'Love Divine.'*[48] Gunter was writing as a Wesley scholar from within the UMC. However, he does explore to some extent Wesley's relationship with the Church of England and, more than some scholars, he acknowledges its influence on Wesley.

---

43   Langford, *Practical Divinity*, p. 12.
44   Langford, *Practical Divinity*, p. 13.
45   Langford, *Practical Divinity*, p. 15.
46   Langford, *Practical Divinity*, p. 25.
47   This point is argued in pp. 24-27 of Langford, *Practical Divinity*.
48   W. Stephen Gunter, *The Limits of 'Love Divine' John Wesley's Response to Antinomianism and Enthusiasm*, Kingswood Books, 1989. However, at a later date, he was the editor of W. Stephen Gunter et al, *Wesley and the Quadrilateral - Renewing the Conversation*, Abingdon Press, 1997 which did give consideration to matters relating to the Quadrilateral.

He does this by looking at some of the controversies in which Wesley was involved. In the chapter on 'Treading on the Boundaries,' for example, he argues that in his later work Wesley was moving steadily away from the Established Church.[49] Gunter comments 'If Wesley had not, through all the conflicts with Charles and the Anglicans, resolutely maintained his ecclesiastical dialectic, if he had not succeeded in treading for fifty years the fine line between church and sect, Methodism would probably have been absorbed into Anglicanism like the other religious societies or fragmented into unidentifiable remains like the followers of Whitefield and Lady Huntingdon.'[50] At the same time, referring to The Minutes of Conference, including those for 1762, Gunter writes 'They bear witness to Wesley's faithfulness to Anglican theology.'[51] Gunter does not spell out the fact that Wesley's Anglican roots were a dominant influence when he came to interpret the Bible.

Gunter frequently refers to Wesley's conflicts with other Anglicans but does not appear to see them as disputes within the Anglican Church, with Wesley constantly constrained by the pressure of the influence of that church and determined to prove that his biblical interpretation was simply that of the church in which he had been brought up.

It has already been shown that the term the Quadrilateral refers not to standards of doctrine but to boundaries within which biblical interpretation takes place within the UMC. This is further illustrated in *Doctrine and Theology in the United Methodist Church*, 1991 to which reference has already been made. The chapters by Schubert M. Ogden, Leroy T. Howe, and Robert E. Cushman illustrate the ways in which the concept of the Quadrilateral emerged in the thinking, and subsequently in the statements, of the UMC.[52]

The four elements within the Quadrilateral are noted and there is debate about the way in which primacy is to be accorded to scripture. Ted Campbell states explicitly that 'the "Quadrilateral" is a distinctively modern tool.'[53] On the previous page he had argued that it was an oversimplification to trace the idea of the Quadrilateral directly back to Wesley.

In the same volume, attempting to demonstrate that the concept of the Quadrilateral is to be found in Wesley's work, Outler made the point that 'It was intended as a metaphor for a four-element syndrome, including the

---

49   Gunter, *The Limits of 'Love Divine'*, pp. 156-180.
50   Gunter, *The Limits of 'Love Divine'*, pp. 179-80.
51   Gunter, *The Limits of 'Love Divine,'* p. 160.
52   For Ogden, see pp. 42-3; for Howe, see pp. 53-4; for Cushman, see pp. 72-4.
53   Ted A. Campbell, 'The "Wesleyan Quadrilateral": The Story of a Modern Methodist Myth' in *Doctrine and Theology in the United Methodist Church*, Kingswood Books, 1991 p. 161.

fourfold guidelines of authority in Wesley's theological method. In such a quaternity, Holy Scripture is clearly unique.'[54] He qualified this by indicating the influence of the other elements within the Quadrilateral. It is clear that what was under discussion was Wesley's theological methodology, not the underlying influences that fashioned his thinking.

Also in the same book Richard P. Heitzenrater drew attention to the resolutions of the General Conference of 1984, which set up the work leading to the statement of 1988. One issue to be addressed was 'the significance and proper use of the so-called Methodist Quadrilateral.'[55] This further confirms the argument that primarily the discussion on the Quadrilateral arose within the UMC as part of its debate on doctrinal standards and the method of theologising. That is not to deny that there was a serious attempt to locate it in Wesley. The extent to which it is of help in determining the sources from which Wesley derived his beliefs is another matter. Langford goes even further in placing the use of the idea of a Quadrilateral in the contemporary UMC with the words: 'This wide, thorough and appreciative acceptance gives the impression that the quadrilateral represents a long-standing self-understanding. Yet, this is not the case.' [56]

In *Outward Sign and Inward Grace: The Place of Sacraments in Wesleyan Spirituality*,[57] Rob L. Staples made a valid point:

> Using Albert Outler's term, many Wesleyan scholars have discussed 'the Wesleyan Quadrilateral' of Scripture, tradition, reason, and experience, which were all authoritative sources for Wesley. The four were not equal partners for Wesley, however, for Scripture had priority. In reality the final religious authority for Wesley was the gospel. But it was the gospel as revealed to us in Scripture, mediated to us through the historic Christian tradition, explicated and made understandable through reason, and authenticated in experience.[58]

Rob L. Staples, has been professor of theology at Nazarene Theological Seminary in America since 1976. He is a past president of the Wesleyan

---

54 Albert Outler, 'The Wesleyan Quadrilateral in John Wesley' in *Doctrine and Theology in the United Methodist Church*, ed. Thomas A. Langford, Kingswood Books, 1991, p.80.

55 Richard P. Heitzenrater, 'In Search of Controversy and Consensus: The Road to the 1988 Doctrinal Statement,' in *Doctrine and Theology in the United Methodist Church*, p.94.

56 Thomas A. Langford, 'The United Methodist Quadrilateral: A Theological Task,' in *Doctrine and Theology in the United Methodist Church*, ed. Thomas A. Langford, Kingswood Books, 1991, p. 232.

57 Rob L. Staples, *Outward Sign and Inward Grace: The Place of Sacraments in Wesleyan Spirituality*, Beacon Hill Press, 1991.

58 Staples, *Outward Sign and Inward Grace*, p. 174.

Theological Society. He is in the Wesleyan/Holiness tradition, not a member of the UMC. His work recognises, more than some others, the Anglican influences on Wesley in his sacramental theology and practice. Although there is emphasis on the importance of the Bible for Wesley, there is need to use the results of modern biblical scholarship to develop further how Wesley interpreted and used scripture.

Thomas C. Oden is a theologian rather than an historian with an interest in showing Wesley as a systematic theologian having a biblical base to his teaching. In 1994 he made a statement:

> The quadrilateral method (the authority of Scripture understood in the light of tradition, reason and experience) may be seen at work in the early parts of The Doctrine of Original Sin, and in the Appeals, and most explicitly in the homily 'On Sin in Believers.'[59]

He comments 'Wesley's primary appeal is to Scripture and only derivatively to tradition, reason and experience.'[60] According to Oden 'This is the principle of the analogy of faith, analogia fidei, which in accord with classic Christian exegesis, Wesley constantly sought to employ. Scripture is the best interpreter of Scripture.'[61] Thus, referring to Wesley's disagreement with the Quaker theologian Robert Barclay, Oden comments on Wesley: 'The Scriptures are the measuring rod for examining all, real or supposed, revelations.'[62] It is clear that Oden saw Wesley as a theologian in his own right who was Bible-based.

On Wesley's use of tradition, Oden writes: 'Wesley recalled that his own father had early given him the model of "reverence to the ancient church" when he was a student at Oxford.'[63] Oden is referring to a letter to William Dodd in 1756 in which Wesley was reflecting on events 30 years earlier. Oden also comments 'The exegesis of the church fathers is especially helpful on the explication of a doctrine that is not sufficiently explained, or for confirmation of a doctrine generally received. When Wesley appealed alternately to "reason, Scripture, or authority," the third of these criteria meant the ancient creeds and councils and consensually received classical Christian writings.'[64] Oden has a section on The Christian Library commenting '[Wesley] felt himself "at full liberty" not only to abridge but to add his own comments and corrections.'[65] Thus Oden implies

---

59   Thomas C. Oden, *John Wesley's Scriptural Christianity*, Zondervan Publishing House, 1994, p. 55.
60   Oden, *Scriptural Christianity*, p. 55.
61   Oden, *Scriptural Christianity*, p. 57.
62   Oden, *Scriptural Christianity*, p. 90.
63   Oden, *Scriptural Christianity*, p. 65.
64   Oden, *Scriptural Christianity*, pp. 66-7.
65   Oden, *Scriptural Christianity*, p. 69.

that Wesley acknowledged tradition and the works of others, but he was prepared to alter such works in order to ensure that they properly reflected what he saw as the teaching of the Bible. Wesley's appeal to tradition goes beyond the early Church fathers.

In referring to Wesley's use of reason, Oden comments 'Reason and Scripture, far from being pitted against each other, are linked intimately in the attempt to find "the plain scriptural rational way."'[66] Reason is seen therefore as having its use, but, according to Oden, as an authority for Wesley, it was subservient to scripture. Oden does not examine what influences led Wesley to a Bible-based position. For Wesley, according to Ogden, tradition, reason and experience were tools by which Scripture was better understood but were not primary authorities in their own right. Commenting on the place of experience in the Quadrilateral and noting the Aldersgate event of 1738, Oden writes 'Experience is more modestly viewed as the appropriation of scriptural authority, than the source of authority, as in some forms of pietism.'[67] However, on the same page, Oden does recognise that Wesley spoke of spiritual senses and denied the concept of innate ideas: 'Spiritual knowledge is discerned with spiritual senses. "Our ideas are not innate, but must all originally come from our senses."'

Oden does not explore the influence of the Church of England on Wesley's thought and teaching. Therefore he does not sufficiently examine the way in which this influence illustrates how he came to understand what he saw as the meaning of scripture.

Referring to the Quadrilateral in 1994, Randy Maddox,[68] makes a helpful comment:

> Wesley himself never used the term, nor explicitly conjoined its four components in any description of his theological method. Rather the term was created by Albert Outler to emphasize that Wesley relied more on "standards of doctrine" in his theological approach than on theological Systems or juridical Confessions of faith.[69]

Note may thus be taken of the point Maddox makes: 'In reality, Wesley interpreted the Protestant sola scriptura (in good Anglican fashion) to mean that Scripture is the primary, rather than exclusive, Christian authority.'[70]

Commenting on the authority of tradition for Wesley, Maddox refers to the (ante-Nicene or pre-Constantine) early Church, and to Anglican

---

66   Oden, *Scriptural Christianity*, p. 71. He also writes: 'reason is useful in making an intelligible reception of revelation.' (*Scriptural Christianity*, p. 75.)

67   Oden, *Scriptural Christianity*, p. 85.

68   Randy L. Maddox, *Responsible Grace - John Wesley's Practical Theology*, Kingswood Books, 1994.

69   Maddox, *Responsible Grace*, p. 36.

70   Maddox, *Responsible Grace*, p. 37.

standards of doctrine. He refers to the considerable volume of literature that
Wesley read, making a perceptive point:

> Wesley valued tradition critically, as a "normed norm" that helped to enlighten
> and apply Scripture. More precisely, he valued primarily the Early Church and the
> Anglican standards. This limitation apparently reflects a common assumption that
> tradition is helpful only when it is correct.[71]

Maddox then argues that, for Wesley, reason was the means by which
knowledge was processed and understood but it was not the source of
knowledge: 'Wesley characteristically restricted the role of reason in
theology to organising and drawing inferences from revelation.'[72] Writing
of Wesley's empiricism, Maddox says 'Wesley self-consciously sided with
the empiricist denial of innate ideas.'[73] Two pages later he also states 'All
knowledge of God must come either through inference from creation or by
direct sensation through our spiritual senses.'

Turning to experience, Maddox makes comment:

> Wesley's discussions of Original Sin conform to the claim that he considered
> experience to be subordinate to Scripture in theological reflection. His typical way
> of expressing this was that experience "confirms" Scripture. Actually something
> more fundamental was taking place; experience was being used to test proposed
> interpretations of Scripture.[74]

As a further example of the way Maddox understands Wesley to use the
Bible, the comment may be noted 'Wesley assumed that the fundamental
core of the Mosaic law was the moral code (epitomized by the ten
commandments), and that this code recapitulated the original moral law.'[75]
Although Maddox clearly accepts that Wesley appealed to scripture, he
does not, at this point, make clear that it was a selective process. It should
be pointed out that Wesley used the Bible-based moral law, but ignored all
the ceremonial and cultic law that surrounded the Mosaic teaching in the
Old Testament for the purposes of his arguments.

Maddox sums up his comments on Wesley's use of the Bible with the
words 'Wesley's so-called "quadrilateral" of theological activities could
more adequately be described as a unilateral rule of Scripture within a
trilateral   hermeneutic   of   reason,   tradition,   and   experience.'[76]

---

71 Maddox, *Responsible Grace*, p. 46.
72 Maddox, *Responsible Grace*, p. 41.
73 Maddox, *Responsible Grace*, p. 27. The extent to which Wesley was influenced by
     Locke will be explored in Chapter 4.
74 Maddox, *Responsible Grace*, p. 46.
75 Maddox, *Responsible Grace*, p. 99.
76 Maddox, *Responsible Grace*, p. 46.

Maddox also writes 'Few of Wesley's theological convictions were initially "chosen" in an unbiased conscious manner; they were imbibed with his familial and ecclesial nurture.'[77] Thus the position of Maddox is to emphasise the role of scripture as Wesley's supreme authority, to set tradition, reason and experience in a subordinate role, and then to offer a hint that these found their place in Wesley's theological thinking from influences in his earlier life. This provides a pointer to the way Wesley came to accept the Bible as his supreme authority and the way he came to interpret Scripture. This quotation relates to the influence of his life in Epworth upon him and the way in which he came to his understanding of the Bible through the teaching of the Church of England. It also indicates the way in which the development of the ideas within the Quadrilateral helps point to a better understanding of Wesley's use of the Bible. From here the next step could well be to use the findings of Reader-Response biblical criticism to investigate further Wesley's work and the way in which he came to read and interpret the Bible. This will be attempted in later chapters.

John B. Cobb is a leading figure among those interested in process theology and his primary concern is to discuss what he sees as the theological problems and needs of the UMC at the time of writing. He does this through a discussion of Wesley's teaching but referring to the UMC's contemporary situation. In 1995 he wrote about a Wesleyan theology for today.[78] His discussion of the Quadrilateral is left to the last chapter. There he writes 'This chapter is about the theological formulation that we have come to call "the Wesleyan quadrilateral."'[79] Cobb notes that this formulation: 'first appeared in the 1972 Book of Discipline of the United Methodist Church and [...] recurs in the 1992 Discipline.' The rest of the chapter looks at Wesley's teaching, but also notes that the twentieth-century American context is different from that of Wesley. He thus wants to draw points from Wesley but to reinterpret them for today. This further illustrates that the concept of the Quadrilateral is primarily one devised by the United Methodist Church in America to meet its own theological needs at the present time, although scholars have tried to understand it in terms of the work of Wesley in the eighteenth century.

Scott Jones examined Wesley's use of the Bible in *John Wesley's Conception and Use of Scripture*. Jones argues that, for Wesley, authority was in fact constituted by a fivefold locus comprising Scripture, reason, Christian antiquity, the Church of England and experience. This is a development from the "Wesleyan Quadrilateral." Jones acknowledges the

---

77   Maddox, *Responsible Grace*, p. 47.
78   John B. Cobb, *Grace and Responsibility: A Wesleyan Theology for Today*, Abingdon Press, 1995.
79   Cobb, *Grace and Responsibility*, p. 156.

special place the Church of England had in the influences on Wesley and this is worthy of note. This present book argues that Wesley's understanding of Scripture was that of an eighteenth-century High-Church Arminian Anglican. Jones also makes a valid point:

> The Quadrilateral is used as a summary of how Methodists understand theological authority. To be faithful to John Wesley, however, this must always be understood as a single locus of authority with four unequal parts. Scripture is primary, and always interpreted in the light of the other three. For Wesley, all four terms are mutually interdependent. Reason correctly employed testifies to the authority of Scripture, and Scripture must always make sense. Not all Christian tradition is authoritative - only the parts where Christians were faithful to Scripture. Only those experiences where the goals of Scripture are actualized count in the theological arguments.[80]

The work of Jones illustrates the manner in which modern American Wesleyan scholarship understands the question of authority to be explained and how it does so with reference to Wesley.

It will be clear by this point that the majority of scholars, especially those in the UMC tradition, accept that the Bible was regarded by Wesley as being the final and supreme authority to which all others were subordinate and it is this claim that is to be tested. In particular, what does it mean to say that Wesley's beliefs were rooted in the Bible? In fact, was Wesley so rooted in the Bible or, in his interpretation of scripture, did he bring to it ideas derived from other sources that had profoundly influenced him? Therefore it must be asked whether Wesley arrived at his teaching by acknowledgement of these sources of authority, or whether they confirmed belief that had been reached by other means.

Kenneth J. Collins, in his work *The Scripture Way of Salvation*,[81] does not refer to the Quadrilateral. As the title of the book indicates, Collins regards the Bible as being the pre-eminent authority for Wesley's thinking and teaching. Wesley's theology is seen essentially in terms of soteriology, but, in its turn, that is seen as the way of salvation as described in Scripture. Collins is an elder in the Free Methodist Church as well as a recognised Wesley scholar. He is not a member of the UMC.

He writes of 'Wesley's basic theological orientation, which considers Scripture to be the ultimate norm or guide for the Christian life.'[82] On the same page, Collins expands on the phrase 'The Heart of Wesley's

---

80   Scott J. Jones 'The Rule of Scripture', W. Stephen Gunter ed., *Wesley and the Quadrilateral - Renewing the Conversation*, Abingdon Press, 1997, p. 42.

81   Kenneth J. Collins, *The Scripture Way of Salvation*, Abingdon Press, 1997. This work has as its subtitle *The Heart of John Wesley's Theology*. It may be noted that in 1999 he published *A Real Christian: The Life of John Wesley*, Abingdon Press.

82   Collins, *The Scripture Way of Salvation*, p. 13.

Theology.' This is seen by Collins as practical. He does not immediately use the word experience but it is clear that Wesley's theology is regarded as describing an experienced religion. Although this does relate to the theme that 'Wesley was a man of one book,' Collins does not indicate the way in which Wesley came to that standpoint.

Thus, in his treatment of Wesley's understanding of the doctrine of original sin, Collins notes the use of biblical texts including Romans 5:12, 5:19, 5:15-21.[83] He also notes Wesley's use, in his teaching, of references to the moral law. This he separates from the ceremonial law, but he does not give any arguments, used by Wesley, that indicated the authority on which the separation was made.[84] Referring to Wesley's sermon 'Salvation by Faith,' preached shortly after the Aldersgate experience, Collins notes that for Wesley the Devils believe: 'all Scripture was given by inspiration of God,' and comments: 'and so mere assent to all that is contained in the Bible, likewise, does not redeem.'[85] Collins implies that, for Wesley, there is a strong connection between the authority of the Bible, doctrine, faith and experience. Then Collins makes the statement 'In addition to Scripture, Wesley appealed to the doctrinal formulations of his own Church, especially as reflected in the Book of Common Prayer.'[86] Collins also writes: 'Wesley was not only well versed in Scripture, but he also looked to this resource as a normative standard to bring order, coherence, and theological integrity to his doctrinal enterprise.'[87] He continues by referring to the 'diverse sources' in the stream of tradition which fed into Wesley's theological formulation. These are identified as coming from Roman Catholic, Eastern, Pietistic, Moravian and Anglican sources.

A further attempt by Collins to reconstruct a systematic theology from Wesley's writings is to be found in his *Faithful Witness: John Wesley's Homiletical Theology*.[88] Collins uses Wesley's sermons, read against the background of the Apostles Creed, in order to show that Wesley wrote out of a consistent theological context. From *Faithful Witness*, it is worth noting that Collins acknowledges the influence of the Church of England on Wesley and he argues strongly for an interpretation of the meaning of the Aldersgate experience as a modified traditional conversionist one, contra Maddox. Wesley's writings are by no means as systematic as some scholars such as Collins argue. They were, of course, produced in the heat of his

---

83 Collins, *The Scripture Way of Salvation*, pp. 32-3.
84 Collins, *The Scripture Way of Salvation*, pp. 51-4.
85 Collins, *The Scripture Way of Salvation*, p. 76.
86 Collins, *The Scripture Way of Salvation*, p. 81.
87 Collins, *The Scripture Way of Salvation*, p. 205.
88 Kenneth J. Collins, *Faithful Witness: John Wesley's Homiletical Theology*, Wesley Heritage Press, 1993.

work in the Methodist societies of his day and the controversies in which he was involved.

Ronald H. Stone is John Witherspoon Professor of Ethics at Pittsburgh Theological Seminary and a member of the UMC. Although not directly referring to the Quadrilateral, he does refer to Wesley's 'own method of using Scripture, traditions of the ancient church, reflection on experience [...] and rigorous use of reason as he understood it as tools for analysis.'[89] Stone also notes that 'Nor would he [Wesley] leave the Church of England. [...] He wanted to remain a society within the Church of England. England and its church were one.'[90] Stone makes the point that for Wesley 'There is no error in scripture.'[91] He immediately adds, however, a point worthy of note: 'The issue is in the interpretation of Scripture.'

The debate about the Wesleyan Quadrilateral has primarily been centred in America, only a few British authors showing awareness of it. At the 1996 Conference of the Wesley Historical Society, Donald English gave a paper entitled 'John Wesley: a Preacher for Today?'[92] In it he states 'I have been helped, in my reading of Wesley and throughout my ministry, by what has come to be called the 'Methodist Quadrilateral', an inter-relationship of Bible, experience, tradition and reason.'[93] English offers a brief discussion on the Quadrilateral, but it remains essentially a debate within American Methodist scholarship.

Stephen Dawes, a leading British Methodist scholar, in an, as yet, unpublished paper 'Revelation in Methodist Practice and Belief' makes similar point, referring to English.

> The only occurrence of the term [the Wesley Quadrilateral] in a Conference publication in the UK is, to my knowledge, Donald English's use of it in the tapes which accompanied the significant 1985 Home Mission Publication, Sharing in God's Mission. The four constituents of the Quadrilateral are, however, found in section D5 of Unit 12 of Faith and Worship where they are called 'the Building Blocks of the Faith.

It is worthy of note that in the literature generated by the debates over the Wesley Quadrilateral in the UMC, there is no evidence of any major input at the time by Frank Baker who is usually regarded as the authoritative scholar for the study of the original texts of Wesley. In

---

89   Ronald H. Stone, *John Wesley's Life and Ethics*, Abingdon Press, 2001, p. 12.
90   Stone, *John Wesley's Life and Ethics*, pp. 210-1.
91   Stone, *John Wesley's Life and Ethics*, p. 110.
92   Donald English, 'John Wesley: A Preacher for Today' in *Beyond the Boundaries, Preaching in the Wesleyan Tradition*, ed. Richard Sykes, Applied Theology Press, 1998, pp. 1-11.
93   English, 'John Wesley: A Preacher for Today,' p. 7.

particular Baker undertook a lot of meticulous work in editing Wesley's letters. Although Baker was English most of his work was based in America. Certainly an argument from silence is precarious but it does seem significant that he did not become involved in the discussions, which would certainly have been expected if they were primarily about Wesley and the authorities he recognised.[94]

The conclusion to be drawn from a study of the work of American Methodist scholars on the Quadrilateral is that they all accept Wesley's claim to be a man of one book in the sense that, for him, the Bible was the supreme authority. However, unlike many nineteenth-century mainstream Methodist scholars, they recognise that Wesley interpreted scripture by the use of tradition, reason and experience. These are the tools by which the Bible was to be interpreted and the method used in theological argument. There may have been some subtle differences of emphasis on the relative importance of the three secondary elements within the Quadrilateral but the supreme authority of scripture remained. The argument here is that, for Wesley, the authority of the Bible and a knowledge of its contents was instilled in him in his childhood in Epworth. It was a 'given' authority to which he brought all the baggage of his eighteenth-century High-Church Arminian Anglicanism. It was this that he then believed that he found reflected in what he regarded as the sacred pages.

This exploration of American Wesley scholarship has also illustrated at some length the way in which the Wesley Quadrilateral emerged and the way in which the authority of the Bible, tradition, reason and experience has been treated by these writers, often to meet the needs of the UMC but with some attempt to locate the approach within Wesley's interpretation of scripture.

Maddox wrote in a way that would gain agreement among most of these authors with the comment

> Wesley identified Scripture as the most basic authority for Christian faith and life; he approached Scripture in terms of the best scholarly principles of his day, he focussed on the major soteriological themes of Scripture and sought to interpret all passages in their light; and he was explicitly aware that Scripture did not definitely address every possible issue.[95]

That is not to deny that there are differences between American Wesley scholars, whether in the UMC or other branches of the Wesleyan tradition. Some of these will become apparent in later chapters.

---

94 A major work of Frank Baker was *John Wesley and the Church of England,* Epworth Press, 1970, second ed. 2000.

95 Maddox, *Responsible Grace*, p. 39.

More Recent British Wesley Scholarship

Before leaving the review of Wesley scholarship, it is necessary to consider more recent British works. In 1993 the British Methodist Conference had a major debate on human sexuality which raised issues about the nature of the authority of scripture. It instructed its Faith and Order Committee to produce a report on the subject and report back to a future Conference. In 1998 it received that report which was then was published.[96]

Its main concern was to examine the contemporary Methodist view on the authority of the Bible but it did contain a number of references to John Wesley. It noted that his works were rooted in the Bible and that he did regard it as his supreme authority. However, the report also noted that Wesley accepted that scripture was inspired through fallible human authors and also that he used his knowledge of the Bible in its original languages to amend the King James Version some 12,000 times. The fact that Wesley produced Notes on the New Testament illustrates the fact that the Bible, according to Wesley, needs interpretation to the reader of a later generation and that this interpretation is according to what he called the 'analogy of faith.' This means that the Bible is to be interpreted in a manner which is consistent with itself and in the light of Christ. The report notes that Wesley set up the first Conferences, from which the modern British Conference is directly descended, to interpret and establish the meaning of the Bible. The report thus notes that Wesley interpreted the Bible in a certain way and that Wesley's doctrines were, according to him, biblically based within certain constraints.

The year 2003 was the tercentenary of the birth of John Wesley. It is therefore not surprising that there were a number of reprints and later editions of previously published books and some totally new works that appeared in 2002/3.

Although Roy Hattersley's book *A Brand Plucked from the Burning: The Life of John Wesley* [97] has been criticised for many errors in detail, the book takes full cognisance of the eighteenth-century context in which Wesley's life was set. He places emphasis on the human weaknesses of Wesley, his ways of relating to women and traces the way in which he, slowly and perhaps reluctantly, saw the movement he founded drift away from the Church of England. Hattersley does not explore the way in which Wesley came to his understanding of scriptural teaching.

---

96   *A Lamp to my feet and a Light to My Path: The Nature of Authority and the Place of the Bible in the Methodist Church*, The Methodist Publishing House, 1998.

97   Roy Hattersley, *A Brand Plucked from the Burning: The Life of John Wesley*, Little, Brown, 2002. There were reprints in 2002/3 and a change of title but no change in his arguments.

John Kent, *Wesley and the Wesleyans: Religion in Eighteenth Century Britain*,[98] challenges what he sees as the Methodist myth that there was an eighteenth-century revival led by the Wesleys. He argues surprisingly that experience was not of the significance for Wesley's understanding of scripture that some Wesley scholars assert. The way in which Wesley used experience to interpret the Bible is examined later in Chapter 4 when the influence of the Moravians and the meaning of the Aldersgate experience is considered.

In 2002 a third edition of Henry Rack's *Reasonable Enthusiast: John Wesley and the Rise of Methodism* appeared. The same year a new edition of John Newton's *Susanna and the Puritan Tradition in Methodism*, of which note is taken in Chapter 3, was published.[99] This is virtually a reprint of the first edition with one extra chapter noting more recent scholarship. Newton does not present any new conclusions. In 2003 a new edition of *The Journal of John Wesley*, Christopher Idle's selection of entries from the full Journal was produced. This, however, added nothing to the earlier edition.

Stephen Tomkins, *John Wesley: A Biography*[100] takes account of modern scholarship and presents a very human Wesley. Tomkins acknowledges the Anglican context of Wesley's work although arguing that separation between Methodism and the Church of England was inevitable. Chapter 19 discusses the pressure on Wesley to separate and his resistance to that pressure. Tomkins tends to regard Wesley as an Evangelical Anglican although there is also some acknowledgement of the influence on him of High-Church Arminianism.

Ralph Waller's *John Wesley: A Personal Portrait* appeared in 2003.[101] Waller comments 'This book is neither a detailed biography of Wesley, nor is it a systematic treatment of his theology; it is rather a series of studies of major points in Wesley's life and work.'[102] In effect it is a useful summary of Wesley's life, work and teaching, treating him as a human figure, sometimes with criticism. Waller uses some of the primary sources, but paints a generally favourable picture of Wesley. He does not deal in any depth with him as a reader of the Bible, nor give much attention to the influences that led Wesley to the interpretation of the Bible which he gives in his works.

---

98   John Kent, *Wesley and the Wesleyans*: Religion in Eighteenth-Century Britain, Cambridge University Press, 2002.

99   John A. Newton, *Susanna Wesley and the Puritan Tradition in Methodism*, Epworth Press, 1968, second ed. 2002.

100 Stephen Tomkins, *John Wesley: A Biography*, Lion Publishing, 2003.

101 Ralph Waller, *John Wesley: A Personal Portrait*, SPCK, 2003.

102 Waller, *A Personal Portrait*, p. ix.

Of much greater note for the argument being developed here is Stephen Dawes's article on 'John Wesley and the Bible' in the February 2003 edition of the *Proceedings of the Wesley Historical Society*.[103] The article draws heavily on the work of Scott Jones discussed above. Dawes comments 'It is the reader who opens the Bible, selects a chosen passage and then quotes and uses it - and without a reader a Bible remains closed and silent.'[104] On the same page, discussing Wesley's methodology and the Quadrilateral, Dawes comments 'Whatever primacy there is lies with the reader.' Thus, finally, biblical Reader-Response criticism has been suggested as a means of studying Wesley's Bible-based theology.

This changing approach is also seen in Johnston McMaster's 'Hermeneutics in the Wesleyan Understanding.'[105] He does make reference to the Wesleyan Quadrilateral. He also makes the point that 'Wesley read scripture from within his Anglican tradition. Though both the Anglican and Puritan streams flow through Wesley's spiritual formation, his basic biblical hermeneutic was Anglican.' McMaster distinguishes between biblical interpretation and biblical authority and states 'The authority of the interpretation can never be equated with the authority of scripture, however that is defined. The truth of the interpretation is never ultimate truth or absolute truth.' Wesley would not have made that distinction but it does help the search for the understanding of the way in which Wesley came to read the Bible.

In April/May 2004 major conference was held arranged by the British Methodist Church Adult Learning Training and Development staff entitled 'The World at Whitby'. This was an exploration of the place of the Bible in modern Methodism and the contributors were distinguished Methodists and acknowledged biblical scholars. It is therefore of note that there were no papers produced that gave any detailed attention to Wesley's use and interpretation of the Bible.

Also in 2004 *Unmasking Methodist Theology* was published.[106] This gives attention in the main to British Methodism and the contributors are representative of mainstream British Methodism. In the attempt to explore and make clear what Methodist's today believe the contributors did not give attention in depth to the way in which Wesley approached the scriptures. The omission of references to Wesley's use and interpretation of the Bible

---

103 Stephen B. Dawes, 'John Wesley and the Bible' in *Proceedings of the Wesley Historical Society*, Vol. 54, February 2003.

104 Dawes, 'John Wesley and the Bible,' p. 9.

105 Johnston McMaster, 'Hermeneutics in the Wesleyan Understanding', 2002, a supporting paper attached to *Finding New Life*, a report of the European Methodist Theological Commission and taken from their web-site, 2003.

106 Clive Marsh, Brian Beck, Angela Shier-Jones and Helen Wareing eds., *Unmasking Methodist Theology*, Continuum, 2004.

may partly be explained by the terms of reference within which the contributors worked and partly by the fact that the Faith and Order Committee of the British Methodist Church had issued its report a few years earlier.

In America, similarly, there has been no major publication concentrating on this theme. David Hempton's *Methodism Empire of the Spirit* may prove to be a significant book for the understanding of Methodism.[107] He does acknowledge the importance of Wesley's *Explanatory Notes on the New Testament* for early Methodist preachers.[108] Although he does give attention to the life, work and teaching of Wesley, he does not take up in detail the particular issue of Wesley's approach to the Bible.

William J. Abraham's *Wesley for Armchair Theologians* has a more popular appeal.[109] Abraham is a native of Ireland but is a professor at the Perkins School of Theology in Southern Methodist University in America. Abraham comments on the inter-relation between the Bible and reason 'Of course, once revelation was available in Scripture, reason was essential for understanding it.'[110] He also writes of Wesley and Calvinism in the words 'He is so sure of his theological ground at this point that he is even prepared to insist that any interpretation of Scripture that backs the Calvinist vision must be wrong; it is nothing short of blasphemy.'[111] Abraham is one who recognises that Wesley comes to the Bible with certain presuppositions as to its teaching.

In summary it may be seen that the work of scholars within Methodism since 2003 have not added very much to those that have written in the late twentieth and early twenty-first centuries.

Conclusions Drawn from the Review of More Recent Literature on Wesley

The conclusions to be drawn from both the previous chapter and this may appear to be very negative. Early, mainly British, biographies began a tradition that looked at Wesley with overzealous veneration, part of which depicted him as supremely a man of the Bible. This neglected the fact, which will be examined in later chapters, that other contemporary figures claimed to use similar authority and came to very different conclusions. George Whitfield and John Newton are examples. It should also be noted that they and many others with whom Wesley was in conflict were also

---

107 David Hempton, *Methodism Empire of the Spirit*, Yale University Press, 2005.
108 Hempton, *Methodism Empire of the Spirit*, p. 74.
109 William J Abraham, *Wesley for Armchair Theologians*, Westminster John Knox Press, 2005.
110 Abraham, *Wesley for Armchair Theologians*, p. 160.
111 Abraham, *Wesley for Armchair Theologians*, p. 175.

members of the Church of England and, on both sides, those in disagreement claimed to be loyal sons of the Church.

In this chapter the beginning of a new approach has been noted. It has been demonstrated that the concept of the Wesleyan Quadrilateral has been developed mainly to meet the needs of the UMC in America in the later part of the twentieth century. The extent to which this concept can be traced back to Wesley himself has been questioned and explored within the critical review of American Wesley scholarship. However, it is now clear that an appreciation of the Quadrilateral as a tool is also helpful, particularly in understanding Wesley's theological methodology. It remains to be argued that the search for the influences that fashioned Wesley's biblical interpretation goes behind and beyond the concepts of the Quadrilateral, whether or not scripture is given sufficient primacy, and particularly involves a study of the influence of the Church of England on Wesley.

The sometimes negative conclusions of this chapter are the starting point for further research into the influences that fashioned the life and thinking of Wesley. How did he come to a belief in the Bible as authority? How did he interpret it? In what ways was Wesley's understanding of the Bible influenced by his understanding of tradition? How much influence did reason have over his interpretation of the texts? To what extent did experience lead him to conclusions about the meaning of scripture? The following chapters take up this task of exploration into the life and teaching of Wesley and the way he came to his beliefs. In attempting to answer some of these questions, it will be necessary to hold in mind some of the work undertaken by biblical scholars in respect of what has been described in the Introduction as 'Reader-Response.' It will also be necessary to consider further the influence of the Anglican Church on Wesley. Therefore the next chapter will give consideration to the young John Wesley together with the influence of the Epworth years and the time spent in Oxford.

Chapter 3

The Young John Wesley

Introduction

The roots of Wesley's acceptance of the Bible as his supreme authority, and
the way in which he interpreted it, were to be found, in the first instance, in
the influence at Epworth of his mother and his father, and were developed
within the eighteenth-century High-Church Arminian Anglican tradition.
This regard for the Bible as interpreted through the teaching of the Church
of England was reinforced during the years he spent in Oxford prior to his
departure for America, especially through the works he read during that
time. It is impossible to disentangle completely the influences of family,
friends and reading as they were all interwoven. They were all of immense
importance as Wesley came to interpret the Bible for himself and others.
This chapter explores these points in more detail.

Early Years at Epworth Rectory

John Wesley was born in 1703, his early years being spent at Epworth in
Lincolnshire. It was then a remote town with a population of approximately
1500 of whom about 100 were Dissenters.[1] As a High-Church Tory,
Samuel Wesley was, on occasion, in controversy with many of the local
residents, including some of the Dissenters. John Wesley was educated in
Charterhouse School, London and proceded from there to the University of
Oxford in 1720.[2]

Many twentieth-century scholars recognise the influence on him of those
early years. His parents' beliefs were the result of the influence of families
that had been Anglican but had, on matters of conscience, gone into dissent.
Then Samuel and Susanna, as young people, had entered the Church of
England through conviction. Susanna made this transition in her early
teenage years. Samuel became a member of the Church of England a short
time before his entry into Oxford University as a student. Indeed, at that

---

1   See Rack, *Reasonable Enthusiast*, p. 45.
2   See Rack, *Reasonable Enthusiast*, pp. 68-9.

time, he could not become a student at Oxford unless he was a member of that Church.

Referring to the influence of the family at Epworth on John Wesley, Richard Heitzenrater aptly comments 'Although the story of Methodism is much more than the biography of John Wesley, the influence upon him of the Wesley household was certainly a formative factor in the rise of the movement that later bore his name.'[3] Heitzenrater also makes the point relating particularly to the family's grounding in scripture 'All the children were given careful training in piety and learning. They learned a traditional theology that combined faith and good works in a fashion that reflected the orthodox doctrinal perspective and Puritan ethical inclinations of Samuel and Susanna.'[4]

The influence of Susanna on John is frequently recognised but, it is argued below, Samuel was of much greater influence than is usually acknowledged. It must also be noted that while Susanna was responsible for her children's early education, Susanna and Samuel held similar views on matters theological and political with certain exceptions.

V.H.H. Green, referring to the time when Wesley was elected a fellow of Lincoln College, Oxford, in 1726, but looking back over the earlier years, makes a good point:

> The influence of his family background, more especially the impact of that dominant personality, was the paramount factor in his early development. The parsonage houses at Epworth and Wroote did not merely provide a family circle, sometimes disturbed by inner tensions but ultimately tied by strong affections: they represented a religious background of mingled churchmanship, of a strong High-Church tradition diluted at source by nonconformity which had been long abandoned by his father and mother.[5]

The influence of Susanna on the young Wesley, and that of his siblings, will be noted before attention is given to the way in which Samuel helped his son to understand the Bible as an eighteenth-century High-Church Anglican.

The Influence of Susanna Wesley

It is the commonly accepted view that Susanna was a major influence in the Rectory on John Wesley, both in terms of his character development and especially in his understanding of the Bible. That is not disputed here. Many Wesley scholars note the extent of this influence. They sometimes

---

3   Heitzenrater, *Wesley and the People Called Methodists*, p. 25.
4   Heitzenrater, *Wesley and the People Called Methodists*, p. 31.
5   V.H.H. Green, *The Young Mr Wesley*, Wyvern Books, 1963, originally published by Edward Arnold, 1961, p. 46.

underestimated the influence of Samuel Wesley on his son and that will be considered later, but it should be recognised from the outset that Samuel never disapproved of Susanna's method of bringing up their children. Henry Rack is one who writes about this influence of Susanna on John.

> Everyone who has studied the Wesley family has been struck by the extent to which the character of the father seems to have been inherited by Charles Wesley and that of the mother by John ... John possessed the cool intelligence and passion for neatness and orderliness of his mother, though time and necessity took him a long way from his High Church origins.[6]

Susanna Wesley deserves to be considered in her own right. As Charles Wallace writes, it would be a pity if she is seen (only) as 'the daughter of a prominent Nonconformist minister, Samuel Annesley; and the wife of an Anglican priest who never quite became prominent, Samuel Wesley; and as the mother of Methodist founders John and Charles Wesley.'[7]

Furthermore John Newton, a recognised authority on Susanna Wesley, makes the point:

> Certainly the most superficial knowledge of the character and career of John Wesley can hardly overlook the enormous influence of his mother on his whole personal development ... It is indeed arguable that this relationship is the vital clue, not merely to his private life [...] but to much of his public life - they were never too far apart in Wesley - and to his whole personal make-up too.[8]

Newton also writes of the influence of Epworth on John and Charles Wesley. 'It [Epworth] did so through the decisive influence of their mother, Susanna, who made them Methodists from the cradle.'[9]

Robert Moore, writing about the relationship between Wesley and his mother comments, 'His personal style as a "Methodist", compulsive, over-organised, perfectionist in his attempts to obey "legitimate", "just", and consistent authority was determined at an early age by this relationship.'[10]

It is sometimes suggested that Wesley was influenced by his parents' Puritan upbringing, which, it is often claimed, they never fully rejected.

---

6   Rack, *Reasonable Enthusiast*, p. 51.
7   Wallace, *Susanna Wesley*, p. 3.
8   John A. Newton, *Susanna Wesley and the Puritan Tradition in Methodism*, Epworth Press, 1968, 2nd ed. 2002, p.11. Note may also be taken of the work of Arnold A. Dallimore, *Susanna the Mother of John and Charles Wesley*, Evangelical Press, 1992, who, although making reference to many other works, makes no mention of Newton's book.
9   John Newton, *The Wesleys for Today*, Methodist Newspaper Company Ltd, 1989, p. 3.
10   Robert L. Moore, John *Wesley and Authority: A Psychological Perspective*, Scholars Press (American Academy of Religion Dissertation Series), 1979, p. 45.

There is no suggestion that the word Puritan carries any overtones of repression. John Newton, in *Susanna Wesley,* makes the point repeatedly that Susanna's upbringing as the twenty-fifth, and last, of Dr Annesley's children was a happy one. For example, he writes 'We might well infer, both from the descriptions of Dr Annesley's cheerful good nature, and from his children's happy reminiscences of their home, that the early years of Susanna and her brothers and sisters were filled with quiet joy.'[11] He also argues that Susanna, a convert to the Church of England, was throughout her life strongly influenced by the Puritanism in which she had been brought up.

In exploring the way in which Wesley's approach to the Bible was influenced by his mother it is helpful to consider Susanna Wesley's views on parental responsibility. In a letter dated July 24 1732, at the request of John, Susanna described the principles which she used in bringing up her family, the strict discipline of the home and the centrality of the Bible in the educational process as well as the time set aside on a weekly basis for individual discussion with the children.[12] This letter was preserved by Wesley. It was used in his sermon 'On Obedience to Parents' which was later published in the Arminian Magazine in 1784. It had been previously included in his *Journal* on August 1 1742. It is clear that Wesley was conscious of the way in which his mother introduced him to early and thorough knowledge of the text of the Bible.

The letter of July 24 laid stress on the need for discipline, respect for authority and the place of the Bible in education. Scripture was the authority she accepted but she did not give any indication in the letter of the way she interpreted it. Respect for the Bible as the supreme authority for religious belief was instilled from the earliest years and this was seen as leading to a good moral life. What is clear is that a knowledge of the text of large portions of the Bible was learned by heart by all the Wesley children at an early age. The letter indicates the seriousness with which Susanna approached the subject and the fact that she was determined to influence the children for what she saw as right and proper reasons.

Charles Wallace further draws attention to references to Susanna Wesley's method of education in her other writings.[13] These include letters to Samuel junior in 1709, Samuel senior in 1712 and various journal entries. She wrote:

---

11   Newton, *The Wesleys for Today*, p. 49.
12   *BE* Vol. 25, pp. 330-1. The information about the sources from which this letter is drawn is to be found on p. 331. This letter is also included by Wallace in *Susanna Wesley*, pp. 369-73.
13   Wallace, *Susanna Wesley*, p. 373, note 1.

In order to form the minds of children, the first thing to be done is to conquer their will. To inform their understanding is a work of time, and must proceed by slow degrees; but subjecting the will is a thing which must be done at once - the sooner the better.[14]

This, of course, is totally at variance with modern child-psychology but it illustrates the way in which Wesley was brought up and the way in which he came to his earliest beliefs and convictions. The strictness of Susanna is obvious. Maldwyn Edwards notes:

It was natural that [...] Wesley should desire the will of the child to be broken in order that it might first be subject to the will of the parent and then to the will of God. In all this he was only faithfully following his mother's precept and example.[15]

The manner in which Susanna dealt with the upbringing of the family was influenced by views of the philosopher John Locke on the education of children as Rack comments:

It is indeed possible that Susanna was influenced by Locke or the attitude he represented, and certainly Charles Wesley (who was much influenced by Susanna in his approach to his own children) wrote later that the most important of Locke's rules was 'that in which the whole secret of education consists' - that is 'make it your invariable rule to cross his will.'[16]

Newton also writes 'She [Susanna] seems here to have been influenced by the educational theory of John Locke, whose works she read and admired.'[17]

It may thus be seen that the earliest formation of Wesley's mind was through strict obedience to his parents and his acceptance of their teaching. The fact that Wesley referred to his mother's letters over a lifetime is an indication that he did not change his views on that method of education. Certainly it is right to argue that Wesley's beliefs, especially with regard to the importance of the Bible, were gained, in part, at an early stage in Epworth, from his parents, especially Susanna.

The work of the Wesley scholars quoted establishes the point that Susanna was a major influence on John. She exercised a discipline and led all her children to understand the supreme authority of scripture. Although it is clear that Susanna instilled, over a number of years, an extensive

---

14   *BE* Vol. 25, p. 330.
15   Maldwyn Edwards, *Family Circle: A Study of the Epworth Household in Relation to John and Charles Wesley*, Epworth Press, 1949, p. 65.
16   Rack, *Reasonable Enthusiast*, p. 56. The influence of Locke's method of education on Susanna is discussed in more detail on pages 55-6 of *Reasonable Enthusiast*.
17   Newton, *Susanna Wesley and the Puritan Tradition in Methodism*, p. 115.

knowledge of the text of the Bible, most scholars do not directly address the manner in which she interpreted the Bible or caused the children to interpret it. The Bible for the Wesley family was the authoritative book and its contents well known. The particular theological meaning of text may well have been grasped at a later date although the High-Church Arminian Anglicanism of Epworth Rectory was undoubtedly an influence.

In an unpublished PhD thesis (1977) Robert Michael Casto examined Wesley's use of the Old Testament.[18] Writing of a later stage in Wesley's life, Casto comments '[Wesley's] exegetical method presumed the absolute authority of the Biblical revelation for determining, not only questions of theological doctrine and ethics, but also biblical interpretation itself.'[19] However, he goes on to say: 'Wesley came to this view of the relative authority of scripture and the traditions of the Church early in his life.'[20] Casto further makes the point 'The importance of the Bible in the early life of the Wesley children must certainly be considered as having affected the respect in which John Wesley held the scriptures throughout his life.'[21] He was making reference to the letter of July 24 1732 to John from Susanna Wesley.

Casto also makes the comment:

> In spite of the demonstrated breadth and depth of his reading, the central and important book in Wesley's life was, and remained, the Bible. This was so from early in his life when his mother taught him and the other children to read, beginning with the first verse of Genesis, until later in life, when he was called upon to defend his practices and preaching.[22]

Therefore it may be seen how the teaching of Susanna and the life in the family home influenced Wesley and led him to accept unquestioningly the supreme authority of the Bible. The children learned the Lord's Prayer as soon as they were able to speak and formal education for John began on his fifth birthday with the learning of the alphabet and beginning to read the Bible. This was only part of the early exposure to scripture.

David Ingersoll Naglee refers to entries in the later *Journal* that Wesley kept to illustrate the fact that 'When a child began to speak, Susanna began to guide the child in memorizing verses of Scripture. By the time the child was five, it knew a large number of biblical passages.'[23] Naglee also points

---

18   Robert Michael Casto, *Exegetical Method in John Wesley's Explanatory Notes on the Old Testament.*
19   Casto, *Exegetical Method*, p. 79.
20   Casto, *Exegetical Method*, p. 80.
21   Casto, *Exegetical Method*, p. 152.
22   Casto, *Exegetical Method*, pp. 84-5.
23   David Ingersoll Naglee, *From Everlasting to Everlasting, John Wesley on Eternity and Time*, Vol. 1, Peter Lang, 1991, p. 3.

out that at the age of five, ten verses of the Bible were covered daily and that

> an older brother or sister read a chapter from the Old Testament and a Psalm before the end of the morning session, and then read a chapter of the New Testament and a Psalm before the close of the afternoon session.[24]

Consequently the young Wesley was made familiar with the content of the Bible. The roots of his acceptance of the authority of the Bible clearly were embedded in the Rectory schoolroom at Epworth and the influence of his mother.

Casto, in his thesis, does not make direct reference to the manner in which Wesley interpreted the Bible but appears to presume that it was rooted in Wesley's early life in Epworth. While it is reasonable to assume that a mother teaching the Bible to her children will have had to give some explanation of the meaning of the text, and while it is reasonable also to assume that the eighteenth-century High-Church rectory life influenced the manner in which the Bible was understood, this needs to be further examined.

Wesley's general approach to the Bible and detailed knowledge of its text was thus directly inspired by his mother, reinforced by the dominating influence she had on his life. It is also of note that, whereas the family had in earlier generations moved between the Church of England and Dissent and back, John Wesley remained a committed Anglican to his death, as is argued throughout this work. He read the Bible in the context of his understanding of Anglican teaching due, in part, to parental influence.

It is noteworthy that Susanna's reading included Roman Catholic mystics, Scottish Episcopalian (Henry Scougal), English Puritans (e.g. Baxter), and Anglicans.[25] It was at Epworth, through the influence of his mother, that Wesley was introduced to a wide range of devotional writers, Roman Catholic as well as Protestant, and that he became familiar with the Articles of Religion, and the Homilies of the Established Church. It is reasonable to assume that the Epworth background was one influence, possibly among others, that helped determine Wesley's later manner of biblical interpretation.

All the influences considered so far are those that Wesley himself acknowledged. It may, however, be claimed he was much more deeply influenced by Susanna than even he realised. This would explain the way in which his acceptance of the authority of the Bible and his Anglican understanding of the text were reinforced. G. Elsie Harrison, like others, argues that the greatest influence on John Wesley was that of his mother.

---

24   Naglee, *From Everlasting to Everlasting*, p. 3.
25   See Newton, *Susanna Wesley and the Puritan Tradition in Methodism*, p. 138.

Her *Son to Susanna* is based on early sources.[26] She wrote highly of Susanna, and disparagingly of Samuel. She sympathised with the female children, but did not have much sympathy for the younger Samuel, and Charles was made the real villain of the story, especially over the relationship between John Wesley and Grace Murray. Nevertheless, she showed clearly the way that Susanna was the dominant person in John Wesley's childhood. Harrison also establishes the point that the influence persisted through the Oxford years and beyond into his later life, particularly in his relationships with certain women.

Mabel Brailsford puts it more simply:

> As John was for nearly half a lifetime the power behind Charles, so was his mother Susanna the power behind John, placing before him an unattainable ideal of womanhood, which caused him three times to draw back on the brink of marriage.[27]

This may be illustrated by reference to the story of his relationship with Sophy Hopkey in Georgia when he was a young Anglican clergyman. The first *Extract* from Wesley's Journal was prepared to give some account to the trustees for Georgia of his work in America. A certain Captain Williams had published an affidavit making accusations against Wesley and his hurried departure from that country in December 1737. Wesley's response was in the form of the published *Extract*.[28] The entry for October 14 1735 gives the reason for going to Georgia as: 'to save our souls, to live wholly to the glory of God.' It is highly likely that Wesley himself did not recognise the influence of his mother on him at this time when he was far removed from the family home.

Brailsford further argued that

> The mother-fixation to which he had been subject from earliest childhood always spoke the last word, and succeeded, if at the eleventh hour, in stepping between him and any new affection. Disguised as "the Will of God" it fought a hard battle with John's "natural man," and each time the matter came to a trial of strength his struggles grew more prolonged and more painful.[29]

Although the manuscript journal for this period was not designed for general publication, it was prepared for certain selected people to read. Wesley was defending himself against accusations that he had not handled his relationship with Sophy Hopkey in a proper manner and was circulating

---

26   G. Elsie Harrison, *Son to Susanna*, Ivor Nicholson and Watson, 1937.
27   Mabel Richmond Brailsford, *A Tale of Two Brothers John and Charles Wesley*, Rupert Hart-Davis, 1954, p.12.
28   See *BE* Vol. 18, pp. 121-2.
29   Brailsford, *A Tale of Two Brothers*, p. 98.

this manuscript journal privately to give his side of the story. Therefore, even if Wesley was aware of his mother's influence he would be unlikely to refer to it. He was, however, aware of what he saw as the dangers of his sexuality. Referring to November 20 1736, he wrote 'I took her [Sophy] by the hand (though I was convinced it was wrong), and kissed her once or twice. I resolved again and relapsed again several times during the five or six weeks following.'[30] Wesley's manuscript journal gives the impression that Wesley did not marry Sophy Hopkey because of his own self-discipline, the providence of God and the dissimulation of Sophy Hopkey herself.

Brailsford's conclusions, and those of other modern writers, that the influence of Susanna was strong at this point, are probably accurate even if they cannot be proved conclusively from the evidence of Wesley's writings. What is clear is that his actions and reactions are consistent with the continuing influence of the experiences of childhood in Epworth and the dominance of his mother in Wesley's life. It may be further noted that, commenting on the fact that neither John nor Charles Wesley married before they reached the age of forty, Brailsford writes 'John's abstention is easier to understand than his brother's and, in spite of the many excellent reasons that he alleged for it, it can be explained as the result of the mother-fixation which had ruled his life from the age of six.' Brailsford also comments 'It is interesting that Grace [Murray], to whom he was twice pledged before witnesses, and Mrs Vazeille, whom he did eventually marry, supplied the Mother element which he looked for, however unknowingly, in the women he loved.'[31]

It may be argued that the influence of Susanna on John in matters relating to such subjects as his relationships with women have no direct relevance to the way in which Wesley read or interpreted the Bible. The point, however, is that he was so dominated by his mother that her work instilling the respect for the authority of the Bible and a knowledge of its contents was reinforced by the way in which she was the dominant figure in his early life in many different ways.

Furthermore, the influence of Susanna was still strong some years later as can be illustrated from the account of the way Thomas Maxfield became accepted as a lay preacher in 1741.[32] Returning to London to forbid Maxwell's preaching, it was Susanna who intervened and changed Wesley's mind. Newton makes the point that Susanna may have been influenced by her own experience when she spoke within devotional

---

30   *BE* Vol. 18, p. 442.
31   Brailsford, *A Tale of Two Brothers*, p. 202.
32   See Rack, *Reasonable Enthusiast*, p.210.

meetings in the Epworth Rectory.[33] Whether or not this is the case, she did undoubtedly restrain Wesley when he was all for banning Maxfield.

The memorial tablet to John Wesley in Epworth Methodist Church names Wesley's parents and then says that: 'by them "he was prayerfully educated in the things of God."' Newton's comment is 'In that prayerful consideration of the Wesleys, there seems small doubt that Susanna bore the major and decisive part.'[34] As Maldwyn Edwards puts it 'Her true memorial was in her children and in their work.'[35] James Fowler also sums up the influence of the family at Epworth on Wesley:

> We can be certain that John Wesley, who throughout his life would be centrally concerned with doing the will of God, responded compliantly to Susanna's firm efforts to instantiate obedience and self-control. Modern sensibilities may reject the suppression of spontaneity and wilfulness implied in Susanna's approach. But we should note that her firmness, clarity, and even-handed consistency in dealing with her children did create for them a sense of order and meaning in what could have been a chaotic household.[36]

Susanna undoubtedly deserves such a memorial but Newton's comment needs to be qualified in the light of the consideration of the influence of Samuel on his son which is discussed below.

The Influence of Wesley's Siblings

Before turning to an exploration of the influence of Samuel Senior on John in respect of his recognition of the authority of the Bible and its interpretation, it is worth commenting that it is not just the influence of Wesley's parents that is to be noted. The fact that Wesley was surrounded by older sisters is not to be overlooked. As a four-year old boy John's companions were all female and older than him with ages ranging from five to sixteen. Any amusements were those of a female community. Susanna kept all the children apart from the other children in the Epworth parish except for the period immediately following the rectory fire. One consequence of this was, as Green observes,

> a decisive streak of femininity in John's character (and to some extent in that of Charles also). His neatness, his meticulous, at times fussy, concern with detail, his

---

33   See Newton, *Susanna Wesley and the Puritan Tradition*, pp. 180-1.
34   Newton, *Susanna Wesley*, p. 129.
35   Edwards, *Family Circle*, p. 86.
36   James W. Fowler, 'John Wesley's Development in Faith' in *The Future of The Methodist Theological Traditions*, ed. M. Douglas Meeks, Abingdon Press, 1985, p. 174.

personal sensitivity, his histrionic approach must have been in part conditioned at this early age.[37]

To a modern reader the words may appear somewhat 'sexist.' However, the influence of Susanna Wesley and John's sisters may be noted and summed up in Green's words: 'These two features, the femininity of his early environment and the thorough training to which he was subjected by his mother, were of the first importance in John Wesley's development.'[38] The influence of the sisters on him is of note because it was their task, under the guidance of Susanna, to read aloud Psalms and other biblical passages during the school time in the nursery. Scriptural passages echoed in his ears as they had been read aloud by his siblings.

John Wesley thus grew up in a secluded atmosphere, protected from exposure to the influences of other families in the town of Epworth. His world was that of the Rectory and the emphasis was on a lifestyle based on authority and what was understood to be biblical moral teaching. In this context it should also be remembered that, in the Rectory, the reading of passages of the Bible and especially the Psalms took place regularly at the end of morning and afternoon school sessions and was shared by the siblings. Thus the respect for the authority of the Bible and the detailed knowledge of the text, though not necessarily its interpretation, were built up in Wesley through the constant contact with his sisters in the life of the Rectory.

The Influence of Samuel Wesley on his Son John

After his graduation Samuel Wesley entered the Anglican priesthood and eventually became Rector of Epworth. A brief booklet on his life is that of Mary and Peter Greetham.[39] His interest in biblical subjects was rooted in his High-Church Arminian Anglican convictions. Samuel is well known for his lifelong work on his commentary on Job. His other known studies were mainly biblical. The interpretation of scripture in the Wesley home, as influenced by Samuel, was that which would be expected in an eighteenth-century High-Church Anglican Rectory.

Although Samuel and Susanna did have much in common in their theological and political views, it should be noted that they did have some political differences and, in this, Samuel appears to have had the greater influence on John. As Rack writes 'In fact John Wesley seems to have adopted his father's Hanoverian Toryism rather than his mother's religious

---

37   Green, *The Young Mr Wesley*, p. 56.
38   Green, *The Young Mr. Wesley*, p. 58.
39   Mary and Peter Greetham, *Samuel Wesley*, Foundery Press, 1990.

Jacobitism.'[40] Gordon Rupp also emphasises the influence of Samuel on
John Wesley.[41] He notes that there was greater warmth in the relationship
of father and son than is sometimes allowed.

Rack further comments 'Samuel had some good qualities. He was
learned, zealous, pious, affectionate when his prejudices were not
aroused.'[42] Among those good qualities was the love for his family and the
interest in the careers of the three sons that survived into adult life, Samuel,
John and Charles. Rack, however, also immediately quotes V.H.H. Green
as saying that Samuel was 'obstinate, passionate, partisan and pedantic.'

In 1951, John C. Bowmer commented 'Methodism's debt to Samuel
Wesley has hardly received its due recognition.'[43] It is the truth of this
statement that needs to be further explored with special reference to John
Wesley's understanding of the authority and interpretation of the Bible.
Bowmer also commented 'Samuel Wesley was not a Non-juror, but the fact
that he had as much in common with them accounts for the influence they
exerted upon his sons, John and Charles.'[44]

1725, the year after his graduation, was the time when John Wesley
began to take religion more seriously. This led to his ordination as deacon
although his ordination as priest did not take place until 1728. Ordination to
Anglican orders was normal practice among many Oxford graduates. In
Wesley's case, however, it is not clear whether seeking ordination led him
to take religion seriously, or taking religion seriously led to his eventual
ordination. He entered into a correspondence with both his mother and
father. He also spent time reading the Bible in preparation for ordination.
On his father's advice, given in the 1725 correspondence, in a letter
preserved by Wesley, he read Grotius on the Old Testament. Hugo Grotius
(or de Groot, 1583-1645) of Holland was interested in both international
and natural law and was also one of the earlier writers to examine some of
the critical questions relating the Old Testament. He was strongly anti-
Calvinist, asserting the freedom of the human will. Thus Samuel may be
seen as an influence that led John to accept the authority of the Bible and
read it. He also pointed him in an anti-Calvinist direction.

The influence of Samuel Wesley on John during this period is very clear.
The possibly indirect influence of father on son is noted by Heitzenrater
when referring to Richard Hooker's *Of the Laws of Ecclesiastical Polity*
(1595) and Samuel Wesley's *Advice to a Young Clergyman* (1735) which

---

40   Rack, *Reasonable Enthusiast*, p. 373.
41   See E. Gordon Rupp, 'Son to Samuel: John Wesley, Church of England Man' in
     Gordon Rupp, *Just Men*, Epworth Press, Epworth Press, 1977, pp. 114-5.
42   Rack, *Reasonable Enthusiast*, p. 49.
43   Bowmer, *Sacrament of the Lord's Supper*, p. 18.
44   Bowmer, *Sacrament of the Lord's Supper*, p. 21.

'assumes that any aspiring cleric will be well-grounded in Hooker.'[45] On that page Heitzenrater notes that Hooker's mediating work presenting a via media referred to: '**Scripture** (but not as used by the Puritans) [...] **Tradition** (but not as used by the Roman Catholics) [...] and **Reason** (but not as used by the Platonists).'[46] Although *Advice to a Young Clergyman* was dated from a later period, it is reasonable to assume that the advice given to, and accepted by, John in 1725 would have been along the lines of that later work.

Heitzenrater also makes the comment:

> John Wesley's own framework for authority owes an obvious debt to the Hookerian perspective that had become pervasive by his day. The tensions between Calvinism and Catholicism that Hooker had addressed were soon superseded by a growing antagonism between Puritans and Arminians - a dispute that first erupted in the Low Countries at the turn of the seventeenth century as an intra-Calvinistic squabble.[47]

The fact that Samuel as well as Susanna was a considerable influence on the young Wesley is also evident when note is taken of three points emerging from the letters of 1725.[48] The first is that during this year Wesley was continuing to seek the advice of both his parents, not just Susanna, and was clearly influenced by them in many ways. Although he made his own decisions, it was natural for him to seek their advice on questions arising from his reading at that time and the understanding and acceptability of the conclusions of books that he was studying.

Second the correspondence in the earlier part of the year with both Samuel and Susanna concerned the approach to ordination in the Church of England. Samuel's letter of January 26 advised delay in seeking ordination, possibly because he was not certain that John was approaching ordination with the right motivation. This advice was changed in a later letter and full support was given. He strongly recommended that John gave detailed attention to the Bible, and to the Bible as the best commentary on the Bible. Samuel further suggested that Wesley might well assist him in the production of a Polyglot Bible with a number of languages compared. [49] The fact that Wesley both kept and later published this letter is an indication that he valued its advice. It is also evidence that the son was influenced by the father when it came to recognising the importance of the study of the Bible. Samuel Wesley used Bible commentaries and wrote works on the Bible. The somewhat odd expression about the Bible being its

---

45   Heitzenrater, *Wesley and the People Called Methodists*, p.10.
46   The words in bold type so emphasised are in the original.
47   Heitzenrater, *Wesley and the People Called Methodists*, pp. 10-11.
48   *BE* Vol. 25, pp. 156-90.
49   See *BE* Vol. 25, pp. 157-9.

own best commentary indicated that Samuel used one Bible passage to help interpret the meaning of another, a practice much used by John in his later work. The interpretation of the Bible was, no doubt, in line with the Anglican biblical doctrine which Wesley had absorbed from his parents during his earliest years at Epworth. This correspondence is thus evidence from a primary source that John Wesley's thought was still being influenced by his father, particularly in the attention he gave to biblical studies.

Not relating directly to Samuel, the third point that emerges in the correspondence is that in the period leading up to his ordination, Wesley was influenced by, among others, the works of Thomas à Kempis. Wesley discussed this with his mother Susanna and it is clear that he was still influenced by her as well as by Samuel. Of course, this particular point relates to the influence of Susanna on John Wesley, but the correspondence between both parents and son at this time is an indication that, although there were many divisions at times between Samuel and Susanna, the fundamental influence of the Anglican Rectory on the thinking of the young ordinand was strong and that Samuel and Susanna had more in common than has sometimes been accepted.

As Christopher Idle points out, the Journal entries written at the time of his Aldersgate experience contain a reflection on his earlier years: 'When I was about twenty-two, my father pressed me to enter into holy orders. At the same time, the providence of God directing me to Kempis's *Christian Pattern*, I began to see, that true religion was seated in the heart.'[50] It is also worthy of note that à Kempis was a Roman Catholic and *The Imitation of Christ* is a work on the spiritual life in the mystical tradition. Book One, Chapter 5 is entitled 'On Reading the Holy Scriptures' and contains the sentences 'Truth is to be sought in the Holy Scriptures, not skill in words. Every Sacred Scripture should be read in the spirit in which it is written.'[51] There are references to the importance of reading the Bible on pages 48 and 209. The work itself contains scriptural quotations and emphasises the need for humility before God.[52]

The reference to Samuel's support for John's ordination illustrates the apparent inconsistency at times between the correspondence and the Journal. In the former there appeared to be some hesitation on Samuel Wesley's part and in the latter strong encouragement. The inconsistency is perhaps not as great as it may appear. It would seem that Samuel was at first cautious about John's desire for ordination because he was not certain of his motivation. Later he warmed to the idea. It is also true that Wesley's

---

50   Idle, *Abridgement*, p. 15.
51   The quotation is taken from the translation of E.M. Blaiklok, Hodder and Stoughton, 1979.
52   Idle, *Abridgement*, p. 15. See *BE* Vol. 18, p. 243.

memory of events written at a later date may have been sometimes confused. In retrospect Wesley recognised that the influence of his father Samuel persisted. Wider reading might help develop the understanding and interpretation of biblical truth, but the roots were deeply embedded in the life in the Epworth Rectory.

The fact that Samuel's influence on John continued well beyond John's ordination is evident from the later correspondence between them. Three letters from John Wesley to his father dated December 19 1729, December 11 1730 and January 15 1731 raise the question of the origin of evil.[53] These are of note in that John Wesley kept copies and that he published the first and the third, slightly edited, in editions of the Arminian Magazine as late as 1780. The letters were not so much seeking advice or guidance as giving his own views on the subject which partly arose from a critical reading of two works, the first Mr. Ditton's *Discourse on the Resurrection of Christ* and the second Archbishop King's *De Origine Mali*. The third letter turned again to *De Origine Mali*.

It is clear that in those days Wesley still had high regard for his father and felt it necessary to share with him his thinking on important matters. It is not necessary here to explore Wesley's views on the origin of evil, but it is noteworthy that he was at that time being influenced by his reading and was using reason to debate the issues arising. In these letters he did not use biblical arguments to establish his case but rather used logic to argue for the points he wanted to make. The use of logic was one of the skills that Wesley acquired at Oxford, but it may also be noted that the eighteenth-century Anglican tradition had a high regard for reason. The Bible itself was usually interpreted through the use of reason.

The fact that Wesley kept copies of the letters he wrote, and then fifty years later published them in a magazine intended for the instruction of the Methodist people, indicates the importance with which he regarded them. They illustrate something of the complexity of the sources that he used to arrive at his beliefs. At the very least it must be concluded that Samuel was a continuing influence on Wesley and that the son obviously thought that his father would appreciate arguments based on wide, but critical, reading and reason. Samuel's influence on John Wesley in these matters must be acknowledged, even if Susanna is seen by many as being the dominant person in John Wesley's early life.

---

53   See *BE* Vol. 25, pp. 240-2, pp. 257-9 and 264-7 respectively.

1725 Onward - The Influence of Thomas à Kempis, Jeremy Taylor and William Law

Christopher Idle, in his abridgement of Wesley's Journal, refers to an extract from 'a letter 'to a friend': Londonderry, 14 May 1765.'[54] In this there are two points to be noted 'In 1725 I met with Bishop Taylor's *Rules of Holy Living and Dying*. [...] In 1730 I began to be homo unius libri.' The significance of this extract is not simply that Wesley confirmed that these were a true record of what happened. They also establish that Wesley recognised that the influences on him in those earlier days were formative and survived into his later life. Of even greater note is the fact that, in a letter with a reference to being a man of one book, he acknowledged the influence of reading other books upon him. The man of one book was also the man of many books.

Others scholars have drawn attention to the extent of Wesley's reading at this time. Nevertheless, care needs to be taken in assessing the influence on Wesley of the works he read. Rack makes reference to a memorandum on the subject entitled 'Not tossed to and fro by every wind of doctrine,' which was dated January 25 1738.[55] He further writes:

> A word of caution is also necessary here, as elsewhere, about laying too much stress on the books Wesley read and their original religious pedigree and meaning. Too many analyses of Wesley's experience and theology have proceeded in this bookish way. It is true that the books mentioned did influence him, some of them (even the mystics) long after his conversion. But he read and abridged them very selectively and built them into patterns of his own.[56]

This warning is to be noted because Wesley did not simply absorb all that he read. He was a very complex person and the influences that fashioned him came from many different sources.

It is sufficient to mention only a few of the scholars who have commented on Wesley's reading at this time. Green points out 'There were few days when he [Wesley] did not devote some hours to the study of the Greek New Testament, and the biblical bent of his interest can already be discerned.'[57] On the same page Green also notes that Wesley was spending time with contemporary theological works including 'Watts on Predestination, Ellis on the Thirty-nine Articles.' Then there is the early evidence of the influence of the Church of England through its Articles. On the following page, Green states that: '[Wesley] was also concerned with the philosophical views of Locke, Hutcheson and the critical problems they

---

54   See Idle, *Abridgement*, p. 17.
55   Rack, *Reasonable Enthusiast*, pp. 96-7.
56   Rack, *Reasonable Enthusiast*, p. 97.
57   Green, *The Young Mr. Wesley*, p. 73.

raised.' Green does not accept that Locke was the major influence on Wesley although, as it will be shown in the next chapter, other scholars have seen him as the source of Wesley's empiricism and his method of theological argument. Heitzenrater also notes that at this time Wesley's reading included Thomas à Kempis, Jeremy Taylor, Robert Nelson, and William Beveridge.[58] One of the consequences of this reading led Wesley to begin to keep a diary. Later this led on to his published Journal and was one way in which he gave account before God and others of his use of time. As Heitzenrater comments:

> Wesley's search during this period [1725] for a meaningful understanding of the demands of Christian living eventually led him to tie together the perfectionism of the pietists, the moralism of the Puritans, the devotionalism of the mystics in a pragmatic approach that he felt could operate within the structure and doctrine of the Church of England.[59]

This gives some indication of the way in which wider reading influenced Wesley's understanding of the meaning of the Bible.

It was during 1725 that Wesley was making frequent visits to Stanton Rectory and developed a friendship with Sally Kirkham, a friendship not approved by his mother. It was through Sally's advice that he came, in the first instance, to read Thomas à Kempis.

As Green notes:

> It has been surmised that Sally Kirkham was the 'religious friend' who introduced him to Thomas à Kempis; Wesley returned to Oxford from Stanton on 28th May, 1725, and the following day wrote to Epworth "I was lately advised to read Thomas à Kempis over, which I had frequently seen, but never so much looked into before.'[60]

The reference to à Kempis was to a paraphrase of *The Imitation of Christ* by George Stanhope, Dean of Canterbury, under the title *The Christian Pattern*. Sally Kirkham may also have introduced him to Jeremy Taylor's *Holy Living and Dying*. These visits illustrate the female influence on Wesley, the parental influence, and the fact that Thomas à Kempis and Jeremy Taylor began to play a large part in his thinking. Susanna Wesley was disapproving of Wesley's relationship with Sally Kirkham, especially after her marriage to another. 'I have many thoughts of the friendship between Varanese [the name by which Sally was known in the group that met at Stanton] and thee, and the more I think of it, the less I approve it.'[61]

---

58 See Heitzenrater, *Wesley and the People Called Methodists*, pp. 85-6.
59 Heitzenrater, *Wesley and the People Called Methodists*, p. 31
60 Green, *The Young Mr. Wesley*, p. 199.
61 Wallace, *Susanna Wesley*, p. 131.

This is in a letter dated January 31 1727. It replicates the feelings expressed in other correspondence referring to the subject.

Referring to the influence of Sally Kirkham, Casto comments 'The Bible gained a new significance for Wesley when he read Taylor. That significance was not confined to the isolated study of Scripture. It became important for the practical concerns of "holy living."'[62] Thus it may be seen that the influence of his friends, the reading of Taylor and the importance for Wesley of scripture are closely inter-related. The introduction of other influences did not diminish the view Wesley had of the importance of the Bible, but it did give him new insights into its interpretation.

William Law's *Serious Call to a Devout and Holy Life* was published in 1729 and Wesley had read it by 1730. As Eric Baker notes 'In respect of humility it is noteworthy that Wesley seems more satisfied with Law's teaching than with that of Jeremy Taylor, his disquiet with the latter's teaching being voiced in a letter to his mother in 1725.'[63] In 1732 Wesley had conversation with Law in Putney and was so influenced by him as to read the mystical medieval work, *Theologia Germanica*.[64]

In order to assess the influence of Law on Wesley, it is necessary to note that Law's thought passed through a number of phases. His earliest known views were those of a High-Churchman as expressed in his letters to the Bishop of Bangor, published in 1717. The later *A Practical Treatise upon Christian Perfection* was published in 1726 followed in 1729 by *A Serious Call to a Devout and Holy Life, Adapted to the State and Condition of all Orders of Christians*. Here, as Baker observes, 'Instead of the ecclesiastical purist of the Bangorian letters, we discover a man dominated by a consuming passion for the ethical implications of his religion.'[65] Law was later strongly influenced by Jacob Böehme and this was reflected in Law's much later works *Spirit of Prayer* and *Spirit of Love* which show the influence of mysticism on Law. *The Spirit of Prayer or the Soul Rising out of the Vanity of Time into the Riches of Eternity* was published in 1749 and *The Spirit of Love* in 1752.

The major influence of Law on Wesley was in Wesley's Oxford years through Law's works on Christian perfection and the *Serious Call to a Devout and Holy Life*. Although he would later disagree strongly with Law, Wesley's search for Christian perfection had its roots in his reading the works of Law. Thus it was Law who introduced Wesley to the mystics who were an influence on him and also a cause, at times, for real concern.

---

62 Casto, *Exegetical Method*, p. 87.
63 Eric W. Baker, *A Herald of the Evangelical Revival*, Epworth Press, 1948, p. 89. Baker's work was published shortly after that by J. Brazier Green, *John Wesley and William Law*, Epworth Press 1945.
64 See Green, *The Young Mr. Wesley*, p. 138.
65 Baker, *A Herald of the Evangelical Revival*, p. 6.

As Heitzenrater comments:

> Madam Guyon, Antoinette Bourignon, Cardinal Fénelon, the Marquis de Renty, and other mystics soon became prominent in his reading lists. Wesley resonated with the spirituality of these writers and was able to look beyond some of what he felt were their theological inadequacies in order to share their concern for holy living.[66]

Wesley was always going to have difficulty with the mystics in his own thinking and yet their influence remained with him and can be traced back to this period in his life.

Wesley was influenced by Law's works. He examined his teaching in the light of scripture and the evidence of the experience of others as much as himself. His later disagreement with Law was not about the requirement to press towards what he sometimes described as perfect love. It was the means to achieve that end that was in question. Possibly even more than Wesley realised, Law remained a determining influence upon his interpretation of biblical teaching with regard to holiness, despite the divergence in the thoughts and ways from this time forward.

As Rack writes:

> A tension was created in some of those who followed the High Church way of perfection adumbrated by men like William Law, which for future evangelicals perhaps had the role of driving men to despair of the doctrine and means proposed.[67]

Reading the works of Law led Wesley to grasp the importance of the holy life without showing him how to achieve it.

Much later, in 1756, Wesley issued an open letter to William Law which was mainly an attack on Law's *The Spirit of Prayer* and *The Spirit of Love*. As Baker notes:

> [Wesley] charges Law with continually blending philosophy with religion more than any other writer in England, instancing in particular *The Spirit of Prayer* and *The Spirit of Love,* 'wherein from these titles of them one would expect to find no more of philosophy than in the Epistles of St. John'.[68]

The point at issue here is that Wesley regarded Law as being unscriptural. As Baker comments,

> Here we should note, what has often been remarked, that Wesley was in no sense an original theologian. He sought neither to expound new dogmas, nor to

---

66 Heitzenrater, *Wesley and the People Called Methodists*, p. 52.
67 Rack, *Reasonable Enthusiast*, p. 103.
68 Baker, *A Herald of the Evangelical Revival*, p. 48.

overthrow existing ones. He himself insisted that what he preached was entirely scriptural and had been preached by Paul in New Testament days, and by Augustine, Luther, and others in later times.[69]

Baker, referring to a somewhat later period in Wesley's life, gives a good summary of the influence of Law on Wesley, commenting:

> The real question should always have been, not whether Law was a Methodist, but how far the Methodists were followers of Law. In all this enquiry we find little evidence of Law being influenced by Wesley or the Methodists. Any influence that was exerted was by Law upon them.[70]

The influence on Wesley of Thomas à Kempis, Jeremy Taylor and William Law was to remain with him throughout his life. Although Wesley's knowledge of à Kempis and Taylor goes back to 1725, his knowledge of Law may be dated about 1730, followed by a meeting of Wesley and Law in 1732. Rack suggests that Wesley's own recollection of the precise dates is possibly in error.[71] In particular it was these influences that led him to interpret the Bible in terms of inward religion and the quest for a holy life. His later criticism was not that this quest was wrong - far from it. His criticism was that these writers did not show him the way to achieve the end he was seeking. Moreover, as Moore comments 'The training of his parents was supplemented and not contradicted by Wesley's reading of Jeremy Taylor, Thomas à Kempis, and William Law.'[72]

It was of this period that Baker commented 'Thus Jeremy Taylor, Thomas à Kempis, and William Law formed a triumvirate jointly responsible for what happened to Wesley in 1725 and the years immediately following.'[73] This implies that Law's works became an influence on Wesley almost as soon as they were published. As Brailsford notes, referring to the Holy Club in Oxford 'In the minds of the four members of the Holy Club, Law kindled a flame that could not be hid.'[74]

The Holy Club

The year 1729 saw the beginning of the Holy Club at Oxford, first with Charles Wesley as its leader, and then with John, when he returned from a time away from Oxford. The fact that it showed the continuing influence of the authority of the Bible for Wesley may be seen in his own words:

69   Baker, *A Herald of the Evangelical Revival*, p. 117.
70   Baker, *A Herald of the Evangelical Revival*, p. 45.
71   See Rack, *Reasonable Enthusiast*, p. 73.
72   Moore, *Psychological Perspective*, p. 103.
73   Baker, *A Herald of the Evangelical Revival*, p. 7.
74   Brailsford, *A Tale of Two Brothers*, p. 67.

In November 1729, four young gentlemen of Oxford, Mr. John Wesley, fellow of Lincoln College, Mr. Charles Wesley, student of Christ Church, Mr. Morgan, Commoner of Christ Church; and Mr. Kirkham of Merton College; began to spend some evenings in a week together, in reading chiefly the Greek Testament.[75]

Wesley claimed that the intention was to read the classics in the week and a book of divinity on Sundays. A clearer understanding of the nature of the Holy Club and its influence on its members is to be found in Wesley's correspondence with Richard Morgan senior.[76] The story behind the correspondence is that William Morgan was an early member of the Holy Club with John and Charles Wesley but that he became physically and mentally ill, dying in August 1732. As a consequence William's father, Richard senior, was strongly opposed to the Holy Club but Wesley wrote to him on October 19 1732 with an account of the group and defending himself and his brother from the charges of causing William's death. Richard senior then sent his younger son, Richard, to Oxford and into the care of Wesley.

The letter to Richard Morgan senior dated 19 October 1732 was used by both John and Charles Wesley, sometimes edited, as a description and a defence of the work of the Holy Club.[77] The importance with which Wesley regarded this letter is shown by the fact that it is also found as part of the preface to the first extract of the Journal.[78] It is evidence that the group was serious and disciplined in its search for a satisfactory religious life. The influences of Bible, Book of Common Prayer, *The Whole Duty of Man*, Church worship, especially frequent attendance at Holy Communion, and works of charity are all clearly illustrated. It is clear that Wesley's thinking was now being influenced within the group and the way he understood the meaning of the biblical text was that of a studious young clergyman accepting Anglican doctrine and formulae.

When Wesley later had difficulty in the responsibility and care of Richard Morgan junior, he consulted a number of people. Thus there are letters to or from Wesley's mother and father and John Clayton, a former member of the group in Oxford but then in Manchester and a close friend of Thomas Deacon, the Non-juring leader. There was also a letter to William Law. This correspondence illustrates the seriousness with which he undertook his pastoral responsibility. It is clear that, at this time, Wesley

---

75 Quoted by Green, *The Young Mr. Wesley*, p. 142. See also a slight variation on this in Wesley's letter to Richard Morgan dated October 18 1732 (See Idle's *Abridgement*, pp. 16-17) and quoted extensively in the Journal, *BE* Vol. 18, p. 124.
76 This is found interspersed with other letters between pp. 335-438 of *BE* Vol. 25.
77 *BE* Vol. 25, pp. 335-44.
78 *BE* Vol. 18, pp. 123-33.

was still open to a number of influences in his attempt to have a biblically-rooted, Anglican and rational basis to his actions.

Green makes the point, referring to Wesley in 1733:

> He still sought an ultimate authority and he believed that he had found it in the traditions and the teachings of the early Church. Fundamentally the members of the Holy Club tried to return to the 'Ancient' practices of the Church. This was where Wesley's own studies, his reading of the High Anglican writers had persuaded him that the life commanded in the Scriptures was in practice carried out.[79]

Correspondence with Mary Pendarves

The correspondence with Mary Pendarves does not directly raise the questions of the influences on Wesley or his understanding of the authority of the Bible. Nevertheless, it does illustrate the development of his use of scriptural language in his written work, even ordinary correspondence.[80] Mary Pendarves was a widow, slightly older than Wesley. At the conclusion of their correspondence he faithfully destroyed the original letters at her request, but first made and kept copies! It is beyond the present purpose to explore the nature of the relationship and its importance to either of them. The first letter quoted is dated in August 1730 and the last from Wesley, which effectively terminated the correspondence, in July 1734, Mary Pendarves having written to him at that time after not responding to a number of earlier letters.

The use of biblical language is a feature of this correspondence which has apparently not been noticed in the scholarly reviews of Wesley's life, but which does appear through a study of the footnotes in the *BE*. In his earlier general correspondence and his first letters to Mary Pendarves there was little, if any, use of biblical language or quotations. The letter of February 1 1731 contained five such quotations and there were six in his letter of April 14 1731. The increasing use of biblical language appears to be a conscious development in Wesley's usage at this time. This was beginning of a development of style which may be noted in the later letters, sermons and other works of Wesley.

Wesley frequently used Latin and Greek quotations, perhaps reflecting the influences of his Oxford education, but the use of biblical language went further. The words were not simply immediately identifiable texts. They were biblical sentences and phrases incorporated into Wesley's own written work. Wesley had begun to use biblical language to express the

---

79   Green, *The Young Mr. Wesley*, p. 167.
80   Copies of these letters may be found, with other correspondence, in *BE* Vol. 25, pp. 246-91.

thoughts that he wanted to communicate, and was using texts selectively to that end. This correspondence is therefore of help in dating the time at which Wesley's literary style developed and scripture became more important in the background of what he was writing.

1733 - Wesley's Sermon: 'The Circumcision of the Heart'[81]

On 1 January 1733 Wesley preached the sermon, prepared in late 1732, 'The Circumcision of the Heart,' at St. Mary's, Oxford. It relates to the theme of holiness and undoubtedly contains the roots of his teaching on Christian Perfection. The fact that Wesley included it in the standard volumes of his sermons later, well beyond his Aldersgate experience, justifies the use of it in the search for the major influences on Wesley's biblical interpretation. Evidence drawn from this sermon illustrates the sources on which Wesley relied in his understanding of scripture. Outler's footnotes in the *BE* draw attention to at least three places where the influence of Law may be discerned and two echoes of Jeremy Taylor. Clearly Wesley's reading of these writers had influenced his thought. It is also of note that in paragraph 2 of the Introduction to the sermon Wesley used the phrase 'spiritual sense.' In that and the following paragraph there is an echo of the Lockean empiricism, although Locke himself would not have written in quite that manner.

No one can read the sermon without being aware that it is biblically based. In the footnotes Outler made reference to over 100 verses from the Old and New Testaments that are used, normally without direct attribution to their sources by Wesley. That fact should be noted with some caution. It is clear that some quotations are taken from memory and many are selective. There is also a freedom of use shown, for example, in the reference to 1 Corinthians 13:13, where, as Outler noted, Wesley used the word charity rather than love and, following Law, he added humility to the three cardinal virtues. Outler commented that in the sermon 'all that he [Wesley] had learned from Taylor, à Kempis, William Law, and the traditions of Christian will-mysticism behind them comes to focus.'[82] Wesley also included Greek and Latin quotations quite freely but not giving them the same authority as the Bible.

Wesley preached this sermon on the day that commemorates the circumcision of Christ and that explains his choice of text. However, his objective was not to expound that theme as such. He later published the

---

81 This sermon, with Outler's Introductory Comment and footnotes, is found as No. 17 in *BE* Vol. 1, pp. 398-414. This was the only sermon preached before 1738 included in Wesley's published collections.

82 See *BE* Vol. 1, p. 403, and especially notes 15 and 16. Outler made a similar point with reference to the teaching about self-denial. See *BE* Vol. 1, p, 412, note 120.

sermon to outline his teaching on Christian holiness. He had also been aware of the need to respond to an article in *Fog's Weekly Journal* on December 9 1732 on 'This Sect called Methodists.'[83] Any study of this sermon to explore the sources on which he drew and the influences on Wesley in his Oxford days will show that it raises very complex questions. Although biblically based, it is clearly not just an exposition of the scriptures but is the result of the many elements that made up his personality and experience. The fact that Wesley published it some years later indicates that, even if there were some changes in his views, there was a real continuity as well. His perfectionist theology in the Anglican tradition had its roots in his understanding of the meaning of the Bible for him and others in his earlier days and was evident in this sermon.

1734 - The Succession to the Living in Epworth

Correspondence concerning the succession to Samuel Wesley's living at Epworth does not illustrate any new influences on John Wesley but it shows the way he dealt with those influences that challenged his own wishes as to future action. As Samuel Wesley's death approached, John Wesley was put under some pressure by his father and his older brother Samuel to apply to succeed his father in the living.[84] In fact Samuel Junior was the preferred son for this task: 'One of the last tokens of the Rector's confidence in Samuel [Junior] was manifest in his strong request for the son to succeed him at Epworth.'[85] John was thus his father's second choice but both Samuel senior and Samuel junior pressurised him. In a long letter to his father dated December 10 1734 Wesley acknowledged the authority of Samuel and yet struggled to say 'no' to this pressure.[86] The greater part of the letter reads as if Wesley was trying to find reasons, or even excuses, for declining his father's will. He also sought the views of Bishop Potter, who had ordained him both deacon and priest, as to whether he had been ordained in order to take the cure of a parish.[87] He accepted the prompting of the bishop when it allowed him to take the line that he had already determined to pursue.

Robert Moore makes a comment

> It is clear that Wesley had developed a sense of personal destiny that required a role which would have the marks of being special or extra-ordinary. And it is equally clear that the general conclusion of the family was that being rector of

---

83   See *BE* Vol. 1, p. 399, and note 70 on p. 408.
84   This correspondence, interspersed with others, is found in *BE* Vol. 25, pp. 395-423.
85   Edwards, *Family Circle*, p. 104.
86   *BE* Vol. 25, pp. 397-410.
87   See the letter from Bishop Potter in *BE* Vol. 25, p. 420 and his use of that letter in his letter to his brother Samuel on p. 421.

Epworth was not a role which facilitated the fulfilment (sic) of the potential of its occupants. [...] Epworth had frustrated the dreams of his father, but he was determined that it was not going to frustrate his own.[88]

The real reason for the refusal to succeed his father had already appeared in his letter of November 15 in which he wrote 'The question is not whether I could do more good to others *there* or *here*, but whether I could do more good to myself; seeing that wherever I can be most holy myself, there, I am assured, I can most promote holiness in others.'[89] It is clear that Wesley was still searching in his own mind how he might best serve God and understand his ways. Epworth was not seen as an attractive option. Samuel Wesley had been a major influence on John in his formative years, certainly in the younger man's acceptance of the authority of the Bible and the manner in which he interpreted it. It was not easy for him to break free from the authority of his father when it affected his future course of action but he was determined to do so.

Conclusion

By late 1734 Wesley was in his thirty-second year. This chapter has shown the way in which he came to his biblical interpretation by a variety of routes, beginning in the family setting in Epworth, continuing in Oxford, influenced by a great variety of reading, but within a traditional High-Church Anglican setting. His roots went back not only into the Nonconformity and Anglicanism of Samuel and Susanna Wesley, but also into the influences of the Oxford years on biblical interpretation until the encounter with Moravianism caused the awakening experiences of 1738. As John Munsey Turner comments, after referring to the influences of Samuel and Susanna Wesley on their son, and to the influence of Puritanism, Caroline Anglicanism and 'men of reason' 'None of the influences of his early days - personal or intellectual - were ever quite forgotten.' [90]

What happened before and after the Aldersgate experience of 1738 undoubtedly led to a consolidation of the earlier sources of belief in Wesley's mind. In the next chapter a consideration of these events is given and an exploration is undertaken of the importance for him of experience as a tool to help in biblical interpretation.

---

88   Moore, *A Psychological Perspective*, p. 60.
89   *BE* Vol. 25, p. 395.
90   John Munsey Turner, 'Wesley's Pragmatic Theology' in *Windows on Wesley, Wesleyan Theology in Today's World*, ed. Philip R. Meadows, Applied Theology Press, 1997, p. 2.

Chapter 4

Moravian Influence, Aldersgate and Experience

Aldersgate – A Turning Point

The events surrounding what has often been described as the 'conversion' of John Wesley on May 24 1738 have been seen by many of his biographers as the crucial turning point of his life. All that he was before that date, they argue, was changed by the heart-warming experience that has been seen as leading to the great evangelical outreach of the following years. Kenneth Collins, for example, argues for a modified traditional position, affirming that Aldersgate was indeed a conversion experience.[1] Randy L. Maddox challenges this view[2]

Here the traditional assumption is also challenged without denying that it was a major experience in his spiritual development. As a consequence the contention is made that Wesley went to Georgia with a theology built on an eighteenth-century High-Church Anglican interpretation of the Bible. His close relationship with the Moravians introduced him to another interpretation. From 1736 to 1738 his understanding of biblical teaching increasingly approached that of the Moravians. Then, from May 1738 onwards, he moved from that position into a revised Anglican Arminian interpretation of the Bible and by 1740 he was, in his own mind, firmly Anglican in his understanding of scriptural teaching.

Henry Rack comments: 'Many of his [Wesley's] pre-1738 High Church practices and prejudices were gradually abandoned or modified'.[3] However, he also shows that this statement is an oversimplification. Wesley's later position was certainly modified as a result of Aldersgate but it did not cease to be that of a member of the Church of England as is made clear later in this chapter. All that he approved and had gained from the Moravians he found to be both biblical and contained within the Formularies of the Church of England. All that he disapproved and rejected he considered to be neither biblically-based nor with any parallel in the Anglican Church.

---

1   See Collins, *A Faithful Witness*, Excursus on pp. 149-61.
2   See 'Introduction,' *Aldersgate Reconsidered*, Kingswood Books, ed. Randy L. Maddox, 1990, p. 13.
3   Rack, *Reasonable Enthusiast* p. 154.

Wesley scholars have not discussed the implication of what happened at Aldersgate for his understanding of the authority of the Bible. If it was a 'conversion' experience, it certainly cannot be described as the time of Wesley's first acceptance of the authority of scripture. That, as has been shown already, was in place long before. Rather it was a time when he came to a new interpretation of the Bible, possibly influenced by the experience of others and then of himself. If, as Maddox and others have argued, Aldersgate represented a new stage in Wesley's development, it is necessary to consider whether this changed the way he read the Bible. Important factors are the influence that the Moravians, particularly Peter Böhler, had on him and the way in which later he distanced himself from certain of their beliefs and practices. Wesley was strongly influenced by the Moravians but then found that aspects of their teaching did not accord with the Anglican context in which his theology was set and hence came to reject it, entering into disputes with members of the Moravian Church. His interpretation of the Bible remained that of an eighteenth-century Anglican.

This chapter will consider the influence of the Moravians on Wesley's understanding of the meaning of the Bible prior to the events of May 1738 and then attention will be given to the Aldersgate experience itself. This is followed by a consideration of the events of the next two years. This naturally leads to an assessment of the place of experience as a tool in Wesley's biblical interpretation. It is argued that this reflects to a large degree Lockean epistemology.

The Influence of the Moravians on Wesley prior to May 1738

Before considering the influence that the Moravians had on Wesley, it is helpful to note their place in England during the earlier eighteenth century, and their policy with regard to mission. There had been a small group of Moravians who came to England in 1728, including David Nitschmann, establishing contacts with the Church of England. In 1734 August Gottlieb Spangenberg was in England trying to arrange for permission for a Moravian settlement in Georgia. Spangenberg was a leading figure within the Moravian community at that time but had no English and did not preach during the visit. He subsequently sailed for America. David Nitschmann went to Georgia two months after Spangenberg's departure.[4] Having been consecrated bishop in 1735, he sailed on board the ship Simmonds as part of the group who happened to be fellow-passengers with Wesley.

Although some have argued that the Moravians were already engaged in a missionary task in England, this view has been challenged by Colin Podmore, an authority on the Moravians of this time. An example of the

---

4   It is slightly confusing in that there were two prominent Moravians at that time with the name of David Nitschmann.

view challenged by him is that of Clifford Towlson.[5] This point needs to be kept in mind as the Moravian influence on Wesley's understanding of biblical teaching developed. It would have been out of character for the Moravians to have deliberately set out to try and convert him. They were more likely to have wanted to discuss the Christian faith and the meaning of scripture with a minister of the Anglican Church with whom they were seeking a closer relationship and from whom they wanted to gain recognition.

Thus Colin Podmore, comments 'The Moravians did not seek people out, and they neither preached nor formed any group in London. This had not been their intention.'[6] Clearly it was not at that time to establish a church in Britain. That came later. In fact, the work of the Moravians was scarcely established in London by 1738. Podmore argues 'C.W. Towlson misunderstands their purpose completely, for it is clear that the Moravians sought fellowship with those who were already children of God; they wanted to tell of God's deeds to people whose eyes were already opened.'[7]

Herbert McGonigle makes the same point, writing '[The Moravians] had no intentions of proselytising; rather their purpose was to find out those who were already in faith and who would be glad to hear of what was happening at Herrnhut.[8] The aim of the Moravians at that time was to seek recognition by the Church of England and to obtain permission to form settlements in Georgia. In 1737 Count Zinzendorf, the leader of the Moravians, visited London when Nitschmann was also present and in January met the Archbishop of Canterbury who recognised the Moravian orders. A small society was subsequently formed in London, but there was no Moravian church and no church members. In February 1738 four Moravians came to London which later led to the founding of the Fetter Lane society. Peter Böhler was part of the group, but was on his way to America and only intended to stay a short time in England.

Wesley gave his main reason for going to Georgia as 'My chief motive, to which all the rest are subordinate, is the hope of saving my own soul.'[9] The first Extract from the Journal began on October 14 1735. In the entry for that day, Wesley made the same point 'Our end in leaving our native country was [...] singly this - to save our souls.'[10] This statement, perhaps,

---

5   Clifford Towlson, *Moravian and Methodist*, Epworth Press, 1957.

6   Colin Podmore, *The Moravian Church in England 1728-1760*, Clarendon Press, 1998, p. 22.

7   Podmore, *The Moravian Church in England 1728-1760*, p. 9.

8   Herbert McGonigle, *John Wesley and the Moravians*, Morley's Print and Publishing, 1993, p. 6.

9   In a letter to Rev John Burton, a founding trustee of the state of Georgia, on October 10 1735, *BE* Vol. 25, p. 439.

10   *BE* Vol. 18, p. 137.

offers some explanation of the fact that he was open to the influence of the Moravians throughout the whole of this period. Their theology was in the Lutheran tradition with a strongly scriptural basis and with an emphasis on personal salvation experienced by the believer.

Wesley sailed for Georgia in 1735. Describing the outward journey, the Journal entry for October 17 notes that there were twenty-six Moravians on board ship. In the entry for October 10 1735, Wesley wrote 'In the afternoon David Nitschmann, Bishop of the Moravians, and two others, began to learn English, O may we be not only of one tongue, but of one mind and of one heart!'[11] The Journal entry for January 25 1736 gives an account of a storm at sea and the fearlessness and the faith of the Moravians. The entry shows that this experience made a deep impression on Wesley.[12] This may partly explain the fact that in the coming months he became increasingly open to be influenced by their interpretation of the meaning of the Bible in terms of personal salvation.

In February 1736 Wesley had his first encounter with Spangenberg,[13] Spangenberg immediately questioned Wesley on the personal nature of his faith, which Wesley appears to have found somewhat disturbing. In the Journal entry for February 9, Wesley gives the substance of Spangenberg's account of his own life and that of the Moravian Church. In the manuscript Journal and the entries for February 8 and 9 there is a slightly different and fuller account of the conversations between the two men.[14] Nevertheless the Journal record of Wesley's subsequent practices in Savannah suggests that he did not feel any challenge to his understanding of the authority of the Bible, nor of his acceptance of Anglican discipline. This is evidenced in his pastoral work and especially in his baptismal practices. He continued as a High-Church Anglican. It was the interpretation of scripture and its meaning for personal Christian salvation that was in question.

The influence of the Moravians was reinforced later in February in a meeting with Spangenberg and Wesley's presence at a Moravian service in which a new bishop was elected and ordained.[15] Brief notes of this also appear in the diary for this date.[16] Wesley had some reservation about the validity of Moravian orders at this time and whether he could allow Moravians to participate in Anglican communions. However, Wesley was to some extent open to Moravian influence, possibly because the Archbishop of Canterbury, who as Bishop Potter at Oxford had ordained Wesley, recognised Moravian orders. Certainly he found the ordination

---

11 *BE* Vol. 18, p. 137.
12 *BE* Vol. 18, pp. 142-3.
13 *BE* Vol. 18, pp. 145-6.
14 Compare *BE* Vol. 18, pp. 146-8 with *BE* Vol. 18, 352-5.
15 *BE* Vol. 18, p. 151
16 See *BE* Vol. 18, pp. 361-2.

service to be a very moving experience. Clifford Towlson comments '[Wesley] was present at the ordination of Anton Seiffart as Moravian bishop of Georgia, and his unquestioning acceptance of this ordination is evidence of his recognition as a High Churchman of the validity of Moravian orders.'[17] The next day, Wesley commented '[God] hath opened me a door into the whole Moravian Church.'[18] At this time the attractions of the Moravian Church were clearly becoming an influence on Wesley but this did alter the way he carried out his duties as an Anglican minister in Savannah. Although he was commenting on his access to the Moravians, the reality is that he was becoming increasingly open to their influence on him, especially in the way they understood the meaning of scripture and the biblical doctrines of personal salvation.

Soon afterwards Wesley wrote to Count Zinzendorf in Herrnhut.[19] Wesley's letter was dated March 15 and Zinzendorf's reply October 23. Baker, in *BE*, notes this as having been dated in Savannah, March 15, 1736 (Old Style). At that time the New Year was reckoned as beginning on March 25, and Wesley arrived in America February 6 1735 in the older reckoning, 1736 in the new. Frank Baker in his note in *BE* commented 'Wesley was led to initiate their correspondence because of the tremendous respect which he had acquired for the Moravians who had accompanied him to Georgia in the Simmonds.' Heitzenrater discusses his spiritual search at this time which he describes as a 'quest for assurance.'[20] He argues that Wesley believed from his contacts with William Law and others that true religion consisted in holiness in the heart, but that he agonised over the way in which a person could be certain of acceptance by God. It was thus an encounter with doubt to which, following the storms on the voyage to America, was added an encounter with fear.

The encounter with the Moravians, according to Heitzenrater, led Wesley to the point where 'He would adopt the Moravians as his tutors in the faith.'[21] In the event they would bring him to the experience of Aldersgate and then would cause him such concerns that he would reject aspects of their biblical interpretation. In the entry for July 27 1737, Wesley recorded another meeting with Spangenberg and a visit to New Ebeneezer to meet 'the Salzburgers.'[22] The Salzburgers and the Moravians were two

---

17   Towlson, *Moravian and Methodist*, p. 42.
18   *BE* Vol. 18, p. 152.
19   See *BE* Vol. 25, pp. 449-50 and pp. 479-483.
20   Richard P. Heitzenrater, 'Great Expectations: Aldersgate and the Evidences of Genuine Christianity,' in *Aldersgate Reconsidered*, ed. Randy L. Maddox, Kingswood Books, 1990, p. 62.
21   Heitzenrater, 'Great Expectations,' p. 62.
22   *BE* Vol. 18, pp. 186-7.

different and distinct communities, not always in agreement.[23] For the present purpose it is not necessary to pursue this except to note that it was the Moravians who were the increasingly greater influence on Wesley. There are also some references to the meeting in the diary and a longer note in the manuscript Journal.[24] This gives further evidence for the fact that Wesley's belief in the authority of the Bible was unchanged but that his interpretation of it was increasingly influenced by the Moravians

Meanwhile Wesley's biblical usage at that time was illustrated in his description of his first service in Savannah on March 7 1736. He contrasted the Gospel for the day, Luke 18, and the prediction of Jesus that he and the believers would encounter opposition in the world, with the large, attentive and serious congregation before him, and commented 'I could scarce refrain from giving the lie to experience and reason and Scripture all together.'[25] This is evidence that, at this early period in his ministry, Wesley recognised the authority of scripture and the place of experience and reason in interpreting it.

Another early reference to Wesley's understanding of the Bible is found in his somewhat naive view of the nature of the Native American community and the work which he hoped to accomplish with them although he never in fact achieved it. Referring to a conversation with certain 'Creek Indians,' including Chigilly, their headman, Wesley wrote:

> I told him, "If red men will learn the Good Book, they must know as much as white men. But neither we nor you can understand that book unless we are taught by him that is above; and he will not teach unless you avoid that which you already know is not good."[26]

Evidently Wesley's teaching was Bible-based but he believed that scripture needed to be explained in some way. The inference is that a Church of England priest could do this although the encounters with the Moravians were challenging his own interpretation of the scriptures.

On the journey home from Georgia in late 1737, Wesley prepared a memorandum on his spiritual condition. In this he noted the scriptural injunction to keep the commandments, but also noted the interpretations of Papists, Lutherans and Calvinists, the English Divines, the Essential Non-jurors and the Mystics.[27] He also noted the way that various sources had influenced him and how his position had moved between them, claiming that the Bible was the fundamental and primary authority for faith. He was clearly struggling with the way to arrive at the meaning of the scriptures.

---

23 See Rack, *Reasonable Enthusiast*, p. 121.
24 *BE* Vol. 18, pp. 530-4.
25 *BE* Vol. 18, p. 153.
26 *BE* Vol. 18, pp. 163-4. This is the entry for July 1 1736.
27 *BE* Vol. 18, pp. 212-3.

The first Extract of the Journal concluded with Wesley's return to England. An entry published after the Aldersgate event, reads 'I who went to America to convert others, was never myself converted to God.'[28] This has been frequently quoted as evidence for the fact that Aldersgate marked the date of Wesley's conversion and that his real spiritual experience was rooted in the influence of the Moravians on his understanding of scripture. However, this ignores the footnote to the entry made by Wesley in 1774: 'I am not sure of this.' The mature Wesley looked at the event with hindsight and gave a more balanced judgement without undervaluing the importance of what had happened to him. It must also be remembered that the later additions to the first Extract from the Journal date from a time when Wesley had largely broken from the influence of the London-based Moravians and that he may, therefore, have wished to present a slightly different account of the events leading up to Aldersgate.

The second Extract from the Journal covers the six months from February to August 1738. It was published in 1740.[29] In the preface, dated September 29 1740, Wesley indicated that his purpose was to put on record certain facts about the Moravians. In July 1740 he finally broke with the Fetter Lane Society and severed his close ties with them. The inference from the Journal is that he retained a high regard for some members of the Moravian Church. However, as this extract of the Journal was published by Wesley after the break, it is necessary to remember that it, like the first extract, recorded the events from Wesley's later point of view and showed the way he wanted people to understand them. It is necessary to ask, in a way that Methodist scholarship generally has failed to do, whether the Journal gives the facts exactly as they happened without bias.

In February 1738 Wesley first met Peter Böhler, perhaps, as Towlson comments, 'the man to whom, more than to any other single person, John and Charles Wesley owed that change of mind and heart which brought about the Methodist revival.'[30] Then Wesley travelled to Oxford with him, it having been part of Böhler's original plan to make contact with the students there. It was during this time that Wesley recorded Böhler as saying to him 'My brother, my brother, that philosophy of yours must be purged away.'[31] In response to Wesley's concern about preaching faith to others when he was sure that he lacked faith himself Böhler gave the advice 'Preach faith till you have it, and then, because you have it, you will preach faith.'[32] What is not usually noted by commentators on this quotation is the fact that the advice runs counter to the Quietism which later affected

---

28   *BE* Vol. 18, p. 214. The entry itself was for February 1 1738.
29   See *BE* Vol. 18, pp. 218-97.
30   Towlson, *Moravian and Methodist*, p. 48.
31   *BE* Vol. 18, p. 226. (Wesley's translation of the Latin.)
32   *BE* Vol. 18, p. 225.

London Moravianism. It was not a question of giving up the ordinances of the Church until receiving faith, but quite the reverse.

In these encounters with Böhler, Wesley did not once hint at any change in his regard for the authority of scripture. For him what was in question was the fact that his experience did not match that of the Moravians. The search for certainty was also a search which included questioning the interpretation of scripture as given by others and by himself. In March there were further conversations with Böhler in Oxford. During these early months of 1738 Wesley was clearly strongly influenced by Böhler whose departure to America had been delayed. Heitzenrater notes that, on Wesley's return from America, he turned to Böhler in his search for faith, writing 'Within this developing framework, Peter Böhler had a fairly easy time during the early months of 1738 convincing Wesley that true faith eliminated all doubt.'[33] Heitzenrater makes the further point 'On 5 March 1738, Wesley became convinced of the necessity of this faith alone for salvation (sola fide) and of his own state of unbelief. He began preaching salvation by faith the following day.' Thus he was preaching faith nearly three months before the Aldersgate experience. The influence of the Moravians challenged Wesley's long held views, not by challenging his understanding of the authority of the Bible, but by questioning his interpretation of it.

On March 22, Wesley met again with Böhler and discussed faith, which Wesley found agreed with Church of England teaching, and instantaneous conversion, which puzzled him. Wesley tested Böhler's teaching against scripture and on the next day was further convinced by the testimony and experience of other witnesses.[34] His views were later modified after Aldersgate as Wesley tried to assimilate them with his new-found experience and as he reassessed the beliefs that he held through his reading, his Anglican traditions and his understanding of the Bible. Thus scripture was being interpreted by experience and experience tested by scripture itself.

This conversation continued on a short journey on March 26. In April Wesley wrote to James Hutton, a neighbour of Samuel Wesley junior who was a bookseller and close friend of John.[35] His words were 'This one thing I do. I follow after, if haply I may attain faith. I preach it to all, that at length I may feel it.' This reflects the earlier conversations with Böhler, to whom reference is made in the Hutton letter and who had advised Wesley on the preaching of faith. Clearly the search for faith was being intensified. It was also in conversation with Böhler that Wesley was finally convinced that conversion and the attainment of faith could be an instantaneous event.

---

33   Heitzenrater, 'Great Expectations,' p. 64.
34   Wesley's account of this is given in *BE* Vol. 18, pp. 233-5.
35   *BE* Vol. 25, p. 537.

This came through the study of the Bible, especially the Acts of the Apostles, and the testimony of others, therefore through their experience confirming scripture.[36]

On May 1 Böhler invited a group to meet at James Hutton's and Podmore claims that Wesley was there by chance.[37] In his Journal Wesley acknowledged the advice given by Böhler, but that probably partly hides the fact that it was Böhler who was the leading figure in the event which preceded Aldersgate by nearly a month. Having grown in size the society moved, in mid-October, to a room in Fetter Lane and so it was the origin of the Fetter Lane Society.[38] Wesley claimed in his Journal to have been at least the co-founder of the society, calling it 'our little society.' However 'the Society was in fact Moravian in foundation and character, even if initially Anglican in membership.'[39] Wesley gave the impression that the society was the joint work of Böhler and himself, suggesting that the rules of the society were 'In obedience to the command of God by St. James, and by the advice of Peter Böhler.'[40] However, it is more accurate to describe the society as primarily Böhler's work. The rules of the society were biblically-based but the influence that led to the interpretation of scripture was Moravian.

Wesley's searching is shown again in a sharp exchange of letters between Wesley and Law in the period immediately preceding Wesley's evangelical experience of May 24, 1738.[41] Although in later years Wesley would refer to Law with the greatest respect, and publish selected extracts from his books, there was a parting of the ways at this time. The dispute centred on the path by which holiness was to be achieved. Wesley was learning from the Moravians the importance of faith as the way to acceptance with God and, 'Why, asks Wesley, had Law never given this advice, when he must have discerned that Wesley lacked this faith.'[42]

Throughout this period, Wesley does not appear to have been in any doubt about the authority of scripture, but he was confronted, in the experience of others and himself, by questions about the method by which the scriptural way of salvation was to be interpreted. Robert Moore writes that 'Just as he [Wesley] had trouble knowing where he stood with his father, even when he had done his very best, he feared that he had not yet

---

36 See *BE* Vol. 18, pp. 233-4 and p. 248.
37 See *The Moravian Church in England 1728-1766*, p. 38. For Wesley's account of the events see *BE* Vol. 18, pp. 235-7.
38 See Podmore, *The Moravian Church in England 1728-1766*, p. 44.
39 See Podmore, *The Moravian Church in England 1728-1760*, p. 40.
40 *BE* Vol. 18, p. 236.
41 A transcript of these letters is to be found in *BE* Vol. 25, pp. 540-50.
42 Quoted by Eric Baker in *A Herald of the Evangelical Revival*, p. 22.

pleased his heavenly father.'[43] May 24 was the date on which many see that problem as having been resolved, although there were many further questions to be raised. Wesley was both indebted to Law and yet able to view his work critically. He, in some ways, broke with Law, but Wesley's later work on Christian Perfection still reflected his influence.

Aldersgate, May 24 1738

On May 24 1738, Wesley records,

> In the evening I went very unwillingly to a society in Aldersgate Street, where one was reading Luther's Preface to the Epistle to the Romans. About a quarter before nine, while he was describing the change which God works in the heart through faith in Christ, I felt my heart strangely warmed. I felt I did trust in Christ, Christ alone for salvation, and an assurance was given me that he had taken away *my* sins, even *mine*, and saved me from the law of sin and death.[44]

Reginald Ward comments that 'Moravian sources [...] suggest that this [the society in Aldersgate Street] was a society that met in Nettleton Court, Aldersgate Street.'[45] If this was a Moravian society, as seems likely, it is further evidence of the fact that Wesley was being strongly influenced at this time by their teaching in his understanding of the meaning of the Bible for personal faith.

Referring to the Journal entry, Ward argues that 'This is a contemporary document.'[46] He suggests that this was written before a visit to his mother on June 8, and that it was the document he then read to her. Ward admits, however, that the document may have been edited before it was published two years later. What does not receive much comment by Wesley scholars is that, even at that later time, the publication of this Extract of the Journal coming very shortly after his final break with the Moravian Fetter Lane Society, he was still prepared to acknowledge his continuing debt to the Moravians for his awakening to faith. It is thus clear evidence that there was a major change in the life of Wesley in May 1738, and that this was due to the influence of the Moravians.

V.H.H. Green makes a valid point, writing 'It was less the beginning of a new phase than a vital and critical stage in a development which he started at Epworth and continued at Oxford.'[47] The concentration of attention on the events of 'a quarter before nine' overlooks the fact that

---

43   Moore, *A Psychological Perspective*, p. 103.
44   *BE* Vol. 18, pp. 249-50. This is part of paragraph 14 of a long account of Wesley's earlier spiritual pilgrimage and the events of the whole day.
45   *BE* Vol. 18, p. 249.
46   *BE* Vol. 18, p. 242.
47   Green, *The Young Mr. Wesley*, p.258.

Wesley, in his Journal entry, saw this in the context of events beginning when he was ten years old, continuing in the experiences of his school days and, perhaps more importantly, his Oxford years, visit to America and return. Even the references to the events of May 24 itself begin with a note of his Bible reading in the morning and the choir singing a Psalm in St. Paul's Cathedral in the afternoon. At this time, and throughout most of his life, Wesley would on occasion simply open the Bible and take the text seen as it were by chance as a message from God to himself. Then again, at this time, according to Green 'The basic element in his [Wesley's] reading was on patristic learning and the teaching of the fathers.'[48]

Wesley's record of the Aldersgate experience requires careful attention. The familiar words describing this event include the reference to an assurance being given to Wesley that his sins were forgiven. This clearly relates to his spiritual state and some scholars have stressed the element of experience in what happened. The Biblical truth was to be understood through experience. At the same time, the Journal entry refers to Paul's Letter to the Romans. Thus some would argue that the reading of the Bible itself was at the centre of all that happened to Wesley. Without the Bible there would have been no experience. However, the actual reference was to someone reading Luther's Preface to his work on the Epistle, not the words of the Bible itself, and it may be argued that tradition, history and interpretation of scripture were all involved. The Bible had to be interpreted for its meaning to be understood by Wesley.

Philip Watson suggests that the passage that was being read was:

> Faith is a living, daring confidence in God's grace, so sure and certain that a man would stake his life on it a thousand times. This confidence in God's grace, and knowledge of it makes a man bold and glad and happy in dealing with God and all his creatures; and this is the work of the Holy Ghost in faith. Hence a man is ready and glad without compulsion, to do good to everyone, to serve everyone, to suffer everything in love and praise of God who has shown in him this grace. And thus it is impossible to separate works from faith as to separate heat and light from fire.[49]

Watson makes the additional comment:

> Not for a moment did they [the Wesleys] leave off any of the tasks that they had assumed before - their Bible-study and constant prayer, attendance at Holy Communion, their visiting of the sick and those in prison, feeding the hungry, clothing the naked, teaching, preaching, exhorting, rebuking, comforting.[50]

---

48   Green, *The Young Mr. Wesley*, p. 261.
49   P.S. Watson, *The Message of the Wesleys*, Epworth Press, 1964, p. 8.
50   Watson, *The Message of the Wesleys*, p. 8.

The influences on Wesley at that moment in time were complex and it would be over simplistic to draw out just one as the cause of all that happened to him on that day.

These influences clearly related to Wesley's experience of God and his understanding of the meaning of scripture for personal salvation. Nevertheless, the Journal entry draws attention to the fact that he did not immediately find joy and that he did not find escape from temptation. At the time when the influence of the Moravians was at its strongest, Wesley was already beginning the movement that would lead him to depart from their theological understanding and scriptural interpretation to discover new truth in Anglican teaching that he had not perceived before. Although the Aldersgate event was catalysed by Moravian influence, it led Wesley to the discovery that teaching about this experience was to be found in the Anglican Formularies with which he had thought that he was familiar.

It may be argued that the sources of Wesley's understanding of Christian doctrine were all in place by 1738. What was changed was not his understanding of the authority of scripture but its interpretation. Aldersgate itself was to have a fundamental affect on his life and work but as he looked back from later life, it appeared to him that there was greater continuity between all that he taught, and the influences that brought him to those conclusions, in the time before 1738 and the time afterwards. Maddox has correctly commented:

> As the Methodist movement took form after Aldersgate Wesley made it clear that he did not see himself advancing any doctrinal claims beyond the established teachings of the Anglican Church. Rather he identified the mission of his movement as transforming nominal Christians into real Christians.[51]

In summary Rack's comment may be noted:

> The task of interpreting the events of 1738 offers an exacting exercise in analysis of a religious event which resulted from the combined effects of biblical models, patterns derived from inherited religious traditions, the stresses of personal psychology and the persistent force of experience felt in the self and observed in others. [52]

---

51   Quotation from transcript of text provided by Randy L. Maddox of a lecture, "Vital Orthodoxy" A Wesleyan Dynamic for 21st Century Christianity, given at Liverpool Hope University College, September 11 2002.

52   Rack, *Reasonable Enthusiast*, p. 157.

Events Subsequent to May 24 1738

Subsequent to the Aldersgate event Wesley attempted to fit the new experience into his understanding of scriptural teaching, his well-formulated traditional evangelical Arminian theology and his Anglican roots. That he wanted to establish the fact that he remained firmly within an Anglican and biblically-based faith is illustrated in the account of a visit Wesley made to his mother in June 1738. John Newton argues strongly that in this meeting he was to some extent seeking his mother's approval and not just correcting any false account she might have heard about the event.[53] Wesley was anxious to acquaint his mother with all that had happened within the greater context of his spiritual development and for her to give approval to it.

Such was the continuing influence of Susanna on John and, as Brailsford notes,

> When she had read the paper in which he [Wesley] gave a brief account of the religious experiences through which he had been passing since his return to England, "she greatly approved it," so he confided to his Journal, "and said she heartily blessed God, who had brought me to just such a way of thinking." He left Salisbury full of hope and confidence, and three days later he preached before the University of Oxford his "great manifesto," as it has been called, on "Salvation by Faith."[54]

These words illustrate the way that the public and private life of Wesley centred in his own experiences and the influence of Susanna. The reference to Wesley's sermon 'Salvation by Faith' is a further reminder that he had formulated his theological position clearly at that time. Ward points out that this was the sermon placed first in the 1746 collection of his Sermons.[55] Clearly Wesley regarded it as worthy of particular note. In this sermon Wesley tried to answer three questions "What faith is it through which we are saved? What is the salvation which is through faith? How may we answer some objections?" Thus in Oxford Wesley was setting his new experience within the context of traditional Anglican and biblical teaching.

Kenneth Collins comments 'The influence of Moravianism and even of the Continental Reformation was evident throughout this sermon.'[56] He suggests that Wesley may have misunderstood the Moravians, but, like many Wesley scholars before him, he assumes that Wesley was correct in his theology. The Moravians may have thought otherwise.

---

53   See Newton, *Susanna Wesley*, pp. 161-168.
54   Brailsford, *A Tale of Two Brothers*, p. 121.
55   *BE* Vol. 18, p. 255.
56   Collins, *A Real Christian*, p. 64.

However, all was not well. Wesley had been greatly influenced by the Moravian understanding of the meaning of the Biblical teaching on salvation but Aldersgate was followed with periods of theological and spiritual malaise. For example, describing the emerging differences between Wesley and the Moravians, Heitzenrater makes the comment:

> The English Moravians had, in Lutheran fashion, collapsed sanctification into justification and, in Pietist fashion, extended forgiveness of sins (**imputed righteousness**) into freedom from sin (**infused righteousness**). This approach resulted in the expectation of a sinless perfection (including a full measure of the fruits of the Spirit) as the necessary mark or evidence of salvation (genuine conversion).[57]

This Wesley did not accept.

Wesley could not deny the influence of the Moravians but he could argue that all that was good in their teaching was to be found in the Formularies of the Anglican Church and were scriptural. All that he denied in their teaching and practice was, in his opinion, both unscriptural and not Anglican as becomes apparent in the unfolding story of the break between him and the London Moravian Society. Undeniably Wesley's Aldersgate experience was due in large measure to the influence of the Moravians, but he found it increasingly difficult to absorb their understanding of scriptural Christianity into the thought forms already within his mind. The weight of influence on him over the years from the family home, the Oxford years and his grounding in the Church of England prevailed.

In the later summer and early autumn of 1738 Wesley visited Herrnhut to see Moravianism at its source and to seek further understanding of what he had experienced in May. This visit made a considerable impression on him but he began to make an increasing criticism of many of their beliefs and practices. Wesley embarked ship for his visit to Herrnhut on June 13 and arrived back in London on September 16. In his Journal, Wesley notes details of sermons preached by Christian David, conversations with Christian David, Michael Linner, David Nitschman, Augustin and Wenzel Neisser, Zacharias Neisser, David Schneider, Christopher Demuth, and Arvin Gradin. Publishing the Extract from the Journal when he had broken with the Fetter Lane society, he still acknowledged his indebtedness to the Moravians he had met in Herrnhut. They undoubtedly influenced his interpretation of scripture, although he would differ strongly from the teaching and practices of the London-based members of that community within a few months.

The fact that this Extract from the Journal ends at the time when Wesley was still in Germany may have added point. The extract was published

---

57 Heitzenrater, *Wesley and the People Called Methodist*, p. 83 - the bold type is from the original.

shortly after the break with the Fetter Lane Society in the summer of 1740 and may well be the reason for placing the notes on these interviews at the conclusion of that extract. It was the practice and teaching of the London Moravian community that, in Wesley's opinion, were both unscriptural and far removed from the Anglican tradition in which he stood firmly as will be seen below.

Heitzenrater comments that:

> While he was in Germany, Wesley met and interviewed several persons who could testify that their experience matched their doctrines. Wesley wrote careful notes on these interviews and later published them in his Journal as evidence of the true doctrines of the Moravian Church in order to clear the Moravians from any aspersion arising from the teaching of the English brethren.[58]

Heitzenrater further notes that 'The conflict between the German and English Moravian positions represented the nub of the problem for Wesley at this point.'

On his return to England, Wesley wrote to the German Moravians. He expressed his approval of much that he had seen, but offered some criticism of the things he did not like.[59] He was assessing what he had seen and heard in Germany.[60] In November he was trying to resolve the questions in his own mind and commented 'I began more narrowly to inquire what the doctrine of the Church of England is concerning the much controverted point of justification by FAITH.'[61] It is clear that Wesley was already trying to set his new experience within the traditional teaching of the Church of England, the influence of which he never escaped in his understanding of scriptural teaching.

On January 1 1739, Wesley attended a love feast in the Fetter Lane Moravian society where there was a Pentecostal type experience, stating that 'About three in the morning, as we were continuing instant in prayer, the power of God came mightily upon us, insomuch that many cried out for exceeding joy, and many fell to the ground.'[62] Podmore has sympathy for the Moravian understanding of Wesley's experience and writes 'Wesley's 'heart-warming' in Aldersgate Street was crucial for him personally, but this lovefeast in Fetter Lane was the turning-point at which the revival's focus moved from devotional realization in London to evangelism

---

58   Heitzenrater, 'Great Expectations,' p. 68.
59   Baker's footnotes suggest that the letter was not actually sent but formed the basis of the letter of August 8 1740. See *BE* Vol. 25, p. 566.
60   A letter to Count Zinzendorf was written on October 14 but not sent until the 30th. See *BE* Vol. 25, pp. 566-7, 571-3, and 573-4 for this correspondence.
61   *BE* Vol. 19, p. 21.
62   *BE* Vol. 19, p. 29.

throughout England.[63] This is probably an overstatement of the case but an appropriate comment is that of Towlson 'The love-feast of 1st January 1739 was the high-water mark of Methodist and Moravian fellowship.'[64]

Wesley was involved in preaching tours throughout 1739. The Journal entry for September 13 contains the answer that Wesley gave to a 'serious clergyman' who wanted to know in what points Wesley differed from the Church of England 'To the best of my knowledge, in none. The doctrines we preach are the doctrines of the Church of England; indeed, the fundamental doctrines of the Church, clearly laid down, both in her Prayers, Articles, and Homilies.'[65] Wesley went on to explain that, in his opinion, the points in which he differed from other clergy in the Church of England were only in matters in which the others dissented from the truth as it was found in the Church. Therefore it is clear that Wesley's interpretation of scripture was that to be found in the Church of England authorities to which he referred. Sixteen months on he was firmly setting his Aldersgate experience within an Anglican context.

Spangenberg and Philip Heinrich Molther visited the Fetter Lane Society in October and Molther was shocked by the groaning, crying, and contortions. Whatever the cause, Molther enjoined "stillness." His advice may have been in part misunderstood by the society. Most of the members ceased to observe the normal means of grace and sacraments. This was part of an emphasis on 'faith alone.' The Moravian stillness contributed to the growing difference between Wesley and many in the society. The significance of this for Wesley as a 'Church of England Man' will be considered in Chapter 5. For him the experience of salvation as described in the Bible did not involve any departure from Anglican practices.

Referring to the controversies over stillness or quietism, particularly during the period following Wesley's experience of May 1738 and the problems within the Fetter Lane Society, Stephen Gunter comments 'Molther was adamant that a person came through Christ to the ordinances of the Church; Wesley preferred to emphasize the path through the ordinances of the Church to Christ.'[66] The controversy was particularly significant during the period in which Wesley reassessed his own faith, but it also affected the way the Methodist societies would relate to the Church of England. Wesley believed that Holy Communion could be a converting ordinance and it is clear that he, in part, came to his views through the worship and sacraments of the Church. Wesley was confirmed in this view by discovering a woman (possibly his own mother) who had come to faith

---

63   Podmore, *The Moravian Church in England 1728-1760*, p. 48.
64   Towlson, *Moravian and Methodist*, p. 77.
65   *BE* Vol. 19, p. 96.
66   Gunter, *The Limits of 'Love Divine'*, p. 90.

through an experience at Holy Communion.[67] Thus things came to a head in Fetter Lane on July 20 1740.[68]

Defending the reputation of the Moravian Church and referring to the move of the Fetter Lane Society away from the Church of England, Podmore claims that:

> It is important to note that this rejection of the Church of England on the part of a section of the society did not result from the growing Moravian influence. Zinzendorf had been shocked by what he had found in London, and argued against any separation from the established church.[69]

The previous December Wesley had founded a new society in London which became known as the Foundery but his final break with Fetter Lane did not take place until the summer of 1740. The Journal for June 20 includes Wesley's summary of a paper that he read to the Society. It is worth quoting the summary in full:

> About nine months ago, certain of you began to speak contrary to the doctrine we had till then received. The sum of what you asserted is this:
> 1. That there is no such thing as weak faith; that there is no justifying faith where there is ever any doubt or fear, or where there is not, in the full proper sense, a new, a clean heart.
> 2. That a man ought not to use those ordinances of God which our Church terms 'means of grace', before he has such a faith as excludes all doubt and fear, and implies a new, a clean heart.
> 3. You have often affirmed that to 'search the Scriptures', to pray, or to communicate, before we have this faith, is to seek salvation by works, and that till these works are laid aside no man can receive faith.
>   I believe these assertions to be flatly contrary to the Word of God. I have warned you hereof again and again, and besought you to turn back to the law and the testimony. I have borne with you long, hoping you would return. But as I find you more and more confirmed in the error of your ways, nothing now remains but that I should give you up to God. You that are of the same judgement, follow me.[70]

Wesley was thus appealing to the authority of scripture, an authority that his opponents would also assert. However, it is clear that Wesley's interpretation of scripture with regard to sacramental practice and the means of grace was that of the Church of England.

It is also worthy of note, in the words of Towlson 'Wesley's doctrine of Christian Perfection was as much a stumbling-block for the Moravians as

---

67   See Rack, *Reasonable Enthusiast*, pp. 203-4.
68   See Gunter, *The Limits of 'Love Divine'*, p.95.
69   Podmore, *The Moravian Church in England*, p. 54.
70   *BE* Vol. 19, p.162.

stillness was to the Methodists'.[71] Wesley was concerned about the consequences of salvation in terms of holy living and about the proper use of the means of grace and the sacraments.

Wesley was, therefore, indebted to the Moravians for the Aldersgate experience, but the influences on his teaching from the Epworth and Oxford days, especially that of the Church of England, had finally reasserted itself, although with new insights gained from his Aldersgate experience. In August 1740 Wesley wrote at length to Count Zinzendorf and the Church at Herrnhut. There was a reply dated October 5.[72] Running through Wesley's letter are phrases such as 'I have heard some of you say.' Wesley was at pains to indicate that his concern was about what some of the English Moravians had said and taught. It clearly echoed the split that had taken place as Wesley had left the Fetter Lane Society. Wesley's concern was particularly related to Moravian teaching about faith, about doctrines relating to salvation, and about the use of ordinances and the means of grace. The Moravians claimed to have a biblical basis as is illustrated in the words 'A religion is an assembly wherein the Holy Scriptures are taught and expounded after a prescribed rule or form, which more or fewer profess.'[73] Indeed it is clear that both Wesley and the Moravians claimed to be scriptural. What was at issue was the interpretation of scripture. After the experience of May 24, Wesley was still highly indebted to and influenced by the Moravians, but was moving increasingly into an understanding of scriptural teaching that was very close to his Anglican roots. Nevertheless, at times, he accused Anglican clergy of neither adhering to it nor preaching it.

Wesley finally broke with the Moravians at that time, although this was by no means the end of his relationships with the Moravians or, indeed, the end of the controversy over the means of grace. Note may be taken of Wesley's sermon 'The Means of Grace.'[74] Outler commented that 'There is no way of dating it exactly [...] What is clear, however, is that a sizeable group of Methodists in 1746 still continued to regard all 'outward observances' as superfluous, or even harmful, in their Christian life.'[75] Wesley stressed the need for the Christian to use all the means of grace in the Anglican sense of the term and placed emphasis on the reading of the Bible.

The extract from the Journal for the period November 1 1739 to September 3 1741 was published in 1744. The Preface to it is headed 'To the Moravian Church, More especially that part of it now or lately residing

---

71   Towlson, *Moravian and Methodist*, p. 114. See *BE* Vol. 9, p. 92.
72   See *BE* Vol. 26, pp. 24-30 and 34-41.
73   *BE* Vol. 26, p. 38.
74   *BE* Vol. 1, pp. 376-397.
75   *BE* Vol. 1, p. 376.

in England.'[76] This Preface is in the form of an open letter found on pages 116-8 of *BE* Vol. 19. Wesley, even in June 1744, was still full of praise for many aspects of the Moravian Church, but determined to set out the differences clearly. From this it may be deduced that the extract was published with a view to setting out Wesley's side of the story of the growing division. It is of note that Wesley made it clear that the difference was with the English section of that Church. From the outset of that section of the Journal, there are references to Molther and Spangenberg, who were the central figures in the differences in teaching that were then emerging between Wesley and the Moravians. These differences begin to appear in the entries of November 1 and November 7 1739.[77]

It is not necessary to pursue here the story of the relationship between Wesley and the Moravians subsequent to the events of 1740. It is clear that by that date Wesley had tested his new found experience against the teaching of the Bible, assessed it in the light of Anglican teaching and found that the tradition in which he had been brought up had, through its Formularies, a biblically-based explanation that satisfied his understanding of the event.

Experience - A Method of Interpreting the Bible

In the exploration of Wesley's relationship with the Moravians and his indebtedness to them it is clear that there was, for him, a search for religious certainty, an exploration of the experiences of others and a reflection on what he did, or did not, experience for himself. Experience was thus a part of the methodology through which Wesley interpreted the Bible. Heitzenrater examines that part of paragraph 12 of Wesley's account of the events leading up to the experience of May 24 in which Wesley was concerned about the search for faith while in debate with Peter Böhler. 'Experience would never agree with the literal interpretation of the Scriptures.'[78] Wesley undoubtedly thought that his doctrine was biblically-based and that he was convinced by the evidence of the testimony and experience of others while remaining within his Anglican tradition. However, in the events of the months following May 1738 it is clear that Wesley's experience did not fit into the pattern outlined in the Moravian teaching that he encountered either in London or Germany.

Thus it was that, one by one, Wesley discarded items of belief in the Moravian interpretation of the Bible because they did not match up to what he found, or could not find, in his own experience. R.A. Knox has a chapter on 'The Parting of Friends,' in which he explores the way in which Wesley

---

76   *BE* Vol. 19, p. 116.
77   See *BE* Vol. 19, pp. 119-20.
78   Heitzenrater, *The Elusive Mr Wesley*, Vol. 1, p. 100.

was drawn into an experience at Aldersgate strongly influenced by the Moravians but yet which did not quite fit into Moravian theology.[79] Knox writes:

> The fact is, I think, that Wesley grew away from, but never quite grew out of, the memory of those early days when Peter Bôhler was his oracle, the days of his conversion. For one moment, Herrnhut had been a dream city to him, and he never quite forgave it for not being a reality. [80]

This emphasis on experience is also found in a comment of Collins:

> When Aldersgate is stripped of its excesses due to the English Moravian influence what remains is the following:
> A. It is the time when John Wesley encountered a gracious God, exercised justifying faith, and received a measure of assurance (occasionally marked by doubt and fear).
> B. Since regeneration, according to Wesley, occurs simultaneously with justification, then Aldersgate must also be the occasion of his new birth.
> C. Given A. and B., Aldersgate was the time when Wesley became a real, proper Christian according to his own mature criteria.[81]

What is missing in the words of Collins is the major point that the experience was that of an Arminian Anglican.

A similar emphasis on Wesley's use of experience as a tool to interpret scripture is found in the work of Gregory Clapper.[82] This too misses the relevance of the fact that the experience was that of an Anglican who happened to be an Arminian. Referring to Wesley's Journal for the much later date of May 14, 1765 and the words homo unius libri, Clapper argues that scripture was supremely important for Wesley. Clapper sees Wesley's teaching about the affections and the importance of experience as arising from his understanding of the Bible. Nevertheless, in a chapter on Wesley's Explanatory Notes on the Old Testament, Clapper refers to texts that could possibly be interpreted in a Calvinist way.[83] For Wesley, scripture could not teach Calvinism, therefore his notes had to explain, and, some may argue, explain away, what appeared to be the literal meaning of the biblical text. Experience was a subordinate authority to that of scripture, but it did have a strong influence on the way scripture was understood.

---

79   Knox, *Enthusiasm*, Clarendon Press, Oxford, 1950 pp. 459-82.
80   Knox, *Enthusiasm*, p. 478.
81   Collins, *A Faithful Witness*, p. 163.
82   Gregory S. Clapper, *John Wesley on Religious Affections: his Views on Experience and Emotion and theirRrole in the Christian Life and Theology*, Pietist and Wesleyan Studies, No 1, The Scarecrow Press Inc., 1989, pp. 2-3. This work was a revision of his doctoral thesis of 1985.
83   See Clapper, *John Wesley on Religious Affections*, pp. 29-30.

Thus Clapper sees Wesley as saying that experience is valid only if it is based on scripture. This is undoubtedly the position that Wesley would maintain but, for Wesley, scripture was seen through the eyes of experience. The experience was that of an Arminian Anglican. This point comes out again in a reference to 1 John 1:5, 'That God is light', and Wesley's comment on it in his Explanatory Notes Upon the New Testament. Clapper states:

> What this means is that to be filled with the love of God, for example, is to have an awareness, a correct knowledge, of that spiritual reality known as "God." To be "inwardly sensible" of this love is to have a spiritual sense.[84]

Wesley's interpretation of Biblical passages was considerably influenced and, perhaps modified, not by experience in general but by his own particular experience. This discussion about the influence of experience on Wesley's interpretation of the Bible raises questions about the influence of John Locke's philosophical teaching on him and it is appropriate to turn to that now.

The Influence of Lockean Epistemology

For Wesley, experience, perhaps more that of others than his own, was recognised as having a considerable degree of authority in the interpretation of the Bible. The question remains, however, is this experience to be understood in terms of Wesley's understanding of empiricism, based on the philosophy of John Locke?

Many scholars have not taken into account the philosophical origin of Wesley's usage of experience as a tool to interpret the Bible. For example, Leslie Church comments on the first generation Methodists 'They had not been taught a theological system; they had caught a spiritual experience.'[85] This book was written to give some account of the early Methodist people who had been influenced by Wesley and the other early Methodist preachers. It was based on research on journals, diaries and local histories relating to the eighteenth-century Methodism. Those who were drawn into early Methodism were attracted by a vital experience. For them the Bible was authoritative but they came to the Bible through the experience that they shared within the fellowship created by the work of Wesley and his colleagues. Although true, this does not adequately account for Wesley's apparent application of Lockean empiricism as a theological tool.

This is even true of Henry Rack who traces the origins of the influence of experience on Wesley to an early stage in his life.

---

84 Clapper, *John Wesley on Religious Affections*, p. 58.
85 Leslie F. Church, *The Early Methodist People*, The Epworth Press, 1948, second ed. 1949, p.96.

One characteristic of Wesley which would have a profound influence on the later development of Methodism was already beginning to show itself spasmodically in Georgia: his ability to respond to the test of experience even against his inherited prejudices, especially when experience appeared to show religious reality in unexpected places.[86]

Then, referring to a later period in Wesley's life, Rack observes 'The appeal to experience in terms of ordinary observation and self-analysis does become more and more important to Wesley in settling doctrine.'[87] In the same paragraph Rack comments: 'Ostensibly experience merely confirmed the teaching of Scripture, but in effect it was needed to ascertain what Scripture 'really' means.' Therefore, referring to the events that occurred after the return from Georgia, Rack writes:

> The task of interpreting the events of 1738 offers an exacting exercise in analysis of a religious event which resulted from the combined effects of Biblical models, patterns derived from inherited religious traditions, the stresses of personal psychology and the persistent force of experience felt in the self and observed in others.[88]

Rack also quotes Wesley's words 'If there be no living witnesses of what we have preached for twenty years, I cannot, dare not preach it any longer.'[89] In this context Rack does not refer to the influence of Lockian empiricism but it is there implicitly, if not acknowledged, in Wesley's words. However, Rack does comment elsewhere that 'Wesley was certainly a Lockean, though not quite a whole-hearted one.'[90] This is a fair and balanced statement.

Two other modern writers took a different view. John Kent denied the Lockean empiricist influence arguing that '[Wesley] interpreted what he saw, or what was reported to him, in terms of a set of biblical texts whose meaning, as far as he grasped it, took precedence over empirical data.'[91] Stephen Long has argued that Welsey's work was far removed from that of Locke.[92] He agreed that Wesley rejected the philosophy of 'innate ideas' but saw his moral theology as more nearly akin to that of Thomas Aquinas.

---

86   Rack, *Reasonable Enthusiast*, p. 121.
87   Rack, *Reasonable Enthusiast*, p. 385.
88   Rack, *Reasonable Enthusiast*, p. 157.
89   Rack, *Reasonable Enthusiast*, p. 385. The end-note indicates that the quotation is taken from Telford's Letters of John Wesley, Vol. V, p. 41 to which he adds a reference to Wesley's Thoughts on Christian Perfection (1759), at the end of *Plain Account*.
90   Rack, *Reasonable Enthusiast*, p. 386.
91   Kent, *Wesley and the Wesleyans*, p. 38.
92   This is argued in D. Stephen Long, *John Wesley's Moral Theology: The Quest for God and Goodness*, Kingswood Books, 2005.

'His world was more like that of Thomas Aquinas than like ours.'[93] Therefore the study of the way in which Wesley used experience as a tool to interpret scripture does raise the question of whether or not he was influenced by the epistemology of Locke.

'An Essay Concerning Human Understanding by John Locke (1632-1704) is often taken to be the first major empiricist work.'[94] Locke rejected the theory that human beings are born with innate ideas and argued that knowledge came through the senses. Hence, according to the article 'Epistemology of: John Locke' in the Encyclopaedia Britannica,

> In Book II of the Essay [Concerning Human Understanding] Locke supposes the mind to be like a blank sheet of paper that is to be filled with writing. How does the paper come to be filled? "To this I answer in one word," says Locke, "Experience."

In Locke's epistemology, experience was the tool by which knowledge was acquired, not knowledge itself. Locke denied Descartes' theory of innate ideas and argued that 'the mind was constructed in the more passive role of receiving, ordering, and reflecting upon the information provided it by the senses.'[95] By these arguments Locke helped prepared the way for the advances of modern science and the experimental methods of apprehending truth.

It has been written of Locke: 'He was a broad, tolerant Anglican anxious to heal the breach in English Protestant ranks.'[96] Locke's understanding of religion was expressed in *The Reasonableness of Religion* where he had argued for two essentials in being a Christian: the accepting of Christ as God's Messiah and living in accordance with the teaching of Christ. What is clear is that although Lockean philosophy may have affected much of Wesley's thinking, Locke's theology did not. Moreover, the article from which the quotation has been taken notes that Locke had reacted sharply against "enthusiasm". Experience was not set up over and against reason, but it was utilised by reason. There is a question as to whether Wesley's recognition of the authority of experience was based on the philosophy of John Locke or in his reading, at Oxford, of the work of Peter Browne who modified Locke's philosophical views.

However, Wesley was not primarily interested in the philosophical debate. He taught that there are spiritual senses that are parallel to physical senses but which 'are attuned to the level of reality the physical senses

93   Long, *John Wesley's Moral Theology*, p. xix.
94   The Encyclopaedia Britannica 2000 CD has a number of articles on Locke. The quotations are taken from one entitled 'Epistemology of: John Locke.'
95   Theodore H. Runyon, 'The Importance of Experience for Faith' in *Aldersgate Reconsidered*, ed. Randy L. Maddox, Kingswood Books, 1990 p. 95.
96   Encyclopaedia Britannica, 2000 CD, article 'Locke, John: Religion.'

cannot penetrate: they are "avenues to the invisible world" which the physical "eye hath not seen, nor the ear heard.'"[97] This, as Theodore Runyon argues, has significance for the interpretation of the meaning of the Aldersgate experience:

> Most importantly, Aldersgate convinced Wesley that "Christian experience" meant participating in an event of reconciliation that was initiated by God. As the source of the event, God remains the Other, the external reference point in the experience, but also transcendent, thus providing not only continuity to the experience but also a point of comparison with the experiences of this same God by others in Scripture, tradition, and "conference," through which reason can critique, evaluate, and correct the understanding of any single experience.[98]

Thus Runyon has illustrated the fact that the source of Wesley's beliefs was to be found in the tension created by scripture, the Formularies of the Church of England, tradition, experience, and reason. All the accumulated baggage of thought, reading and experience in the Epworth Rectory, at Oxford, in his relationships with his contemporaries, including the Moravians and, not least, the events of May 24 1738 inter-related in the forming of his views.

However much Wesley may have protested that his views did not change, it is clear that his understanding of the Christian faith was wrought out in the resolving of the tensions which he both faced and experienced. The Moravians were an undeniable major influence on Wesley but at the end of the day he remained an eighteenth-century Arminian Anglican. As Stephen Gunter writes 'If it was justification by grace alone that unlocked the door to his famous "Aldersgate experience," it was the potential consequences of fideism in rejecting good works that moved Wesley more in the direction of classical Anglicanism.'[99]

Gunter makes the point 'Experiential validation was to become an ever present component in Wesley's method, and would eventually lead in pragmatic and enthusiastic directions which Wesley himself could not have anticipated.'[100] He also quotes Susanna's letter to John dated August 18 1725 in which she wrote 'Divine faith is an assent to whatever God has revealed to us, because he has revealed it.'[101] He then gives Wesley's reply 'I am therefore at length come over to your opinion that saving faith

---

97 Runyon, 'The Importance of Experience for Faith,' p. 97.
98 Runyon, 'The Importance of Experience for Faith,' pp. 99-100.
99 Gunter, *The Limits of 'Love Divine'*, p. 38.
100 Gunter, *The Limits of 'Love Divine'*, p. 66.
101 Gunter, *The Limits of 'Love Divine'*, p. 71.

(including practice) is an assent to whatever God has revealed because he has revealed it and not because the truth of it is evinced by reason.'[102]

Gunter also refers to the work of Richard Fiddes which Wesley had read. On p. 24 of Telford's edition of Wesley's Letters, the editor gives Fiddes' definition of faith as 'An assent to a proposition on reasonable (or rational) grounds.' This phrase is, of course, an echo of the way scientific truths were tested and is also an echo of Lockean empiricism. Although Wesley posited a spiritual sense, it was, in his judgement, preserved from mere subjectivism by being regarded as part of the work of the Holy Spirit in a person and subject to the supreme authority of the Bible.

This exploration of the Lockean influence on Wesley's way in which he used experience to determine the meaning of scripture may be concluded by noting that, as Maddox argues, experience was fundamentally important for Wesley but that he saw its consequences in practical terms:

> There is no disputing the common assertion that experience plays a prominent role in Wesley's overall theology. However, it is important to recognize that a major portion of his actual appeals to experience were not directly concerned with either formulating or testing doctrinal claims. They reflected instead his emphasis on the contribution of experience to providing the assurance that empowers us for Christ-like living.[103]

The question remains, however, whether, for Wesley, scripture or experience came first and what was the interrelation of scripture, experience and the events of the eighteenth century.

The interaction between these three elements in the life and work of Wesley gave rise to his biblical interpretation. In the Preface to the first volume of Sermons on Several Occasions, Wesley wrote 'I have endeavoured to describe the true, the Scriptural, experimental religion, so as to omit nothing which is a real part thereof and to add nothing thereto which is not.'[104] It is of note that here Wesley put in juxtaposition the words scriptural and experimental. In these words Wesley was clearly setting out the basis for his teaching. The words do not, however, of necessity indicate the way that Wesley came to his belief in that teaching.

In Chapter 2 and the discussion on the Wesley Quadrilateral it was noted that Outler argued that Wesley placed experience alongside scripture, tradition and reason, although subservient to the Bible itself, as an

---

102 See *The Letters of John Wesley*, Vol. 1, ed. John Telford, Epworth Press, 1931, p. 25.

103 Randy L. Maddox, 'The Enriching Role of Experience,' in *Wesley and the Quadrilateral - Renewing the Conversation*, ed. W. Stephen Gunter, Abingdon Press, 1997, p. 117.

104 From paragraph 6 of the Preface to the First Volume of *Sermons on Several Occasions*, 1746, quoted in Heitzenrater, *The Elusive Mr Wesley*, Vol. 1, p. 149.

authority. Note was also taken, among others, of the works of Langford and Oden as emphasising the importance of experience as a tool wherewith to interpret scripture. The exploration in this present chapter confirms that experience was, for Wesley, a method to explore the meaning of the Bible. It should, however, be noted that the argument needs to be taken further. For Wesley, experience itself was subsumed into the Anglican faith, practice and teaching which became the key to explain both the meaning of the Bible and the understanding of the Aldersgate event.

The Charge of Enthusiasm

In using experience as an authority to interpret scripture, Wesley faced criticism from those who dismissed his work with the term 'enthusiasm.' For a study of enthusiasm in the technical sense in which the term is used here it is helpful to refer to R. A. Knox's work, *Enthusiasm*. Knox looks at the evidences of enthusiasm in the early church and later with extended reference to the phenomenon in the seventeenth and eighteenth centuries and has good coverage on Wesley. He writes of the phenomenon in the words 'If I could have been certain of the reader's goodwill, I would have called my tendency 'ultrasupernaturalism'. For that is the real character of the enthusiast; he expects more evident results from the grace of God than we others.'[105] The word enthusiast was used in Wesley's time to describe the person who exalted the authority of emotional aspects of experience above tradition and reason. The person could even set the content of experience alongside or above scripture as authoritative. In the context of the eighteenth-century evangelical revival, the physical and emotional manifestations in the congregations that accompanied preaching were often regarded as dangerous enthusiasm by those who were unsympathetic towards them.

In his analysis of enthusiasm, Knox comments:

> Our traditional doctrine is that grace perfects nature, elevates it to a higher pitch, so that it can bear its part in the music of eternity, but leaves it in nature still. The assumption of the enthusiast is bolder and simpler; for him, grace has destroyed nature, and replaced it. The saved man has come out into a new order of being, with a new set of faculties which are proper to his state. [...] That God speaks to us through the intellect is a notion which he may accept on paper, but fears, in practice, to apply.[106]

However, Knox argues 'The term 'enthusiast' was used in Wesley's day, and by Wesley himself, with singular want of accuracy.'[107] Knox defends

---

105 Knox, *Enthusiasm*, p. 2.
106 Knox, *Enthusiasm*, p. 3.
107 Knox, *Enthusiasm*, p. 449.

Wesley against the charge of being a fanatic, but shows him to have been a man for whom experience was of considerable importance, discussing the relationship between the Church of England and Wesley.[108] He traces the ways in which the Anglican hierarchy criticised Wesley and the way in which Wesley insisted that he remained loyal to that Church to the end of his days.

The nub of the problem, in this analysis, is found in the understanding of experience and the charge of enthusiasm made against Wesley. Knox points out that there was a controversy with Bishop Lavington and also with Bishop Butler, among others within the Established Church.[109] It is clear that the authority accorded to experience was a point of contention and that Wesley's understanding of Christian doctrine and the meaning of the scriptures was strongly influenced by it. In this context, note may be taken of Wesley's letter of 1762 to William Warburton. Wesley defended himself and the Methodist people against the many criticisms made by Bishop Warburton, writing 'What reasonable assurance can you have of things whereof you have had no personal experience?'[110]

Alexander Knox, a younger contemporary of Wesley wrote 'Another charge against Mr. Wesley I cannot equally dispute, namely, that of enthusiasm. Still he was an enthusiast of no vulgar kind; as Nelson was an enthusiast for his country, so was John Wesley for religion.'[111] On the same page, he added: 'Singular as his course was, he no more supposed himself raised above the guidance of his reason than of his conscience.' Further, referring to the Aldersgate experience, he made the point: 'I must repeat, however, that I dispute the enthusiasm of John Wesley's mind only in the gross and palpable sense of the term nor can I say that it was through dislike of strict and proper enthusiasm that he escaped its influence: I even think he would have been an enthusiast if he could.'

A. Knox had known Wesley only in his later years, not at the time of the Aldersgate experience, and was writing well into the following century, but it is clear he did understand Wesley to have accepted the authority of experience alongside that of reason. Aware of the strong Anglican leaning of A. Knox, it is also clear that, for him, Wesley's emphasis on experience was seen to be contained within his commitment to the Church of England and its authority.

Under the heading of enthusiasm, consideration has to be given to the attitude of Wesley towards the more unusual events that followed some

---

108 See Knox, *Enthusiasm*, pp. 503-12.

109 Knox, *Enthusiasm*, p. 505.

110 *BE* Vol. 11, p. 537.

111 Alexander Knox in Southey's work *The Life of Wesley*, p. 356. In order to distinguish Alexander Knox from R.A. Knox references to him are normally given as 'A. Knox.'

evangelical preaching including his own. Note may be taken of the paroxysms that first attended the work in Bristol, especially in 1739 and the early 1740s. These shocked Bishop Lavington and others.[112] R.A. Knox notes that '[Wesley] attached great importance, also, to the inward experiences of the people concerned, and shows obvious disappointment when they can give 'no rational account' of these.'[113] Wesley was clearly in a dilemma. He wanted to avoid the charge of enthusiasm, but in a time of increasing rationalism, he wanted to place emphasis on the evidence of genuine religious experience, even where some of the signs were of a bizarre nature. The experience that he believed in was set in a rational context and he wanted this to be seen within the context of Anglican teaching.

Enthusiasm may have been unattractive to those involved in the leadership of more formal acts of worship and may have appeared to contradict reason and sound biblical interpretation. This is why Wesley felt compelled to defend his position and to use experience as a tool in scriptural interpretation.

Evidence from Wesley's Sermons of the Way in which He Used Experience to Interpret Scripture

The way in which Wesley argued for the importance of experience as an authority but, at the same time, defended himself against the charge of enthusiasm is illustrated in three sermons which date from different periods in his life. However, these were placed together by him in the collections of published sermons.[114] In the sermons Wesley was attempting to steer a middle course between not accepting the authority of experience and the dangers of the excesses of enthusiasm. He did this by quoting the words of scripture to argue his case.

Thus, in Sermon 10, he claimed that Romans 8:16, 'The Spirit itself beareth witness with our spirit, that we are the children of God,' was evidence that experience was not merely subjective. The Holy Spirit's presence rescued the Christian from subjectivism and enthusiasm.[115] In Section I, paragraph 8, Wesley argued that 'this 'testimony of the Spirit of God' must needs, in the very nature of things, be antecedent to 'the

---

112 See Knox, *Enthusiasm*, p. 521.

113 Knox, *Enthusiasm*, p. 522.

114 Sermon 10 'The Witness of the Spirit I' was published in 1746. Sermon 11 'The Witness of the Spirit II' was published in 1767. Sermon 12 'The Witness of our Own Spirit' was published in 1746, a postscript being added in 1771. These sermons, together with Outler's comments on them are found in *BE* Vol. 1, pp. 257-313.

115 See, for example, the beginning of the main Section I in Sermon 10, *BE* Vol. 1, pp. 270ff.

testimony of our spirit." This reflects the way in which Wesley was influenced by Lockean epistemology but was using it in a theological way and a way in which Locke may not have done. He was assuming that there was a spiritual sense and that this contained direct objective experience of the Holy Spirit.

In Sermon 11, Wesley quoted from the earlier sermon, stating 'I can see no cause to retract any part of this.'[116] Wesley related the authority of experience and scripture in these words:

> It is objected, first, 'Experience is not sufficient to prove a doctrine which is not founded on Scripture.' This is undoubtedly true, and it is an important truth. But it does not affect the present question, for it has been shown that this doctrine is founded on Scripture. Therefore experience is properly alleged to confirm it.[117]

This is the classic statement that experience is subject to scripture, but it is also indicative of the fact that, for Wesley, experience interpreted scripture. He remained, as he saw it, a loyal Anglican, a man of one book. Experience had its right and proper place in the interpretation of the Bible.

In Sermon 12, Wesley defined the term conscience as used by Paul as 'a faculty or power, implanted by God in every soul that comes into the world, of perceiving what is right or wrong in his own heart or life, in his tempers, thoughts, words, and actions.'[118] Thus experience, for Wesley, contained within it a direct awareness of God. He argued for the authority of experience, avoiding the excesses of enthusiasm, and doing so within the context of the teaching of the Church of England.

A further sermon relevant to this is 37, 'The Nature of Enthusiasm.'[119] This dates from 1750. Here again Wesley had to defend Methodists against the charge of being enthusiasts while maintaining a proper place for experience. Wesley noted that the word enthusiasm was understood in his day in a bad sense. 'The generality of men, if no farther agreed, at least agree thus far concerning it, that it is something evil; and this is plainly the sentiment of all those who call the religion of the heart enthusiasm.'[120] On the following page it is stated: 'Every enthusiast is thus properly a madman. Yet this is not an ordinary, but a religious madness.'

Wesley then attacked those who accused the Methodists of being enthusiasts by arguing that they supposed themselves to be Christian but were not, and that was real enthusiasm. Underlying his argument was Wesley's assumption that Christianity was a religion of the heart. In this that he distinguished experience from enthusiasm. Outler took note of

---

116 *BE* Vol. 1, p. 287.
117 *BE* Vol. 1, p. 293.
118 *BE* Vol. 1, p. 302.
119 *BE* Vol. 2, pp. 44-60.
120 *BE* Vol. 2, p. 49.

where within the *Sermons on Several Occasions* Wesley placed this sermon, commenting 'The logical next step was a stocktaking of the impact of the Methodist Revival within the Church of England and a positive delineation of the terms for a fruitful coexistence of the Methodists with the ecclesiastical establishment.'[121]

Thus again it is shown that the debate about the authority of experience and the charge of enthusiasm are to be seen as set within Wesley's position within the Church of England.

Conclusion

It has by now been shown that Wesley was strongly influenced both by the theological teaching of the Moravians and his Aldersgate experience. The way in which he later separated from their practice and teaching in his understanding of the meaning of scripture has also been explored. Experience of others as well as himself both drew him towards the Moravians and then separated him from them. As Towlson says 'It was not merely, or mainly, a matter of theological opinion.'[122] Towlson also argues that on 'Justification by Faith, instantaneous conversion, Assurance - John Wesley departed from his teachers.' While continuing to acknowledge the importance they had played in his life, by 1740 he had moved away from their position. He discovered a new understanding of biblical interpretation in the Anglican tradition.

Runyon asks the question 'How did the mature Wesley's understanding of experience differ from that of the Moravians - at least those with whom he had contact in 1738, particularly Böhler and Molther?'[123] On the same page he answers 'I believe that they tended to understand experience primarily as "feeling", whereas Wesley ultimately understood religious experience as an epistemological event between the Divine and human participant.' This comment does help in understanding the post-Aldersgate Wesley. He did not have the continuing and unbroken feelings and assurance for which he had longed. Nevertheless, he had had a real experience. His epistemology, whether based on Locke or not, combined with the Anglican interpretation of scripture enabled him to argue for an objective rather than subjective element in the way that experience helped in the understanding of biblical truth.

Thus Heitzenrater draws attention to Wesley's rediscovery that in the Anglican Homilies dealing with salvation, faith and good works there was discussion of the doctrine of justification by faith. The point he makes is worthy of note:

---

121 *BE* Vol. 2, p. 44.
122 Towlson, *Moravian and Methodist*, p. 61.
123 Runyon, 'The Importance of Experience for Faith,' p.94.

Although he could not then sense how close he would eventually come to reiterating the doctrine of the Church of England, he immediately recognised that the answer to most of his theological problems with the English Moravians were contained in those homilies, of which he hastened to publish and extract.'[124]

Heitzenrater refers to *The Doctrine of Salvation, Faith, and Good Works: Extracted from the Homilies of the Church of England* which was published in 1738 and reprinted many times. He also refers to Wesley's letter to James Hutton on May 8 1739 containing the comment that the pamphlet was 'better than all our sermons put together.'[125]

It is also possibly true, as Towlson suggests, 'that the most lasting cause of the rift between the Methodists and the Moravians lay in the personalities of the two leaders, John Wesley and Zinzendorf. Each was too dominating - which need not mean 'domineering' - to tolerate a rival.'[126]

That, however, does not alter the fact that there were doctrinal differences and that Wesley was both influenced by the Moravians and then returned to an acceptance of an Anglican interpretation of scripture. Thus Towlson concedes:

The foundation of these differences was a different emphasis on the doctrine of Justification by Faith, Wesley maintaining that the Christian life at all times needed support from the ordinances of Christian Church and especially from Holy Communion, and expression in 'good works'. The Moravians fearing that this support and this expression might tend to take the place of the unique power of salvation in Christ Jesus.[127]

It is clear that the influences on Wesley were complex. It is an oversimplification to say that he was a man of one book interpreted by experience. His biblical interpretation was rooted in the understanding of Christian truth gained from home, the Anglican Church, tradition, the experience of others and himself, from his reading at Oxford and elsewhere. The contacts with the Moravians and the events of May 24 1738 led him in the end to a rediscovery of his Anglican roots from which he never escaped. Ultimately Wesley saw all that was good in the Moravian position as being also expressed in the Formularies of the Church of England. All that he rejected in their teaching he saw as unbiblical and not Anglican. His use of experience as a means of interpreting the Bible became that of a convinced High-Church Arminian Anglican of the eighteenth-century. The distinction between enthusiasm and experience may, at times, be a fine one but Wesley avoided the one and valued the other as a convinced member of the Church

---

124 Heitzenrater, 'Great Expectations,' p. 70.
125 This is found in *BE* Vol. 25, p. 645.
126 Towlson, *Moravian and Methodist*, p. 82.
127 Towlson, *Moravian and Methodist*, p. 117.

of England. The claim of Wesley to be a Church of England man is explored further in the next chapter.

Chapter 5

'Church of England Man'

Introduction

Wesley remained loyal to the Church of England throughout his whole life and interpreted the Bible accordingly. J. Munsey Turner, draws attention to the fact that less than three years before his death, on May 6 1788, Wesley wrote to Henry Moore stating 'I am a Church of England Man and as I said fifty years ago, so I say still, in the Church of England I will live and die, unless I am thrust out.'[1] The allegiance was expressly to the authority of the Homilies, Articles and Formularies of the Church. Wesley was often in controversy with the contemporary Anglican hierarchy although claiming still to be a good member of the Church. Certain of his practices, notably his ordinations and his use of lay preachers, appear to deny the assertion of loyalty to the Church of England and these are given consideration in this chapter. It is further contended that Wesley's use of tradition and reason in order to interpret the meaning of scripture are consistent with contemporary High-Church Anglicanism.

In Wesley's own words, he was a 'Church of England man.' Nineteenth-century Wesley biographers played down the Anglican element within Wesley's thought, confusing the earlier High-Churchmanship with the Anglo-Catholicism of the nineteenth century. The eighteenth-century evangelical movement was itself of mixed theology, much Calvinist but some, especially Wesleyan, Arminian. This is well argued by Peter Nockles.[2] However, the eighteenth-century High-Church Anglican should not be confused with the nineteenth-century Anglo-Catholic. Most of the former were Tory in politics, loyal to the monarch and believed in an established Church. They disagreed strongly with ecclesiastical dissent and

---

1   J. Munsey Turner, *Conflict and Reconciliation: Studies in Methodism and Ecumenism in England 1740-1982*, Epworth Press, 1985, p. 13. See *The Letters of John Wesley,* Epworth Press, 1931 edition, Vol. VIII, p. 58.
2   See Peter Nockles, *The Oxford Movement in Context, Anglican High Churchmanship 1760-1857*, Cambridge University Press, 1994.

they did not have any conception of a broader-based political suffrage. They were patriarchal in affairs of Church and state.

In an appendix to this chapter there is a review of Wesley's attitude towards the Roman Catholic Church and an assessment of his indebtedness to it, showing that this did not change either his allegiance to the Established Church nor the Anglican influences on his biblical interpretation.

John Wesley and the Authority of the Church of England

It should be noted that the Church of England in the eighteenth century was still strongly influenced by Richard Hooker. His major work *Of the lawes of ecclesiasticall politie* was not completed before his death in 1600. Details about Hooker may be obtained from articles in the 2000 CE edition of Encyclopaedia Britannica CD where the comment is made:

> In the *Politie*, Hooker defended the Elizabethan church against the Roman Catholics and Puritans alike. He upheld the three-fold authority of the Anglican tradition - Bible, church and reason. Roman Catholics put Bible and tradition on a parity as the authorities for belief, while the Puritans looked to Scripture as sole authority. Hooker avoided both extremes, allowing Scripture absolute authority when it spoke plainly and unequivocally; where it was silent or ambiguous, wisdom would consult the tradition of the church, but he insisted that a third element lay in man's reason, which should be obeyed whenever both Scripture and tradition needed clarification or failed to cover some new circumstance. (Article 'Hooker, Richard: His major work.')

Hooker was opposed to Roman Catholicism, but also to Calvinism and set out the basis for the Church of England becoming the via media in doctrine.

It has already been noted concerning the Wesley family that 'The Bible played a prominent part not only in church worship and in family prayers, but in their private education at their mother's knee.'[3] Hence it was a family in which the Bible was central, but its authority was recognised from within the traditions of the Church of England.

Undoubtedly Wesley regarded the Bible as his final authority but Frank Baker draws attention to Wesley's own comment that 'He recognised quite clearly that "scarce ever was any heretical opinion either invented or revived but Scripture was quoted to defend it." Therefore some secondary authority or authorities were needed to supervise the interpretation of the Bible.'[4] For Wesley, the Bible was to be interpreted through the guidance of the Church to which he gave his allegiance throughout the whole of his life.

---

3   Baker, *John Wesley and the Church of England*, p. 8.
4   Baker, *John Wesley and the Church of England*, p.20, quoting Wesley's *Works*, Vol. VII, p. 470.

Thus Baker can write of the way Wesley prepared to enter Holy Orders when 'more and more he emphasized the role of the Church of England as the interpreter of God's word for his own nation.'[5]

By 1739 Wesley was involved in setting up religious societies and working with other evangelists, such as Whitefield. Undoubtedly there were similarities between these evangelists but there were major differences. Baker notes that 'Two factors distinguished Wesley's followers from the remainder - their Arminian teaching and their firm resolve to stay within the Church of England.'[6] Baker does not here sufficiently acknowledge the fact that many of Wesley's opponents claimed, in their Calvinism, to be more loyal to the Anglican Church than Wesley himself. Staying within the Church of England, however, could mean different things to different people. Furthermore, as will be shown below, Wesley's own practices were seen by his opponents as being not entirely true to the Anglican Church. Itinerancy, which involved preaching in other men's parishes, lay preaching and the later ordinations of certain of Wesley's assistants were glaring instances of this. Rupert Davies argues that 'Wesley created a society within the Church of England and was its perpetual president, and in a non-technical but valid sense, its 'episcopos'.'[7] Referring to this, Davies also commented that Wesley:

> laid upon all its [Methodist Societies'] members the duties of professing the faith of the Church of England, of attending the parish church (and therefore of not holding their own services at times which conflicted with this duty), of obeying their bishop and the Book of Common Prayer, of disowning all thought of separation, and the additional higher duty of working and praying for the reform of the Church in matters where it was defective or corrupt.[8]

Heitzenrater also comments 'Wesley says many times over that the Methodists preach the doctrines of the Church of England, as clearly laid down in her Articles of Religion, Homilies, and the Book of Common Prayer.'[9] His footnote gives a number of supportive references to Wesley's writings to establish the fact.

Ted Campbell makes a similar point:

> To the extent, then, that Wesley explicitly acknowledges the authority of the Church of England, it is clear that (at least after 1738) the authority he

---

5   Baker, *John Wesley and the Church of England*, p.22.
6   Baker, *John Wesley and the Church of England*, p.81.
7   *BE* Vol. 9, p. 24.
8   *BE* Vol. 9, p. 27.
9   Heitzenrater, *Mirror and Memory*, p. 175.

acknowledges was that of the foundational documents of Anglicanism, not so much the living authority of the Church as it existed in his day.[10]

The influence of the Church of England on Wesley, particularly in the interpretation of the Bible, may be best illustrated by reference to his own works. The instances examined below show how this influence remained all through his life.

In 1742 Josiah Tucker published a pamphlet critical of Wesley who responded in *The Principles of a Methodist.*[11] Here Wesley sought to rebut the charge that he denied the moral element in Christian life and salvation by preaching justification by faith alone. Wesley acknowledged that he did preach what he regarded as a biblical doctrine, although he argued that Tucker partly misunderstood it. What is of note here is that Wesley answered the charge by drawing references extensively not so much from the Bible as from the Homilies as Rupert Davies's footnotes show. Davies also comments 'Tucker pointed out Wesley's dependence on William Law and the Moravians, his combination of Calvinist and Arminian ideas, and charged him with serious inconsistency.'[12] This was a charge that Wesley rejected.

The first part of Wesley's *Farther Appeal to Men of Reason and Religion* appeared in 1744 and in it he referred to 'Our Articles and Homilies.'[13] Wesley saw himself as in dispute with three Anglican bishops, Gibson, Herring and Smalbroke.[14] In a footnote Gerald R. Cragg, editor of Volume 11 of *BE*, draws attention to the fact that these three bishops were behind the criticisms being directed at Wesley at this time. He had to defend his preaching of justification by faith against an accusation in which he said 'it is vehemently affirmed (1). That it [justification by faith] is not a scriptural doctrine, (2). That it is not the doctrine of the Church of England.'[15] Wesley defended himself against both charges, stating 'There is neither one text produced [...] to prove the doctrine unscriptural, nor one sentence from the Articles or Homilies to prove it contrary to the doctrine of the Church.' Wesley was extensively quoting the *Book of Common Prayer* and the Articles of the Church of England as Cragg's footnotes

---

10 Ted A. Campbell, 'The Interpretive Role of Tradition,' in *Wesley and the Quadrilateral - Renewing the Conversation*, ed. W. Stephen Gunter, Abingdon Press, 1997, p. 71.

11 See *BE* Vol. 9, pp. 47-66.

12 *BE* Vol. 9, pp. 47-8.

13 *BE* Vol. 11, p. 108. Wesley's *Earnest Appeal to Men of Reason and Religion*, 1743, is found in *BE* Vol. 11. His *Farther Appeal to Men of Reason and Religion* was published in 1745, although part 1 was written in late 1744. It is found in *BE* Vol. 11.

14 See *BE* Vol. 11, p. 96.

15 *BE* Vol. 11, p. 109.

show. Wesley's teaching was rooted in the Church of which he was an ordained minister.

The same point was made in Part III of the *Farther Appeal*. Defending the doctrines held by the Methodists, Wesley wrote:

> It has been shown that every branch of this doctrine is the plain doctrine of Scripture, interpreted by our own Church. Therefore it cannot be either false or erroneous, provided the Scripture be true. Neither can it be enthusiastic, unless the same epithet belongs to our Articles, Homilies and liturgy. Nor yet can these doctrines be termed new. No newer, at least, than the reign of Queen Elizabeth; not even with regard to the way of expression, the manner wherein they are proposed.'[16]

Here again Wesley is seen to be aligning his doctrine not only with the Bible but also with the foundational documents of the Church of England.

Another example is the exchange of treatises that took place in 1744-5 between Thomas Church and Wesley and a further exchange in 1746.[17] Church had charged Wesley with being too much under the influence of the Moravians. In his response to Church, Wesley was forced to define more clearly his attitude towards the Moravians and then defend his position as an Anglican priest.

A key passage, not relating directly to Wesley's interpretation of the Bible, where again Wesley is seen to be clear regarding the Church of England and his attachment to it, reads:

> I dare not 'renounce communion' with the Church of England. As a minister, I teach her doctrines. I use her offices. I conform to her rubrics. I suffer reproach for my attachment to her. As a private *member* I hold her doctrines. I join in her offices, in prayer, in hearing, in communicating. I expect every reasonable man, touching these facts, to *believe his own eyes and ears*. - But if these facts are so how dare any man of common sense charge me with *renouncing* the Church of England?[18]

Wesley might possibly have argued that his attachment to the Church of England was because that church was true to the Bible. However, the quotation strongly suggests that his beliefs came from the Bible as interpreted within the Church of England. The difference between these two views is subtle but of note for this study.

Another occasion when Wesley may be seen as defending himself, not with the use of scripture but with a claim to fundamental Anglican allegiance, is found in 1748 when Thomas Ellis, an Anglican clergyman,

---

16   *BE* Vol. 11, p. 290.
17   See *BE* Vol. 9, pp. 160-237, *The Principles of a Methodist Farther Explained.*
18   *BE* Vol. 9, p. 195.

urged Wesley to write a pamphlet to 'advise the Methodists not to leave the Church, and not to rail at their ministers.'[19] This resulted in a small publication, written in English and translated into Welsh. Very much later it was translated back into English for the Bicentennial Edition of Wesley's Works.[20] Wesley adopted the suggestion and, within the pamphlet, wrote:

> How much less should any one of us bring an accusation against the Church of England, all of whose doctrines we subscribe and hold, whose Common Prayer Book we love, and in communion with whom we have received so many blessings from God.[21]

In response to Ellis, as in the correspondence with Tucker, Wesley refers again to his general attitude towards the Church of England. It is in that context that his biblical interpretation was set. His claim to be a man of one book is the claim of a person fully committed to the Church of England and his readiness to quote the Homilies and Articles of the Church indicates that he interpreted scriptural truth through those traditional statements and expositions of belief.

Wesley presented a document to the Conference of 1755 with the title 'Ought we to Separate from the Church of England?' The strong argument of the paper was that it was neither right nor expedient so to do. In the course of it he raised the question of the authority of the Bible with the question 'But is not the Bible the only rule of Christian worship?' To this he responded:

> Yes, the only *supreme* rule. But there may be a thousand rules *subordinate* to this, without any violation of it at all. For instance the supreme rule says, 'Let all things be done decently and in order'. Not repugnant to, but plainly flowing from this, are the subordinate rules concerning the time and place of divine service. And so many others observed in Scotland, Geneva, and all other Protestant churches.[22]

For Wesley the Church of England was an authority from which he could not, even if he wanted, escape. Certainly, in this quotation he claimed that it was subservient to scripture. However, although this was the position Wesley claimed to take, it is to be noted that in his biblical interpretation the Anglican influence helped determine the meaning that he found in the biblical text.

---

19   See Davies's comments, *BE* Vol. 9, p. 238.
20   See *BE* Vol. 9, pp. 239-246 for this under the title *A Word to a Methodist*.
21   *BE* Vol. 9, p. 245.
22   The document is given in full by Baker in *John Wesley and the Church of England*, pp. 326-40. The quotation is from p.330.

In 1756 Wesley produced *A Short History of Methodism*.[23] Writing
about the Holy Club of the earlier Oxford days, Wesley commented 'They
were all zealous members of the Church of England, not only tenacious of
all her doctrines, so far as they knew them, but of all her discipline, to the
minutest circumstances.'[24] Having referred to their obedience to the
university statutes, Wesley continued:

> But they observed neither these nor anything else any further than they conceived
> it was bound upon them by one book, *the Bible*, it being their one desire and
> design to be downright *Bible Christians* - taking the Bible, as interpreted by the
> primitive Church and our own, for their whole and sole rule.

This quotation stands out as an example of the way in which Wesley
referred to the authority of the Bible but then immediately linked that with
both the traditions of the early Church and the authority for him and his
friends of the Anglican interpretation of the Bible. Later in the tract he
added: 'At present those who remain with Mr. Wesley are mostly Church of
England men. They love her Articles, her Homilies, her Liturgy, her
discipline, and unwillingly vary from it in any instance.'[25]

Further evidence for Wesley's attitude towards the Church of England is
his *Reasons Against a Separation from the Church of England*, published
1758. This stated 'Whether it is *lawful* or no [...] it is by no means *expedient*
for us to separate from the Church of England.'[26] It may also be noted that
Rev Dr John Free was another who made strongly critical comments about
Wesley and the Methodists, especially in 1758-9. He wrote a number of
works on the subject. Wesley responded in two letters to Dr Free in 1758.[27]
Davies's comment in *BE* is that Wesley: 'shows without difficulty that
Methodists do not contradict the Thirty-nine Articles.' In the second letter
Wesley wrote: 'That we call ourselves members of the Church of England
is certain. Such we were, and such we are at this day.'[28]

Rev. George Horne preached before the University in Oxford in 1761 on
justification by faith. Wesley responded giving extracts from the *Farther
Appeal*, quoting from the Church of England: 'Liturgy, Articles or
Homilies.'[29] The quotations from *Farther Appeal* twice used the phrase
'our Articles and Homilies.' Wesley was thus clearly identifying himself
with the Anglican position, as he saw it. As Cragg comments '[Wesley]
undertook to prove that justification by faith alone is both scriptural and

---

23   *BE* Vol. 9, pp. 367-72.
24   *BE* Vol. 9, p. 368.
25   *BE* Vol. 9, p. 371.
26   *BE* Vol. 9, p. 334.
27   See *BE* Vol. 9, pp. 315-330.
28   *BE* Vol. 9, p. 326.
29   Quotation from *BE* Vol. 11, p. 445.

Anglican, proclaimed by St. Paul and expounded in the Homilies and the Thirty-nine Articles.'[30] Again Wesley is to be seen as fighting his battle on two fronts. Doctrine must, of course, accord with the Bible, but, also, for him, with the Formularies of the Church of England.

In 1777 Wesley preached a sermon at the laying of the foundation for the New Chapel in City Road. In response Rowland Hill made highly critical comments, to which Wesley responded in *An Answer to Mr. Rowland Hill's Tract*.[31] This related specifically to Hill's acceptance of the doctrine of predestination as being both biblically based and Anglican. Wesley was in dispute with him over it. He quoted Hill and made comment to the effect that: '"[Wesley] denies the doctrines of the Church of England." That is absolute predestination. Mr. Sellon has abundantly proved that this is not doctrine of the Church of England.'[32] Sellon had been appointed by Wesley as classical master at Kingswood School. Wesley resisted any suggestion that he was not loyal to the Church of England and argued strongly that his teaching was both Anglican and biblically based.

Further examples of Wesley's concern to show that what he taught was in keeping with Anglican doctrine could easily be given, but such is hardly necessary as already the main point has been clearly and abundantly established. For Wesley the Bible may have been, theoretically at least, the supreme standard, but it was not the only one. Time and time again he can be seen to go out of his way to 'prove' his views on the basis of *The Book of Common Prayer*, the Homilies, the Thirty-nine Articles and the doctrines of the Church of England.

It is, therefore, undoubtedly beyond contradiction by now that Wesley claimed that the Articles, Homilies and Formularies of the Church of England were to be regarded as subservient to the authority of scripture. Nevertheless, he took to scripture those doctrines in which he had been brought up and which were still influencing his thinking. He read the Bible with eyes and mind trained in the traditions of the Established Church. He faced a tension between fulfilling what he regarded as his God-given task within Methodism, his loyalty to the Church of England and his understanding of scriptural authority. The interaction between these influences led to Wesley's understanding of biblical doctrine and practice. Further evidence of this tension is found in an article 'Some thoughts on an important Question' written in 1781, published in the *Arminian Magazine* in 1782.[33] In it Wesley acknowledged the difficulties of certain Methodists who had followed his advice to continue worshipping in the local parish

---

30   *BE* Vol. 11, p. 438.
31   See *BE* Vol. 9, pp. 402-18. Davies's comments on the dispute are given on pp. 402-3.
32   *BE* Vol. 9, p. 408.
33   See *BE* Vol. 9, pp. 518-9.

church where they found teaching totally at variance with all that they believed. Wesley was reluctant to give up the connection with the Church of England although he understood the problems of those concerned.

It is also of note that many of the Wesley's works quoted were his responses in arguments with others, often leading figures, in the Church of England. Wesley never escaped from the influence of the Church in which he was brought up.

A further illustration of the influence of the Church of England on Wesley, which is not pursued in depth in this study, is his understanding of the sacraments of baptism and Holy Communion. This is explored by Rob Staples in *Outward Sign and Inward Grace*. Staples notes that Wesley's definition of a sacrament was 'an outward sign of inward grace, and a means whereby we receive the same.' On page 87, Staples notes that this is an abridgement of the definition given in the Anglican Catechism in the *Book of Common Prayer*. Staples also makes reference to Wesley's sermon on *The Means of Grace* on page 98 and Wesley's 'Twenty-five Articles of Religion, Article XIII which was copied from the Anglican Articles on page 100. Although not directly relating to Wesley's interpretation of the Bible the references do illustrate the way in which Wesley claimed to be consistently Anglican in his teaching and practice.

It has thus been demonstrated that Wesley claimed to be loyal to the teaching and practice of the Church of England. Wesley's understanding of Christian antiquity and his interpretation of scripture came through that form of Anglicanism in which he had been brought up. That is not to deny that, in his contacts with other traditions, including the Moravians, there was, at least from 1738 onwards, a growing recognition of the fact that they too embodied Christian truth. Baker makes the comment:

> Wesley came to place less importance on speculative theology and ritualistic practice, much more on a conscious personal experience of a living God. Testing their teaching by Scripture, reason, and experience, he himself had sought in prayer, along with continued use of the divinely appointed means of grace, a personal assurance of salvation by faith in Jesus Christ as "the one thing needful."[34]

This did not weaken his allegiance to the Church of England.

Wesley and the Problems Posed by Ministry, Ordination and Lay Preaching

It is sometimes assumed that Charles Wesley was in a minority within the Methodist societies in standing firm, resisting separation from the Church

---

34   Baker, *John Wesley and the Church of England*, p. 139.

of England and that the majority wanted to be independent of the Established Church. Gareth Lloyd has challenged this view, arguing that the majority, not the minority, of eighteenth-century Methodists wanted to remain within the Established Church.[35] Lloyd makes his point well. Charles Wesley was undoubtedly influenced by the pressure from the minority, especially the lay preachers, but did not therefore immediately side with that more vocal element. He was very strong in his allegiance to the Church of England and his desire was to keep the Methodist societies within that Church.

That, however, does not mean that John Wesley did not also have a strong conviction that he, and the Methodist communities, should remain within the Church of England. Therefore, for the purpose of the present argument, further comment needs to be made on Wesley's attitude to ministry, ordination and lay preaching in so far as it illustrates Wesley's understanding of biblical teaching in these matters. It may appear that his resolve to reman loyal to the Church of England was weakening but this is not the case.

Wesley was greatly influenced in 1746 by reading Peter King on the Primitive Church and concluded that in origin bishops and priests were of the same order.[36] Certainly he came to believe this was true of both biblical teaching and the practice of the early Church. At about the same time he read Edward Stillingfleet's *Irenicum* and concluded that no one form of Church government was divinely ordained.[37] Albert Brown Lawson comments on the influence of these two books and points out that Wesley appears, at a relatively early period, to have been convinced by their arguments that, in biblical teaching, bishop and priest were fundamentally of the same order.[38] Lawson notes that Wesley read Peter King's *Account of the Primitive Church* in 1746 and Edward Stillingfleet's *Irenicum* no later than 1755.[39] He also notes that both these works were written when their authors were young and that they amended their views at a later stage.

Therefore, according to this view, every priest was able to perform a valid ordination service to create new deacons and priests. However, this did not lead Wesley into any action to ordain priests until later in his ministry. He was convinced that the clear teaching of the New Testament

---

35   See Gareth Lloyd, *Charles Wesley: A New Evaluation of his Life and Ministry*, 2002, an unpublished doctoral thesis in Liverpool Hope University College.

36   Peter King, *An Inquiry into the Constitution, Discipline, Unity and Worship of the Primitive Church*, J. Robinson , 1691.

37   See, for example, Rack, *Reasonable Enthusiast*, pp. 291-2.

38   Albert Brown Lawson, *John Wesley and the Christian Ministry*, SPCK, 1963, pp. 47-70.

39   Edward Stillingfleet, *Irenicum : a Weapon-salve for the Churches Wounds : or, the Divine Right of Particular Forms of Church-government Discussed and Examined*, Henry Mortlock, 1661

and the practice of the Primitive Church would allow him to ordain others but he resisted those who urged him to do so. His allegiance to the Anglican Church appears to have stopped him doing what he believed to be biblically correct. While he retained his belief that the episcopal form of church government, as in the Church of England, was expedient and valid, he no longer argued that it was essential to continue this practice to remain loyal to scriptural teaching.

This was the seed-change in his thinking that later enabled him to proceed with ordinations, for America, for Scotland and, finally, for England. Without in any sense minimising the influence of King and Stillingfleet, it is important to see the influence of the two books in the wider context. Wesley from childhood had accepted the Anglican form of ministry. He was ordained deacon in 1725 and priest in 1728. From that time forward he never wavered in his belief in the validity of his own orders, continually affirming that he would remain in the Church of England until his death.

As the number of Methodist societies increased, so the number of lay preachers, itinerant and local, also increased. Wesley contravened the practice of the Church of England in two respects. First, although there were precedents for lay preaching, it was not common practice in the mid-eighteenth century. Second, he was constantly challenged about the propriety of preaching, uninvited by the incumbent, in other people's parishes, whether in preaching houses, chapels, private houses, or the open air. Obviously, in England, it was impossible to preach anywhere without being in someone else's parish! Wesley frequently argued that he was in an extraordinary situation and that the salvation of many depended upon his response. Thus he contravened normal Anglican practice when he felt it to be essential to do so in order to continue the advance of the work of Methodism, or rather what he would have regarded as the work of the Kingdom of God. In these instances he responded to the pressure placed upon him in what he saw to be an extraordinary situation. The work of God took precedence even over Anglican practice here.

When it came to the sacraments, it was a different matter. He opposed those who disregarded the importance of the sacraments, and those who advocated the practice of 'stillness.' Wesley insisted that regular attendance at Holy Communion was of the highest importance, a practice that he personally followed all his life. Nevertheless, he strongly resisted the many attempts by his lay assistants and by the members of the societies for the lay preachers to conduct such services. As Lawson comments 'The necessity of ordination for the administration of the sacraments was always a fixed principle with Wesley.'[40] Lawson adds, referring to a letter to Lord Dartmouth in April 1761, 'That this ordination should necessarily be

40   Lawson, *John Wesley and the Christian Ministry*, p. 83.

episcopal, he was no longer convinced.' Wesley may have become convinced that episcopal ordination was not essential, but he did not abandon his conviction that ordination was essential if a person was to administer the sacraments. Lawson refers to Wesley's sermon on "The Ministerial Office" and argues that Wesley accepted that often the roles of evangelist/preacher and administrator of sacraments were combined. Nevertheless, they were separate and distinct. Lawson also makes the point that for Wesley 'Ordination implies the conveyance of a ministerial commission, not the transmission of grace.'[41]

Towards the end of his life, in 1784, perhaps under pressure from others, Wesley felt he had to ordain preachers as priests for America and provide a superintendent (Thomas Coke) to continue the work there. Up to the last minute, he sought ordination for preachers to go to America from the Bishop of London and others. It seems clear that if such ordinations had been forthcoming, he would not have proceeded as he did. Wesley was trying to adhere to the Church of England even when he appeared to have been of the view that scripture allowed ordination by a priest. The inner conflict in himself and his reticence are evidenced by the fact that, even then, it was done without great publicity. Charles Wesley and others who would have vehemently opposed the action only heard about it after the event. Lawson notes 'Wesley's regard for the Church of England is shown on Coke's ordination certificate. He appointed Coke to adhere to "the doctrine and discipline of the "Church of England."'[42]

This may appear inconsistent, but is further evidence that Wesley's beliefs were deeply rooted within the Anglican Church. The influence of King and Stillingfleet was accepted with a degree of reluctance. Subsequently Wesley ordained certain preachers as ministers for Scotland who were not permitted to act as such when in England. Finally there were ordinations for England. The nature of all these ordinations is of note. They were not episcopal, except in the sense that Wesley was acting, as he thought, as presbyter/bishop. They were not presbyterian in co-operation with other presbyters. They were not in some way acts of the Methodist Conference which had not been consulted. Those ordained were to use the orders of service of the Church of England, but Wesley could hardly have believed that they would be recognised by members of that church or its bishops.

Wesley appears to have believed that he was acting within his rights as a presbyter in the Church of England and that his actions, highly questionable in the eyes of many, did not separate him from that Church. It may be argued that the needs of the situation and the pressures upon him from members of society, lay preachers in particular, and the needs of the

---

41   Lawson, *John Wesley and the Christian Ministry*, p. 92.
42   Lawson, *John Wesley and the Christian Ministry*, p. 151.

advancement of the gospel combined to force him into action. It would seem that Wesley could be convinced by arguments, by reason, by the practice of the early Church and by what he saw to be the meaning of scripture, but he found it hard to act in any way that was not in accord with what he had come to accept as normal practice from the earliest days of his life. Wesley did not regard himself as having broken with the Church of England and continued his work as though he was in every respect still a good member of it. It is also of note that his status as a priest within the Church of England was not officially challenged. Despite the fact that he, as a presbyter, had ordained others to the priesthood, and apparently entirely on his own initiative, Wesley was allowed to continue as a minister within the Church of England and regarded himself as such for the remainder of his life.

What is remarkable in the case of Coke is that he was already ordained priest. Wesley set him aside as a superintendent of the work in America, studiously avoiding the word bishop. In fact he reacted in disgust when he heard that Coke had called himself a bishop. Wesley was not always consistent! The others ordained at this time were laymen who, in Wesley's judgement, became priests by his action.

The matter of the ordinations may not appear to be directly relevant to Wesley's understanding of the Bible but in fact it is. It is directly illustrative of his struggle to remain within the Church of England, to serve the needs of the growing Methodist societies and to be a biblically based person within the teaching and practice of the Established Church. It is also evidence that he accepted an interpretation of the Bible at one time but over many years he tried, because of his loyalty to the Anglican Church, not to do anything about it. It was the great pressure of the situation in America that forced his hand.

This is a major point in the argument being pursued in this book and may be summarised as follows. First, Wesley read King and Stillingfleet. Second, he concluded that they were correct in their biblical view of the identity of bishop and priest. Third, he still tried to obey the Church of England (not the Bible) in the matter of ordination for many years. Fourth, he reluctantly, and under pressure, gave way. He ordained priests and even a superintendent for America although he made every attempt to do so in as quiet as possible manner, avoiding any publicity. To this it may be added that even when the matter came known and Charles Wesley had made the utmost objection, the Anglican hierarchy of their day took no action. Wesley was allowed to remain a priest within the Church of England.

The Church of England and the Authority of Tradition

Before examining Wesley's use of early Church Fathers and the extent to which tradition was an authority for him, it is worth taking note of the more general eighteenth-century Anglican attitude and usage. Ted Campbell writes: '"Christian antiquity" was in fact the focus of intense study and debate in the British Christianity of Wesley's age, and had been for at least a century.'[43] Thus Campbell notes that Hooker 'asserted that ecclesiastical practices could be grounded in ancient Christian teachings so far as they did not *contradict* scriptural teachings.'[44] As Campbell further comments, 'John Wesley was born into an age in which Christian antiquity, far from being a subject of merely historical interest, had been a focal point for theological, ecclesiastical, and moral discourse for more than a century.'[45] Although this attitude towards Christian antiquity is evident in the eighteenth-century Anglican Church, it would not have been accepted in the same way within many Dissenting Churches.

Wesley used tradition as a means of interpreting the Bible, his attitude towards the early Church fathers being entirely consistent with an eighteenth-century Anglican approach. He argued for the supremacy of the Bible, placing tradition under the judgement of scripture.

There is clearly a vast difference in theological method between those who regard the Bible as their sole authority and those who recognise more than one authority. What is sometimes not recognised is that there is also a difference between those who regard the Bible as their sole authority and those who regard it as their supreme authority. This point is made by Donald Thorsen in *The Wesleyan Quadrilateral*.[46] Drawing attention to the 'Reformers emphasis on *sola Scriptura*,' he comments:

> Later Anglican theologians such as Richard Hooker sought to develop a *via media* (middle way) between theological overemphases they perceived in Continental Protestantism and in Roman Catholicism. They hoped to avoid the episcopal structures of Roman Catholicism and the system-building tendencies of Protestantism, both of which they viewed as hindering a comprehensive and vital understanding of Christian belief. In explicitly appealing to tradition and reason along with Scripture for religious authority, the Anglicans did not consider themselves particularly innovative, but instead they believed they had brought greater integrity to their endeavors.[47]

Wesley's position is seen in an article, 'Farther Thoughts on Separation from the Church,' written in 1789, published 1790 in the *Arminian Magazine*, which began:

---

43 Ted A. Campbell, *John Wesley and Christian Antiquity - Religious Vision and Cultural Change*, Kingswood Books, 1991, p. 9.
44 Campbell, *John Wesley and Christian Antiquity*, p. 12.
45 Campbell, *John Wesley and Christian Antiquity*, p. 21.
46 See Thorsen, *The Wesleyan Quadrilateral*, pp. 23-4.
47 Thorsen, *The Wesleyan Quadrilateral*, pp. 23-4.

> From a child I was taught to love and reverence the Scripture, the oracles of God, and next to those to esteem the primitive Fathers, writers of the first three centuries. Next after the primitive Church I esteemed our own, the Church of England, as the most scriptural national Church in the world. I therefore not only assented to all the doctrines, but observed all the rubric in the Liturgy, and that with all possible exactness, even at peril of my life.[48]

John Munsey Turner refers to this quotation in *John Wesley: The Evangelical Revival and the Rise of Methodism in England.*[49] His chapter on 'The Church of England and John Wesley' traces some of the developments throughout which Wesley both tried to remain loyal to the Church of England and yet saw the Connexion drifting away from that church.

Thorsen argues that Wesley 'lived in the context of eighteenth-century Anglican theology.'[50] On the same page Thorsen also claims that the Anglican appeal to tradition and reason 'did not contradict the Continental Reformation principle of *sola Scriptura.*' He then states 'Scripture remained the primary source of religious authority, but other sources were specifically named as essential - albeit secondary and contingent on the primacy of inspired Scripture - to theological reflection.' This, however, is not the same as *sola scriptura* in the strict sense of that term.

In a chapter on 'The Authority of Tradition,' Thorsen takes special note of the sermon 'On the Laying of the Foundation of the New Chapel,' where Wesley took the opportunity to review the growth and development of Methodism.[51] The sermon is of note because Wesley was planning to move the centre of the Methodist Connexion from the Foundery to what was going to become the Mother Church of Methodism in City Road, London. Outler, in his notes on the sermon commented that Wesley traced Methodism back to 1725 and that 'Wesley has blotted out all memory of the early influence of the Moravians.'[52] Furthermore, there is no reference to Aldersgate.

In Section II of the sermon he wrote 'Methodism, so called, is the old religion, the religion of the Bible, the religion of the Primitive Church, the religion of the Church of England.'[53] Wesley devoted paragraphs to the religion of the Bible, the religion of the Primitive Church, and the religion

---

48   *BE* Vol. 9, p. 538.
49   John Munsey Turner, *John Wesley: The Evangelical Revival and the Rise of Methodism in England*, Epworth Press, 2002, p. 97.
50   Thorsen, *The Wesleyan Quadrilateral*, p. 18.
51   *The Wesleyan Quadrilater*al, pp. 151-68. The sermon, dating from 1777, is found in *BE* Vol. 3, pp. 579-92.
52   *BE* Vol. 3, p. 578.
53   *BE* Vol. 3, p. 585.

of the Church of England. Clearly he did not see these phrases as being in any sense contradictory. Rack, for example, makes the point:

> His guides were, in his own mind, Scripture as primary, but also tradition, reason and experience. The balance of these 'authorities' varied from time to time. [...] Yet the Bible has always to be interpreted, and Wesley never entirely abandoned the use of tradition, especially for apologetic purposes, and he was a thoroughly eighteenth-century man in his desire to appeal to 'reason' and, increasingly, to experience: his own but even more that observed in others.[54]

The use of tradition was, in part, due to the influence of his home and the Church of England. Furthermore, Campbell argues that it was from his father that 'John Wesley received the impetus to study Christian antiquity in the context of Anglican writers who had appealed to Christian antiquity in order to vindicate the doctrines and practices of the Church of England.'[55] However, Campbell also argues that, from 1732 onwards, Wesley's serious studies in the early Church and its practices were developed at Oxford within the Holy Club and that John Clayton, the Non-juror, was the influence that led to this.[56]

It remains to be determined what elements within tradition Wesley recognised as having authority, what period of tradition it was to which he referred, and whether it was authoritative in its own right or subordinate to the supreme authority of the Bible. Ted Campbell has examined some of these questions. He shows convincingly, without difficulty, that Wesley was aware of and used tradition to a considerable extent. He does not claim that the list of references he gives is exhaustive, but it does cover a number of Wesley's major works and thereby gives an insight into the way Wesley used Patristic authors in his own works.[57] Thus he establishes Wesley's extensive knowledge of Patristic writers but does not go on to discuss the degree of authority that Wesley gave to these writings or the way in which he used them although he states that he would deal with the way in which Wesley *conceived* of authority and how Wesley *used* authority. It is the question of the influence of tradition on Wesley's thinking that is of interest here.

It would be equally easy to establish that Wesley also had an extensive knowledge of other writers, especially Latin authors, from the classical period making a large number of references to them. This does not imply that he ascribed them any authority. Thus, in the sermon on *Spiritual Idolatry*, he quotes Horace in the Latin in order to criticise him.[58] Another

---

54   Rack, *Reasonable Enthusiast*, p. 383.
55   Campbell, *John Wesley and Christian Antiquity*, p. 25.
56   Campbell. *John Wesley and Christian Antiquity*, pp. 27-9.
57   See Campbell in *John Wesley and Christian Antiquity*, Appendix 2, pp. 125-134.
58   *BE* Vol. 3, p. 105.

instance is found in the sermon on *The Reward of Righteousness* where Wesley quotes Virgil in what he describes as a 'beautiful passage.'[59] These passages were quoted for literary effect or to make a point. However, it is clear that Wesley accepted that early Christian writers did have at least a degree of authority accorded to them.

Campbell makes a helpful comment by writing:

> John Wesley's view of early Christianity and its authority derived from a variety of interests and influences. His father had urged him to study early Christian writers and conservative Anglican theologians who had appealed to them. While at Oxford, he came under the influence of a peculiar group of nonjurors who stressed the authority of the so-called *apostolic canons* and *constitutions*, and pressed an unusual program of liturgical and disciplinary reform based on these.[60]

Reference has already been made to Wesley's *Farther Appeal to Men of Reason and Religion*. It is also of note that it illustrates his use of Patristic writings in biblical interpretation within the Church of England. Two pamphlets had appeared criticising the Methodists. A question had been raised concerning 'unction from the Holy One' (1 John 2:20 and 27). Was the gift of the Holy Spirit to be regarded as a phenomena of the New Testament Church or was the assistance of the Spirit for Christians in all ages?[61] In Wesley's response, possibly to Bishops Gibson and Smalbroke, he wrote 'I presumed you would have produced so numerous authorities that I should not easily be able to consult them all. But I soon found my mistake, your lordship naming only Chrysostom, Jerome, Origen, and Athanasius.'[62] Wesley spent a number of pages answering the criticisms by appealing to the very Patristic authors cited by his opponent.

Not all scholars recognise that, in this instance, Wesley was responding to his critics' use of these authors from Christian antiquity. Campbell, for example, writes that 'Wesley cited Jerome, Augustine, Chrysostom and Athanasius.'[63] It would be more accurate to state that Wesley accepted that his critics cited these writers, and responded to them. It is clear that Wesley would have been prepared to examine the writings of other authors of this early period because, in this instance, he saw them as having authority in interpreting the meaning of the biblical texts.

For Wesley, the value of tradition was to be found particularly in the writings of the earliest post-apostolic authors. Thus, referring to his letter to Conyers Middleton in 1749, Campbell writes 'Wesley frequently

---

59   *BE* Vol. 3, pp 410-1.
60   Ted A. Campbell, 'The Interpretive Role of Tradition,' p. 68.
61   The question is raised in *Farther Appeal* in *BE* Vol. 11, pp. 153 -4.
62   *BE* Vol. 11, pp. 154-5.
63   Campbell, *John Wesley and Christian Antiquity*, p. 110.

recommended "Ante-Nicene Fathers" or "the writings of the first three centuries," the esteem of which, he claimed "never carried any man yet into dangerous errors, nor probably ever will."[64] Although Wesley maintained that the purest tradition was that closest to the apostolic age, he came to see that error could be found even there and that some purer forms of Christianity still existed post-Nicea. Nevertheless Campbell rightly comments:

> Wesley consistently represented the early Church as being the purest when it was nearest to its apostolic roots, and as degenerating from that time, with a particularly precipitous decline in morals coming in the age of Constantine, when corruption 'poured in upon the Church with a full tide.[65]

This point is evident in Wesley's sermon 'On Laying the Foundation' where he wrote the following words:

> This is the *religion of the primitive church*, of the whole church in the purest ages. It is clearly expressed even in the small remains of Clemens Romanus, Ignatius, and Polycarp. It is seen more at large in the writings of Tertullian, Origen, Clemens Alexandrinus, and Cyprian. And even in the fourth century it was found in the works of Chrysostom, Basil, Ephrem Syrus, and Macarius. It would be easy to produce a cloud of witnesses testifying the same thing were not this a point which no one will contest who has the least acquaintance with Christian antiquity.[66]

Outler's footnote, on the same page, reads 'Note the omission here of Irenaeus, otherwise this is Wesley's standard roster of 'the fathers of the church' who represented for him, the primitive Christian tradition; it is typical of Anglican patriology in general.'

It should be noted that Wesley's usage of the 'fathers of the church' did not challenge the supreme authority of the Bible. For him these works illustrated the meaning of scripture in the practice of his own day. Wesley used the fathers to interpret the Bible in the manner of an eighteenth-century Anglican, confirming his own views. Thus, as Campbell makes clear, Wesley believed tradition remained subordinate to scripture. Its authority was a derived one and not original in itself. As Campbell further comments, Wesley 'regarded the writings of Christian antiquity as having authority for subsequent Christian teachings; not, indeed, the authority which he ascribed to scripture alone, but a "subordinate" authority which he found nonetheless helpful.'[67] This, however, must be understood alongside

---

64   Campbell, *John Wesley and Christian Antiquity,* p.47.
65   Campbell, 'The Interpretive Role of Tradition,' p. 69.
66   *BE* Vol. 3, p. 586.
67   Campbell, *John Wesley and Christian Antiquity*, p.75.

the fact that Wesley was selective in the quotations he used from within the Patristic writings. Wesley's interest in Christian antiquity was not simply that of academic research. It was a study that inter-related with his interests in mission and worship in the eighteenth century.

Campbell also writes that Wesley

> utilized his vision of Christian antiquity in a polemical manner in order to refute his opponents, in a conservative manner in order to defend certain Anglican customs and teachings, and in a distinctively programmatic manner in order to restore certain ancient customs, beliefs and moral standards which he felt to be desirable for the church in his age.[68]

Wesley accepted the authority of tradition selectively, not just to defend the Church of England as it was. Christian antiquity was seen as evidence for the way the Church should be.

Campbell pulls this argument together in the words:

> In summary, then, Wesley did ascribe an authority to Christian antiquity, not as replacing in any sense the authority of Scripture, but as faithfully interpreting and illustrating scriptural truths, and as faithfully suggesting and confirming Christian teachings and practices not specifically enjoined in scripture.[69]

The fact that Wesley used the writers of Christian antiquity to interpret the Bible is of note. This may be further illustrated, for instance, by a quotation from Wesley's letter to Rev. George Horne in 1761, in which he wrote 'That we are justified only by this faith in Christ, speak all the ancient authors: especially Origen, St. Cyprian, St Chrysostom, Hilary, Basil, St. Ambrose, and St. Augustine.' This, in fact, is a quotation from *Homilies*, 'Of Salvation', Pt. II.

It is worth going further to ask whether Wesley's use of tradition was precisely as described by Campbell and other scholars. Undoubtedly there were passages within the early Church writings that Wesley brought to the text of scripture and these influenced his interpretation of the text. Wesley's understanding of the traditions of the Church was in turn influenced by the advice received from his father, the experience of the life in the family home in Epworth, the carefully chosen reading in Oxford and the work of John Clayton and the Non-jurors. These were the ways in which Wesley's work in the eighteenth century interacted with tradition and scripture.

It is appropriate to conclude this section on Wesley and the authority of tradition with the words with which he introduced the section in *Christian Library* that contained extracts from S. Clement, S. Ignatius and S. Polycarp:

---

68   Campbell, *John Wesley and Christian Antiquity*, p.105.
69   Campbell, *John Wesley and Christian Antiquity,* p.111.

The plain inference is, Not only that they were not mistaken in their interpretation of the gospel of Christ, but that in the necessary parts of it, they were assisted by the Holy Ghost, as to be scarce capable of mistaking. Consequently, we are to look on their writings, tho' not of equal authority with the Holy Scriptures (because neither were the authors of them called in so extraordinary a way to the writing of them, nor indeed with so large a portion of the blessed Spirit) yet as worthy of a much greater respect, than any composures which have been made since. However men have afterwards written with more art, and a greater sense of human learning, than is to be found not only in the following pieces, but even in the New Testament itself.[70]

These words are those of an eighteenth-century Anglican and not those of a Dissenter. From this quotation it is clear that Wesley would always assert the primacy of scripture while acknowledging the importance of tradition and the teaching of the Church of England.

Wesley, Reason and Biblical Interpretation

In the last chapter the influence of Lockean epistemology and the authority of experience for Wesley were considered. Here the subject is further explored in the light of the way in which reason was an authority in Wesley's method of biblical interpretation.

As has been already noted, Wesley was influenced by Locke at least to the extent that he too denied the existence of innate ideas. Wesley, however, posited the existence of a spiritual sense through which religious truth was apprehended and in this he went beyond the teaching of Locke. John Locke's *The Reasonableness of Christianity* had been published in 1695 and his *Essay Concerning Human Understanding* had been published early in the eighteenth century. These works had considerable influence within the Church of England. Within Dissent there was a growing movement towards deism with some leading ministers and congregations of Presbyterian and other churches drifting into Unitarianism.[71] Here note may be taken of Richard Brantley's summary of Locke's philosophical position:

Locke's philosophy teaches, first, that ideas are the mind's record of what the senses bring; second, that the mind works on these ideas to produce general propositions; third, that these propositions take their place, with ideas, as what the mind works on; fourth, that the mind applies these propositions to problems it confronts; and fifth, that solutions to these problems occur.[72]

---

70   Wesley, *Christian Library*, Vol. 1, Preface, para. 11, p. iv.
71   See, for example, Gerald R. Cragg, Volume 4 of *The Penguin History of the Church, The Age of Reason 1648-1789*, Penguin Books, 1990, first published 1960.
72   Richard E Brantley, *Locke, Wesley, and the Method of English Romanticism*, University of Florida Press, 1984, p. 12.

As Rupert Davies says 'John Locke (1632-1704) claimed to be a perfectly sound Christian, and was widely accepted, even hailed, as such.'[73] Therefore Wesley's acceptance of empiricism was not considered unusual in Oxford. Rack writes:

> The Lockean tradition was more concerned with discovering truth in scientific and religious matters; and truth for Locke comes through experience and observation. We shall see that Wesley, though he kept the capacity for the older kind of point-scoring and clever syllogisms which annoyed more than they convinced, was also much influenced by Lockean empiricism.[74]

The eighteenth century was one of rationalism and deism. Wesley maintained throughout his life that his work was scripturally based. Therefore he had to refute both rationalism and deism, while arguing that Christianity was not contrary to reason, contending for the validity of revelation while showing that reason helped in the interpretation of the Bible.

Wesley's use of reason, derived from his Anglican roots, came through his acceptance of a form of empiricism, influenced to a large extent by John Locke and Peter Browne. An example of this is to be found in Gordon Rupp's work *Just Men*, where in a chapter on 'Son to Samuel: John Wesley, Church of England Man,' he discusses Wesley and reason. In this Rupp quotes Wesley as setting his use of reason in the context of the Church of England. He quotes from a letter by Wesley defending himself against the charge that his *Christian Library* contained too much material from Dissenters with the words:

> In the first ten volumes there is not a line from any Dissenter of any sort; and the greatest part of the other forty is extracted from Archbishop Leighton, Bishops Taylor, Patrick, Ken, Reynolds, Sanderson, and other ornaments of the Church of England.[75]

Wesley regarded the authority of both reason and experience as subservient to the authority of the Bible but the manner in which he used them was the result of his upbringing in Epworth and the Oxford years. They confirmed him in his theological position and were used by him in argument to defend the position he had already adopted with regard to the meaning of the text of the Bible. Wesley was well educated in philosophy and skilled in logic and this was used by him in many of his sermons and other writings.

---

73 Davies, *Methodism*, p. 29.
74 Rack, *Reasonable Enthusiast*, p. 65.
75 See Gordon Rupp, 'Son to Samuel; John Wesley, Church of England Man,' *Just Men*, pp. 120-3. The quotation is from p. 123 and the reference is to Telford's edition of Wesley's Letters, Vol. iv, p. 122.

Cragg comments: 'He consistently showed himself a formidable debater. His training at Oxford, both as an undergraduate and as a don, had equipped him with considerable dialectical skill.'[76] In the Introduction to this book reference was made to biblical Reader-Response criticism. This may be applied to the understanding of Wesley's method of interpretation of the Bible and is to be seen, in part, through his use of a theological methodology which included both reason and experience. These two came together in Wesley's epistemology which was thoroughly Anglican, even if his conclusions differed from those of some of his contemporaries.

Brantley comments 'Wesley [...] was decidedly philosophical, or at any rate philosophically theological: his theology, if not his faith, relates to the empirical philosophy in *An Essay concerning Human Understanding*.'[77] Brantley then summarises his thesis, the first part of which reads 'Locke's theory of knowledge grounds the intellectual method of Wesley's Methodism.' Brantley also claims that '[Wesley's] understanding of revelation, for example, some thirteen years before Aldersgate, was expressed in terms of Locke.'[78] Brantley also notes Wesley's letter to his mother on June 18 1725 in which he 'wanted to "perceive" the graces and "be sensible of" the "indwelling spirit of Christ."' Brantley sees the use of these words as evidence of Lockean influence. In view of Susanna Wesley's familiarity with the works of Locke, it is therefore of note that the influence of Susanna on John and the influence of Locke combine at this point.

Peter Browne, *The Procedure, Extent, and Limits of Human Understanding* (1728), was strongly influenced by John Locke. Browne was Bishop of Cork and Ross, who died in 1735. Wesley completed a manuscript abridgement of Browne's work in 1730 and was considerably influenced by it. Brantley makes the point that 'Young Wesley, then, understood rational and sensationalistic method as an indirect access to God and even as a precondition of belief in the Bible.'[79]

The significance of this point is that Wesley's use of the Bible as his supreme authority was rooted in his philosophical method. The quotation is taken from a chapter on 'Young Man Wesley's Lockean Connection.' Brantley establishes that Wesley knew Locke's *Essay*, that he knew and had abridged Browne's *Procedure*, and that he had discussed them in correspondence with Samuel and Susanna. He also makes the point that the term 'sense' has a double meaning. There is an objective use of the word to describe revelation known through scripture and a subjective spiritual experience. Even in the case of spiritual experience Wesley would consider

---

76   *BE* Vol. 11, p. 3.
77   Brantley, *Locke, Wesley, and the Method of English Romanticism*, p. 1.
78   Brantley, *Locke, Wesley, and the Method of English Romanticism*, p. 27.
79   Brantley, *Locke, Wesley, and the Method of English Romanticism*, p. 37.

that there was an objective element in that it was an encounter with God through the Holy Spirit and that God had taken the initiative in the matter.

The influence of Locke and Browne on Wesley is also referred to by Thorsen.

> Wesley developed his own empirical or experimental methodology, following the lead of Peter Browne's interpretation of Locke, by expanding the arena of acceptable sense experience to include spiritual knowledge of that which transcends mere empirical facts. Browne shared Locke's rejection of innate ideas, but desired to incorporate religious experience as "some extraordinary way of communication," which Locke and his followers were unwilling to recognise.[80]

It is also of note that Rack writes, with a degree of hesitation 'But in philosophical terms something much more specific can be said about Wesley. Apparently he was thoroughly imbued with the contemporary fashion for empiricism and followed Locke in his approach to questions of knowledge.'[81]

Locke and Browne had provided Wesley with a methodology for his theological and biblical studies that was within the Anglican tradition. Note may also be taken of Brantley's comment:

> Lockean-Brownian analogy underlies Wesley's conception of language. His works, of course, besides being unavoidably metaphorical, are metaphorical in being deliberately scriptural "The Bible is my standard of language" (Telford, 5:8): but his favourite biblical style is that of 1 John, which he singles out for the easy words and obvious sense of its "plain," i.e., unmetaphorical, language (Telford, 6:15.)'[82]

For Wesley reason was a tool to be used in the discovery and establishment of truth and not the source of truth in itself. As Rebekah Miles observes 'For Wesley, reason was limited not only by sin, but also by its own nature and only processes data and knowledge that originate in experience. It is a tool, not a source.'[83]

The influence of the Lockean empirical approach on Wesley is evident. However, Wesley would have insisted that this experience was that of others as well as himself; it was objective and not simply subjective, being a contact with reality in the form of the Holy Spirit. Miles further comments: 'Wesley believed that God had given the spiritual senses to all people through the additional gift of restored grace but the "eyes" of the

---

80   Thorsen, *The Wesleyan Quadrilateral*, p. 117.
81   Rack, *Reasonable Enthusiast*, p. 385.
82   Brantley, *Locke, Wesley, and the Method of English Romanticism*, p. 95.
83   Rebekah Miles,'The Instrumental Role of Reason' in *Wesley and the Quadrilateral - Renewing the Conversation*, ed. W. Stephen Gunter, Abingdon Press, 1997, p. 79.

spiritual senses are opened in the believer only by the work of the Holy Spirit.'[84] Miles also writes 'Empiricists insist that *all* human knowledge, not just knowledge of mulberries and cottonwoods, begin with our experience. For Wesley, even our knowledge of God comes from experience.'[85]

Arthur Skevington Wood, a relatively conservative Methodist biblical scholar, deals with some of the issues of reason in a more traditional way in *Revelation and Reason, Wesleyan Responses to Eighteenth-Century Rationalism.*[86] Without using the term, he infers that reason, for Wesley, was a tool and did not have the same authority as scripture. He comments 'Wesley and his colleagues [...] appealed to reason and sought to show that, while revelation is above reason and goes beyond it, it is not contrary to reason and therefore irrational.'[87] He also makes the point '[Wesley] stoutly rebutted those who ventured to suggest that he or his Methodist people were committed to irrationality.'[88] After making reference to Wesley's sermon on "The Case of Reason Considered", Wood comments:

> Wesley was not only suspicious of overweening reason: he was also on his guard against spurious revelation which cannot be confirmed by Scripture. His aversion from the excesses of eighteenth-century rationalism was matched by his fear of religious fanaticism.[89]

As Rack comments 'Ostensibly experience merely confirmed the teaching of Scripture, but in effect it was used at least to ascertain what Scripture 'really' means.'[90] Thus Rack argues that, although Wesley by no means fully accepted all of Locke's position on reason, he was clearly influenced by it. Wesley developed the idea that the human mind has spiritual senses as a tool by which spiritual truth is discerned.

Brantley makes the point:

> From the 1740s, when Wesley first formulated his thought, to the last year of his life, when he spoke Lockean language with the ease of exhalation, he more or less consciously followed the Brownean procedure for making Lockean method the method of theology. [91]

84   Miles, 'The Instrumental Role of Reason,' p. 91.
85   Miles, 'The Instrumental Role of Reason,' p. 89.
86   Arthur Skevington Wood, *Revelation and Reason, Wesleyan Responses to Eighteenth-Century Rationalism*, The Wesley Fellowship, 1992.
87   Wood, *Revelation and Reason*, p. 9
88   Wood, *Revelation and Reason*, p. 23.
89   Wood, *Revelation and Reason*, p. 26.
90   Rack, *Reasonable Enthusiast*, p. 385.
91   Brantley, *Locke, Wesley, and the Method of English Romanticism*, p. 48.

The continuing influence of Locke and Browne on Wesley's theological method and biblical interpretation is clear.

Wesley was undoubtedly influenced to a considerable degree by Locke although he also argued for spiritual senses by which spiritual truth could be apprehended. This provides a clue to the way Wesley came to his scriptural theology. The soteriological doctrines that he had absorbed from the Epworth Rectory and the Church of England were brought to scripture and his interpretation of scripture was strongly influenced by them because they were in accord with reason. Noting that Wesley read Locke's *Essay Concerning Human Understanding* in 1725, Thorsen also comments 'That Locke's experimental philosophy influenced Wesley's thinking throughout his life cannot be dismissed and needs to be pursued in unraveling characteristics of Wesley's theological method.'[92] These and other points concerning John Wesley and reason will become clearer by means of an examination of some of the primary texts.

Wesley faced increasing opposition to his work in the early 1740s. Much has been written, for instance, about the Wednesbury riots of 1743-4, but there were periodic bouts of physical violence against the Methodists throughout long periods of Wesley's lifetime. Alongside the physical violence, pamphlets were published that were critical of the new movement. Cragg observes:

> Some of those who represented the best side of the Hanoverian Church - its sober learning, its decent and orderly ways, its hatred of irrational extremes, its devotion to the parish system - felt outraged by what they heard about the teachings and the methods of the new evangelists. [93]

Some authors were easily identifiable Anglicans. Wesley needed to respond in an appropriate manner. Thus, in *An Earnest Appeal to Men of Reason and Religion*, Wesley showed that reason was a tool to interpret scripture, disputing as a member of the Church of England with scholarly representatives of that Church in a thoroughly eighteenth-century manner. Cragg comments on the *Earnest Appeal* 'In few of his works did Wesley reveal himself so clearly as an eighteenth-century English divine. He appealed confidently to 'men of reason' because he was convinced that he himself was a man of reason. He was prepared to defend the essential rationality of faith.'[94] However, Cragg adds 'The acid test of a religious man could be found in his submission to Biblical authority. But the Methodist doctrines to which their 'orthodox' critics objected were drawn straight from the Bible.'

---

92   Thorsen, *The Wesleyan Quadrilateral*, p. 171.
93   *BE* Vol. 11, p. 37.
94   *BE* Vol. 11, p.40.

Wesley's use of reason both brought to the Bible the theology he had already acquired and defended that particular interpretation of scripture. However, he made it clear from the outset where he thought his ultimate authority lay: 'We believe Scripture to be of God. [...] We cannot but believe the Scripture is of God; and, while we believe this, we dare not turn aside from it, to the right hand or to the left.'[95] He could also write 'We join with you in desiring a religion founded on reason and everyway agreeable thereto.'[96] In the same paragraph Wesley asked what the reader meant by reason. He defined reason in terms of 'The nature of God and the nature of man, with the relations necessarily subsisting between them.' He then comments 'Why this is the very religion *we* preach.'

Wesley outlined his preached message, defining it in terms of love experienced through faith. He then wrote 'Will you object to such a religion as this that it is not reasonable? Is it not reasonable then to love God?'[97] Wesley was simply arguing that what he understood to be the biblical faith was something that was reasonable to accept. In the previous paragraph, Wesley wrote about the unreasonable man in the words 'So far as he departs from true genuine reason, so far he departs from Christianity.' Nevertheless, these words were written in the context of Wesley's understanding that Christianity and true religion were based on biblical teaching. In paragraph 30, Wesley went further concerning the denial of reason 'But we can in no wise agree with this. We find no authority for it in Holy Writ. So far from it that we find there both our Lord and his apostles continually reasoning with their opposers.'[98]

The influence of the philosophy of Locke and Browne is evident: 'You cannot *reason* concerning spiritual things, if you have no *spiritual insight*, because all your ideas received by your *outward senses* are of a different kind.[99]

He also wrote:

> Seeing our ideas are not innate, but must all originally come from our senses, it is certainly necessary that you have senses capable of discerning objects of this kind - not those only which are called 'natural senses', which in this respect profit nothing, as being altogether incapable of discerning objects of a spiritual kind, but by *spiritual* senses, exercised to discern spiritual good and evil.[100]

This, of course, goes beyond Locke in that Wesley posits spiritual senses to discern spiritual truth, but the Lockean influence is clear.

---

95   Wesley, *An Earnest Appeal*, Para 13, *BE* Vol. 11, p. 49.
96   Wesley, *An Earnest Appeal*, Para 28, *BE* Vol. 11, p. 55.
97   Wesley, *An Earnest Appeal*, Para 20, *BE* Vol. 11, p. 51.
98   *BE* Vol. 11, p. 56.
99   Wesley, *An Earnest Appeal*, Para. 34, *BE* Vol. 11, p. 57.
100 Wesley, *An Earnest Appeal*, Para. 32, *BE* Vol. 11, p. 56.

The argument asserting the importance of spiritual senses is continued in the three paragraphs following this quotation. Wesley, in using reason in this way, met his Anglican opponents on Anglican ground. Explicitly Wesley wrote 'It is undeniable we neither undermine nor destroy the Church.'[101] Wesley, claiming to be a member of the Church of England, used reason in his approach to scripture in a way that was in accord with contemporary Anglican methods of debate. The Anglican Church was thus an authority for Wesley in interpreting scripture.

Cragg makes the point that these controversies were serious because

> Wesley's parents and teachers had instilled in him a keen awareness of the duty of submitting to constituted authorities: it was therefore no light matter for him explicitly to criticise those whom God had set over the household of faith.[102]

Cragg also argues that Wesley 'insisted, however, that the kind of religion he encouraged was rational as well as scriptural; it is pure from enthusiasm as from superstition.' For Wesley, as a good Anglican of the eighteenth century, reason was the tool to open the meaning of scripture. Reason was an important tool to interpret scripture and was recognised in scripture as of importance in Christian teaching. It is, therefore, not surprising to find a little later in the treatise that Wesley strongly affirmed his own loyalty to the Church of England. Addressing his opponents he wrote 'You are a member of the Church of England. Are you? Then the controversy is at an end. Then hear the Church.'[103] Wesley quoted from the Formularies of the Church of England.

One of the features that had accompanied Wesley's preaching in the earlier days of the revival had been physical manifestations, in which some in the congregations had shouted, screamed, and had been physically affected in a number of ways. Wesley quoted his critic in *Observations on the Conduct and Behaviour of a Certain Sect, Usually Distinguished by the Name of Methodists* as having queried:

> Whether a due and regular attendance on the public offices of religion paid by good men in a serious and composed way, does not answer the true ends of devotion, and is not a better evidence of the co-operation of the Holy Spirit, than those sudden agonies, ravings and madnesses, into which their hearers have been cast?[104]

Although Wesley defended these practices in *A Farther Appeal*, he did not dismiss more conventional acts of worship in which he himself felt more at

---

101 Wesley, *An Earnest Appeal*, Para. 78, *BE* Vol. 11, p. 78.
102 *BE* Vol. 11, p. 97.
103 Wesley, *An Earnest Appeal*, Para. 60, *BE* Vol. 11, p. 69.
104 *BE* Vol. 11, p. 121. Cragg points out that this is quoted from *Observations*, p. 10.

home. However, he preferred not to set the more unusual manifestations and conventional worship in opposition to one another. He defended himself and claimed to be able to reconcile all 'to both Scripture and reason.'[105] Having quoted his own *Journal* on the matter, he added the comment 'Are these the words of one who is beside himself? Let any man of reason judge!' Wesley was anxious to show that he was able to defend himself in reasonable terms. Reason here was not so much a tool to unlock the meaning of scripture, but rather the method by which debate could be conducted. Wesley's claim was that all that had happened could be justified, there being adequate and acceptable reasons that explained all. In this Wesley was consciously acting within what he understood to be the acceptable Anglican way with the proper use of human reason.

A similar point was made by Wesley in 1750 in a letter to Bishop George Lavington of Exeter, 'I am not above either reason or Scripture. To either of these I am ready to submit. But I cannot receive scurrilous invective instead of Scripture; nor pay the same regard to low buffoonery as to clear and cogent reasons.'[106]

In 1762 Wesley wrote an open letter, published 1763, to Bishop Warburton of Gloucester. Warburton had been highly critical of Wesley and Methodist teaching and practice. This was part of a controversy in which Wesley felt it necessary to defend his position with some vigour. He stated:

> *I* do not 'divest faith, either of truth or reason'; much less do I 'resolve all into *spiritual mysticism and ecstatic raptures.*' Therefore suppose *purity* here means *sound doctrine* (which here no more means than it does a sound constitution) still it touches not *me*, who, for anything that has yet been said, may teach the *soundest doctrine* in the world.[107]

This emphasis on the fact that Wesley's teaching was in accord with reason was linked with the comment on the following page where he rebutted the argument that 'Mr Wesley so grossly misrepresents his adversaries as to say that when they speak against Methodism they speak against the *plain, old doctrine* of the Church of England.' Whatever was true of his adversaries, or of Wesley's view of them, it is clear that he set store upon reason and understood that to have a central and authoritative place within the teaching of the Church of England.

In a letter to Rev Dr Rutherford in 1768, Wesley affirmed 'It is a fundamental principle with *us*, that to renounce reason is to renounce religion; that religion and reason go hand in hand, and that all irrational

---

105 *BE* Vol. 11, p. 123.
106 *BE* Vol. 11, p. 370.
107 *BE* Vol. 11, p. 481.

religion is false religion.'[108] Scripture may have had pre-eminence as the authority for Wesley but clearly reason, as understood within the Church of England, had a recognised place and was not to be discounted.

The Bible remained Wesley's supreme authority and reason was a tool to be used to understand its meaning. The rationalists and deists had raised, in their view, the importance of reason and Wesley had to balance the supremacy of the Bible against claims of reason. In this connection note may be taken of his sermons *The Case of Reason Impartially Considered* (1781) and *The Imperfection of Human Knowledge* (1784).[109] As Outler noted 'These two sermons are [...] intended as antidotes and alternatives to what Wesley regarded as a false rationalism.'[110]

In *The Imperfection of Human Knowledge* Wesley commented on the limitation of human knowledge about God, stating 'How astonishingly little do we know of God!'[111] In Section I of the sermon, Wesley was thinking about God as creator and pointed out that human knowledge of God and the world that He created is very limited. He also argued that human knowledge is limited in respect of what he termed 'works of providence.' In Section II Wesley pointed out how little the human mind can grasp of God's dealings with people in different lands, times and places. Then Wesley dealt with what he termed the lack of human understanding of God's 'works of grace.' In Section III Wesley raised questions that he stated he could not answer relating to God's grace. This sermon is of note because, in it, Wesley did not attribute the limitations of human knowledge directly to the consequences of sin. It was the person as a finite human being with all the limitations of being finite who could not understand questions that were obviously of considerable fascination to Wesley.

Nevertheless, he did not counter ignorance just with a range of biblical texts or doctrines to be accepted without thought. Reason was limited and yet a tool to be used. The implication was that a person should acknowledge the limitation of reason and acknowledge the greatness of God and the vastness of knowledge that was beyond full comprehension. Wesley wrote as an Anglican of the eighteenth century, faced with the challenges of the growth of knowledge, yet resisting deism and what he saw as the false rationalism of his day.

In *The Case of Reason Impartially Considered*, Wesley engaged in debate with two very different kinds of opponents. There were those that

---

108 *BE* Vol. 9, p. 382.
109 They were printed in reverse order in *Sermons on Several Occasions* Volume VI in 1788 and subsequently. See Outler's notes in *BE* Vol. 2, pp. 567-8. The two sermons are to be found on pp. 568-86 and 587-600.
110 *BE* Vol. 2, p. 568.
111 *BE* Vol. 2, p. 569.

'despise and vilify reason.'[112] He then referred to those: 'who lay it down as an undoubted principle that reason is the highest gift of God.' The former he saw as those with whom it was almost impossible to have an argument because they rejected reason as a tool for debate. They were often antinomians who were certainly resting their case solely on biblical texts and experience. In the terms of the day they were those dubbed as being enthusiasts. The latter undervalued the authority of the Bible itself. Their theological and philosophical discussions became the deism and the growing rationalism of their day. He defined reason as 'argument,' 'understanding,' and as a tool by which knowledge was gained, writing 'Is it not reason (assisted by the Holy Ghost) which enables us to understand what the Holy Scriptures declare concerning the being and attributes of God?'[113] At the same time Wesley asserted that reason 'cannot produce faith.' It also cannot produce 'scriptural hope, whereby we "rejoice in hope of the glory of God," and cannot produce either the love of God or the love of the neighbour.'

Here he was attempting to steer a middle course between what he saw as the excesses of two extreme views of reason. For Wesley, reason was authoritative within certain limitations but scripture remained supreme.

Conclusion

It is an oversimplification to describe Wesley as a 'man of one book.' He regarded tradition, and the Formularies of the Church of England, as subordinate to the teaching of the Bible. Nevertheless, he was an Arminian Anglican of the eighteenth century and this was evident in much of his work. He interpreted scripture with the help of tradition and the Articles and Homilies of his own church. Additionally he came to the writers of Christian antiquity and to Roman Catholicism and its various writers strongly influenced by his own Anglican background which he never consciously rejected.

This can be seen in much of Wesley's work but there are some particularly clear examples of it. His anguish over the 1784 ordinations is a good case in point. Here, as has been shown above, Wesley had no 'biblical' reason not to ordain but nevertheless his strong Anglican allegiance held him back until his hand was forced in the matter. His understanding and use of tradition enabled him to interpret the meaning of scripture in accordance with the context of the Church that he believed he would never leave. His view of reason, and the way in which it served as a tool in biblical interpretation, was set within the context of contemporary Anglican practice.

---

112 *BE* Vol. 2, p. 587.
113 *BE* Vol. 2, p. 592.

However, there were different traditions within the Church of England in the eighteenth century. The next chapter gives a critical exploration of the dispute between Arminians and Calvinists within the Established Church. It shows that Wesley was strongly opposed to the latter and embraced the beliefs of the former. He was an Arminian within the Church of England in his interpretation of the Bible.

Appendix to Chapter 5

John Wesley's Use of the Bible and the Roman Catholic Tradition

Through most of Wesley's adult life Jacobitism was a live issue and with it that of Roman Catholicism, its place in the country and the attitude of the Church of England towards it. This extended from when Charles Stuart landed in Scotland and invaded England in 1745, posing a serious threat until defeated at Culloden Moor, to the Gordon riots which took place in 1780. Throughout his life Wesley and his followers were sometimes accused of being Jacobites. Hence the attitude of Wesley towards Roman Catholicism was a live issue. It was also more complex than first appears. David Butler discusses this subject in some depth.[114] Butler is a scholar who has extensively researched the attitude of Wesley towards Roman Catholicism and is interested in the issues relating to Methodism and the Roman Catholic Church in the modern world. Of special note is his comment 'Wesley's opportunities for meeting members of the Catholic Church in England seem to have been severely limited,'[115] a point that is missed, for example, by Maldwyn Edwards in his *John Wesley in the Eighteenth Century*. Edwards regards it as: 'comical to think that so many people suspected Wesley of Romanism.'[116] He notes that Wesley reflected the common attitude towards Roman Catholicism in his day, sometimes in quite bitter words, but that when he met members of that Church he could be courteous and kind. He also notes that some of his reading included Catholic authors.

Wesley's attitude towards the Roman Catholic Church is not explored here in detail except inasmuch as it illustrates further Wesley's Anglican approach to the interpretation of scripture. It has already been seen that John Wesley claimed that his ultimate authority was to be found in scripture. The Roman Catholic Church also does so but has been seen as placing greater emphasis on tradition and the authority of the Church than does the Church of England. The claim, challenged by Wesley and others,

---

114 David Butler, *Methodists and Papists*, Darton, Longman and Todd, 1995. The subtitle of his work is 'John Wesley and the Catholic Church in the Eighteenth Century.'

115 Butler, *Methodists and Papists*, p.21.

116 Edwards, *John Wesley in the Eighteenth Century*, p.99.

that there was an unbroken succession of authoritative teaching from the apostolic age onwards, the Bible itself being interpreted not by private opinion but by the Church as the successor of the apostles, especially Peter, led to a sharp divide between the Protestant and Roman Catholic understanding of authority.

Contrasting with much eighteenth-century Protestant comment was the attitude shown by Wesley in his sermon on *The Catholic Spirit* and in his *Letter to a Roman Catholic*. The sermon and the letter date from 1749. It should be noted that Wesley did not weaken his own convictions. As Butler points out 'It does not imply 'speculative latitudinarianism', by which he means having no fixed doctrines and halting between two opinions.'[117] Wesley held strongly to his understanding of the authority of the Bible while pleading for a better relationship between the Methodists and members of the Church of England on the one hand and the Roman Catholics on the other. The *Letter to a Roman Catholic* is a document in which Wesley maintained his own strongly held beliefs, argued that Protestants should try to understand the views of the Roman Catholics and pleaded for mutual toleration and goodwill. It is significant in that in it Wesley acknowledged that some Roman Catholics were both Christian and assured of a place in heaven, a view to which not all Protestants of his day would have subscribed.

The Bible, as interpreted by Wesley, as an Arminian Anglican, remained for him the supreme authority but the sermon and the letter are evidence of an open attitude towards Roman Catholicism that was remarkable in the eighteenth century. By way of contrast, however, there was a polemical element in Wesley's attitude. Butler's work traces, through Wesley's writings, the way that Roman Catholicism was regarded with suspicion and was even regarded as Antichrist. Butler comments:

> In his tract *Popery Calmly Considered,* written in 1779, Wesley argues that the principles of Popery destroy the love of God, the love of our neighbour, and then all justice, mercy and truth. This is an extremely serious accusation and Wesley, despite admitting that there have been holy men in the Church of Rome, states clearly that their goodness has been seen in them *despite* their principles.[118]

Throughout his work Butler illustrates the way that Wesley was bitterly opposed to Roman Catholic teaching and practice. For the purpose of the present discussion it is to be noted that much of this strong disagreement centred on the authority of scripture. Butler states 'The basic problem is that the Romanists have departed from the proper use of the Scriptures and replaced the priority of Scripture with the priority of Scripture with

---

117 Butler, *Methodists and Papists*, p.175.
118 Butler, *Methodists and Papists*, p.159.

Tradition.'[119] As a Protestant and an Anglican, Wesley could not accept this. These words are noted in connection with the Roman Catholic teaching on a number of issues such as the veneration of relics, the priority of the Church of Rome, the supremacy of the Pope, and especially transubstantiation and purgatory.

In the same paragraph, Butler cites Wesley as having quoted from the Council of Trent the words '[The Church] requires that the traditions be received with the like pious regard and veneration as the Scriptures; and whosoever knowingly condemns them, is declared by her to be accursed.' The word Romanist is a strongly anti-Catholic term and here Butler is quoting Wesley, not necessarily indicating that he would use it himself.

In this connection and worthy of comment are Wesley's words published in 1742 in *The Character of a Methodist*.[120] He wrote 'We believe this written Word of God to be the *only and the sufficient* rule both of Christian faith and practice; and herein we are fundamentally distinguished from those of the Romish Church.'[121] In a footnote to this quotation, Rupert Davies points out that the words in italics do not appear in that form in the Book of Common Prayer or the Homilies, but argues that they are Wesley's attempt to summarise Article VI ('Of the sufficiency of the Holy Scriptures for Salvation'). Thus Wesley's regard for the Bible, and his differences from Roman Catholicism, were rooted in his Anglican heritage. It is clear that the point of division between Protestant and Roman Catholic views, according to Wesley, was centred on the questions of authority and the supremacy of scripture.

Against this must be set the fact that Wesley was clearly indebted to Roman Catholic spirituality and certain Catholic writers. It may be too much to argue with Jean Orcibal 'We are thus led to look to Catholic authors for the origins of Wesley's doctrine of sanctification.'[122] Nevertheless, Orcibal does establish Wesley's indebtedness to a number of Catholic authors in his earlier (pre-1738) days. R.A. Knox also draws attention to the influence of certain Roman Catholic authors on Wesley, even though he 'expressed a lively horror of mysticism.'[123] Knox then refers to Gregory Lopez, St. Francis of Sales, M. de Renty and Madam Guyon, in addition to the influence of à Kempis. He certainly goes too far in suggesting that there was a time when Wesley was drawn towards Roman Catholicism but there can be no doubt about the influence of a

---

119 Butler, *Methodists and Papists*, p.107.
120 See *BE* Vol. 9, pp. 31-42.
121 *BE* Vol. 9, p. 34.
122 Jean Orcibal, 'The Theological Originality of John Wesley and Continental Spirituality', translated by R.J.A. Sharp, in *A History of the Methodist Church in Great Britain*, Vol. 1, ed. Rupert Davies and Gordon Rupp, Epworth Press, 1965.
123 Knox, *Enthusiasm*, p. 434

number of Catholic writers upon him. Although he became critical of these writers in many ways, he remained influenced by them and selective abridgements of their works appeared in his *Christian Library*.

On this Butler writes:

> It has been claimed that John Wesley was able to combine successfully the 'Catholic' elements of his theology and spirituality with the 'Protestant' elements. While he spoke the language of evangelical Protestantism, he commended to his people the use of Catholic writers and, with certain reservations, the examples of Catholic lives such as Gregory Lopez and the Marquis de Renty.' [124]

Not surprisingly, it is in the area of Wesley's teaching on the doctrine of Christian Perfection that this influence is most obvious.

Undoubtedly there were inconsistencies in Wesley's attitude towards the Roman Catholic Church. In part this was caused by the lack of any direct or personal knowledge that he had of any Roman Catholic individuals or churches. It was also a common attitude within the Anglican Protestant tradition in which he himself stood. At root there was the question of authority which Wesley saw as being supremely in scripture. He believed that the proper and supreme authority of the Bible was denied in Roman Catholicism. Underlying all this was Wesley's recognition of the importance of the authority of experience where it did not conflict with scripture, and the recognition in certain Catholic writers of a spirituality that was close to that of his own.

Wesley's teaching on Christian perfection aroused strong opposition by many Anglican and Dissenting evangelicals. His attitude towards Roman Catholicism was thus a complex one in which Wesley tried to remain loyal to his understanding of the primacy of the authority of scripture, his Anglican roots, the recognition of what he regarded as unscriptural practices within Catholicism and yet equally the recognition of elements of profound spiritual insight and truth which could not be denied.

---

124 Butler, *Methodists and Papists*, p.141.

Chapter 6

Arminians and Calvinists

John Wesley and the Calvinist Controversy

Wesley maintained that he had remained a Church of England man throughout his life and that he believed that authority was to be found in one book and one book only. That book was the Bible. In the Calvinist controversy he faced a severe challenge to this position. Article 17 of the Church of England is crucial to the debate:

> Predestination to life is the everlasting purpose of God, whereby (before the foundations of the world were laid) he hath constantly decreed by his counsel secret to us, to deliver from curse and damnation those whom he hath chosen in Christ out of mankind, and to bring them by Christ to everlasting salvation, as vessels made to honour. [...] Furthermore, we must receive God's promises in such wise, as they be generally set forth to us in holy Scripture: and, in our doings, that Will of God is to be followed, which we have expressly declared to be the word of God.

The most obvious reading of these words is that of scripturally based Calvinism. It is possible to support this with reference to texts in the Letter to the Romans such as 'For whom he did foreknow, he also did predestinate to be conformed to the image of his Son, that he might be the firstborn among many brethren.' (Romans 8:29 KJV)

The question, therefore, that became more pressing, in Wesley's interpretation of the Bible and his understanding of the Aldersgate experience, was what aspects of Anglicanism were the root of Wesley's belief? Consideration will be given now to the evidence that can be obtained from Wesley's arguments with Calvinists who also claimed to find their authority in scripture, experience and, in many cases, the Church of England. These conflicts are of particular note as they were controversies between those who appealed to similar authorities for their beliefs.

John Calvin (1509-1564) was born in France but his most influential period was spent in Geneva. The elements in his teaching most emphasised by the eighteenth-century English evangelicals were his emphasis on the absolute kingship of God, the irresistible grace of God and the doctrine of predestination.

Arminianism is a term that is used to describe those who held to a doctrine that all people who believe in Christ may be saved by grace through faith. It is named after Arminius (1559-1609), a Dutch theologian, who was strongly opposed to Calvinism and the doctrine of predestination. There were earlier Cambridge critics of Calvin who were not directly influenced by Arminius. The teaching of Arminius came into England partly through the work of the Caroline divines. Although Calvinism was a strong influence in Dissent, it also gained a firm hold in evangelical Anglicanism, particularly with its doctrine of predestination.

The long-running eighteenth-century disputes between Arminians and Calvinists divided evangelicals engaged in mission during that century. Wesley's participation in the debates illustrates his continued adherence to the Arminian Anglican theological tradition in which he had been cradled. It also shows clearly the way in which he read the Bible, bringing to it those views which he subsequently claimed were rooted in scripture. Of particular note is the way in which he dealt with biblical evidence which others claimed disproved his position. Any evidence from the Bible, Anglican teaching or spiritual experience that appeared to contradict his teaching was explained in such a way as to maintain the position with which he began. This is also true of the way in which he dealt with items within Anglican Formularies that appeared to support views other than those he held.

Many Anglican evangelicals were Calvinists who claimed to possess a true interpretation of the Bible and also claimed to be loyal to the doctrines of the Established Church. They pointed to biblical texts and the Anglican Articles of Religion in support of their position. Although the doctrines of Calvin consisted of far more than just that of predestination, in this chapter special attention is given to Wesley's conflicts with Calvinists over that particular teaching. However, other points of disagreement are noted, including Wesley's own teaching on Christian Perfection which caused considerable concern to Calvinists.

A good account of the relationship between Arminians and Calvinists and the controversy between John Wesley and certain Calvinists is to be found in Herbert McGonigle's work *Sufficient Saving Grace*.[1] This does not deal directly with the question of the way in which Wesley read and interpreted the Bible but it does give a clear account of the dispute between Wesley and those who took a different view from his.

There are two major points made in this chapter. The first is that Wesley was an Arminian Anglican, although he did not use the term Arminian to

---

1   Herbert Boyd McGonigle, *Sufficient Saving Grace: John Wesley's Evangelical Arminianism*, Paternoster Press, 2001.

describe himself until later in his life. Following his death, his earlier biographers, and indeed many later biographers as well, portrayed him as a Bible-based Arminian but this is inadequate. His Arminianism was rooted in his Anglicanism. Second is that, whatever the source of his beliefs, the Bible and the Formularies of the Church of England were used in argument to defend his position and attack his opponents. However, this was a selective use of biblical texts and a selective use of Anglican sources. It does not mean that he came to his convictions by reading scripture or studying the Articles of the Church. As has been argued throughout this work, he brought to the Bible the beliefs that he afterwards claimed to find there.

The major contention in this chapter is that Wesley came to the interpretation of scripture and the understanding of Anglican teaching through a High-Church Arminian Anglican, as opposed to a Calvinistic influence and that can be seen in the way he used scripture. It may be noted that Arminianism was associated with eighteenth-century High-Church Anglicanism whereas Calvinism was more associated with evangelical Anglicanism. Wesley came to his position early in life, strongly influenced by his upbringing in the Epworth Rectory and his reading in the Oxford years. This was of a High Church character, in eighteenth-century terms, with Arminian influences and Wesley, at times, had to ignore, modify or explain certain aspects of the Anglican tradition and the Bible in order to interpret scripture in the way that he did. His controversy with Calvinists may have hardened his views but, on this point, did not change them fundamentally.

In *John Wesley and the Anglican Evangelicals of the Eighteenth Century*, A. Brown-Lawson examines both the co-operation and the divisions that developed in the relationships between Wesley and the contemporary Anglican evangelicals.[2] In the earlier chapters, Brown-Lawson notes the fact that the Anglicans who could be described as evangelical had come to their experience by diverse routes. They were not all the product of the same revival of religion, although they were contemporaries of one another. Some, especially Whitefield, were not troubled at the breaking of ecclesiastical law relating to preaching in the parishes of other clergy or using lay-preachers. Others were more concerned to remain within their own parishes and unwilling to allow others to come into their territory. The itinerancy of certain preachers was another divisive issue. Wesley too was open to criticism from fellow Anglicans because of his use of lay preachers, the fact that he and his

---

2   A. Brown-Lawson, *John Wesley and the Anglican Evangelicals of the Eighteenth Century*, The Pentland Press, 1994. It should be note that the author A Brown-Lawson is the same as A Brown Lawson to one of whose books an earlier reference was made.

preachers went into other clergy's parishes and, later in life, he ordained men for his work. All these are points that were given consideration in Chapter 5.

Brown-Lawson devotes the second, and larger, part of his work to the controversy over Calvinism, showing that both Wesley and his opponents appealed to the same authorities but came to very different conclusions. Attention therefore will now be given to the way that Wesley's interpretation of the Bible differed from many of his Anglican contemporaries.

It must also be noted that in controversial works it is sometimes difficult to be certain what one or more of the disputants actually believes. It is sometimes even harder to determine why a person holds the view that is being strongly expressed. Stephen Gunter makes a valid point, writing 'The emphasis that Wesley underscored depended on the party with which he was engaged in dialogue or against which he was polemicizing.'[3] Stephen Gunter also makes the observation

> A vital factor that has clouded the picture we have of early Methodism is an unwillingness to admit that Wesley was responsible for many of the controversies in which Methodism was engaged. [...] The reader of the Wesley corpus looks in vain for a single instance in which John Wesley accepted any significant responsibility for the many consequences in which Methodism became embroiled.[4]

One other scholar who has examined in some detail the disputes in which Wesley was involved is Martin Schmidt.[5] Schmidt is a German Lutheran and his treatment of Wesley's relationships with the Moravians reflects his interest in the doctrine of justification by faith. Although Schmidt goes into considerable detail in his analysis of the controversies, and although he illustrates the different ways in which Wesley argued his case with different opponents, he does not discuss the question of the sources of the beliefs of Wesley or his opponents, many of whom would have claimed the support of similar authorities to those claimed by Wesley.

In what follows a consideration will be given of the way Wesley refused to embrace Calvinism at an early age, then the course of the dispute will be traced with reference to George Whitefield, James Hervey, the furore aroused by the minutes of the Conference of 1770 and the relationship between Wesley and John Newton. To conclude attention will be given to Wesley's *Plain Account of Christian Perfection*

---

3   W. Stephen Gunter, *The Limits of 'Love Divine,'* Kingswood Books, 1989, p. 105.
4   Gunter, *The Limits of 'Love Divine,'* p. 12.
5   Martin Schmidt, *John Wesley A Theological Biography*, Vol. 2, Part One, translated by Norman P. Goldhawk, Epworth Press, 1971. The original was first published in Zürich, 1966.

Wesley and Predestination - 1725

As Wesley prepared to be ordained deacon in 1725 he showed evidence that he had become more aware of the doctrine of predestination and the problems that it caused him. He was strongly opposed to it. Note was taken of Wesley's correspondence with his mother on the subject in Chapter 3 above.

Wesley's claim to have been consistent in his views from his Oxford days is asserted in his *Plain Account of Christian Perfection* where he also outlined the history of the way he had taught the doctrine of Christian Perfection. The opening paragraphs trace the influences on Wesley from 1725 onwards as he came to embrace the doctrine of Christian Perfection. Although not dealing directly with the question of predestination, the doctrine of Christian Perfection, or entire sanctification, as embraced by Wesley offended the Calvinists. Although there are references to events in 1738, there is no direct reference to the Aldersgate Experience. On this point it is helpful to see paragraphs 7-8. *A Plain Account* dates from 1767.[6]

That his opposition to Calvinism dates from an early period is also illustrated in the comment of Brown-Lawson:

> It can, with certainty, be stated that the theological ideas of the Wesleys were shaped by two important factors - the views of their parents and the influence of books. Both of these were far more decisive in the realms of theology than in that of ecclesiastical order.[7]

Brown-Lawson demonstrates the influence of Susanna Wesley on John by making reference to their correspondence in 1725.[8] This shows that Wesley was struggling with the Formularies of the Church of England and that both his mother and his father were strong influences on his beliefs. The correspondence also indicates that while scripture and the traditions of the Church were the major source for his beliefs, anything to which his reason could not assent caused Wesley to reassess the evidence and offer alternative explanations of what he saw as the meaning of scripture and tradition. Brown-Lawson quotes in full Susanna's letter dated 18 August 1725. Note should be taken of the words:

> The doctrine of predestination, as maintained by the rigid Calvinists, is very shocking, and ought utterly to be abhorred; because it directly charges the most

---

6   The Epworth Press published a version of *A Plain Account* in 1952, subsequently with a number of reprints.

7   Brown-Lawson, *John Wesley and the Anglican Evangelicals of the Eighteenth Century*, p. 135.

8   See, for example, *John Wesley and the Anglican Evangelicals of the Eighteenth Century*, pp. 136-8. Brown-Lawson uses, for reference purposes, Curnock's edition of *The Journal* and Telford's edition of *The Letters*.

h[oly] God with being the author of sin. And I think you reason very well and justly against it. For 'tis certainly inconsistent with the justice and goodness of God to lay any man under either a physical or moral necessity of committing sin, and then punishing him for doing it.[9]

The letter concludes:

This is the Sum of what I believe concerning Predestination which I think is agreeable to the analogy of faith, since it does in no wise derogate from the glory of God's free grace, nor impair the liberty of man. Nor can it with more reason be supposed that the prescience of God is the cause that so many finally perish, than that one knowing the sun will rise tomorrow is the cause of its rising.[10]

Brown-Lawson further comments 'This is a long letter and the necessity to quote it in full will be obvious when it is realized that John adopted his mother's views on this subject which was to be such a bone of contention for the greater part of his ministry.' Additionally, Stephen Gunter makes the comment

There never was much inclination toward Calvinism on the part of Charles and John Wesley, probably due to the parsonage in which they were raised, but they certainly had to deal with the issue as priests in the Church of England.[11]

To that extent it may be noted that Wesley was strongly influenced by home and parents on the point. He had to take note of the Articles of the Church of England and resolve his antipathy towards Calvinism at that early stage. Thus Wesley's problems with Calvinism, especially the doctrine of predestination, were an issue that emerged in his thought during the time spent in Oxford and was discussed in correspondence with his mother. It is of note that the subject was not discussed with direct reference to biblical texts. It was a debate in which the exercise of reason prevailed. Wesley's unhappiness with the doctrine, despite its place in Anglican Formularies, and despite the biblical evidence some advanced for it, was based on the exercise of reason.

Henry Rack also notes Wesley's correspondence with his mother on this point and that she distinguished between predestination and God's foreknowledge of what would happen without determining that it should. It therefore appears that Wesley was influenced strongly by both reason and the thoughts of Susanna Wesley. Although the correspondence was with

---

9   *BE* Vol. 25, p. 179.
10 Brown-Lawson, *John Wesley and the Anglican Evangelicals of the Eighteenth Century*, p. 138.
11 Gunter, *The Limits of 'Love Divine,'* p. 227.

Susanna Wesley, there can be little doubt that she reflected also the views of Samuel and the interpretation of the Bible and the theology that was current in the parish church at Epworth.

Rack observes that 'Wesley worried away at problems of knowledge and faith. [...] So what about predestination. He cannot believe in this because it affronts God's justice and mercy and makes him the author of sin.'[12] Thus Wesley may have considered his theology to be based on scripture, but he could not accept that the Bible said something which, to him, seemed unreasonable and irrational. Nevertheless, Rack makes the point

> It seems doubtful whether predestination was of the same order of concern for him at the personal level; like his mother, he instinctively adopted the anti-Calvinist stance which was now normal for Anglicans. As an intellectual problem it recurred occasionally later, but Wesley never wavered in his revulsion against it, and we shall see that for practical as well as theological reason he would react violently against its resurgence among evangelicals.'[13]

The doctrine, for Wesley, was unreasonable and to be rejected. It was also not part of the Anglican tradition in which he had been brought up. He later searched scripture to find arguments against it, or to explain it away in some form. Rack also makes the point:

> By the 1770s [...] [Wesley] was boldly, if not always plausibly, claiming that Scripture and the Articles rule against predestination, though conformity to the Articles on this point was always a strong point in the Anglican Calvinist's case and one which Wesley had obviously found difficult in 1725.[14]

Therefore, as early as 1725, Wesley was troubled over the question of predestination. Scripture was used selectively to support a previously embraced theological position and was not of necessity the ultimate source from which Wesley's theology and biblical interpretation was drawn. The Bible was interpreted through views already held by those in dispute. Wesley brought to the Bible and also to the Anglican Formularies the views which he then claimed to find in them.

Wesley and Whitefield

Brown-Lawson traces three stages in the controversy over Calvinism. In the first the dispute was between Wesley and George Whitefield. Whitefield (1714-1770) was a younger contemporary of Wesley. His mother and

---

12   Rack, *Reasonable Enthusiast*, p. 74.
13   Rack, *Reasonable Enthusiast*, p. 75.
14   Rack, *Reasonable Enthusiast*, p. 452.

stepfather were innkeepers in Gloucester, and he became a servitor at Oxford where, in October 1733, he met Charles Wesley, subsequently joining the Holy Club. Whitefield's background was thus very different from that of the Wesley brothers. One popular biography of him is that of John Pollock.[15] The works of Arnold Dallimore on Whitefield are also of note and reference will be made to them in this chapter.[16]

Brown-Lawson points out that 'in 1733, when he was 19 years of age, the light dawned on Whitefield.'[17] This was an evangelical awakening but he did not embrace Calvinist doctrines until later. The immediate cause of the experience arose from reading Henry Scougal's *The Life of God in the Soul of Man*. Scougal was one-time Professor of Divinity at Aberdeen University. His work had already been read by John Wesley and the copy read by Whitefield had been lent to him by Charles Wesley. Dallimore notes that Whitefield struggled for a considerable period, even after reading Scougal, before finding the answer to his quest for understanding, in particular in his prolonged studies of the Bible (King James Version), the Greek New Testament and Matthew Henry.[18] Although Scougal was a Calvinist, Whitefield moved only slowly in that direction, being influenced by the works of Richard Alleine and Richard Baxter as well as Scougal. Brown-Lawson points out that, when he wrote to Howell Harris in 1739, he acknowledged that he was a Calvinist.[19] Whitefield had been ordained deacon in 1736 by Bishop Benson of Gloucester and priest in January 1739. While the Wesleys were away in America, Whitefield had exercised a leadership role in the Holy Club.

It will be noted that Whitefield's evangelical awakening predated Wesley's Aldersgate experience. Rack draws attention to the state of confusion in Wesley's mind in early 1738.[20] He notes the problems of authority and faith and works and the way that scripture for Wesley was supreme but that he was concerned at the way in which various writers of many traditions interpreted it. Nevertheless, as Rack argues, too much significance should not be attached to the books that Wesley had read as he was capable of abridging them to come to the point that he wanted to establish. From this it may be seen that there is a difference between the

---

15 John Pollock, *George Whitfield and the Great Awakening*, Lion Publishing, 1982.

16 See Arnold Dallimore, *George Whitefield*, The Wakeman Trust, 1990, which is a condensation of *George Whitefield: The Life and Times of the Great Evangelist of the Eighteenth-Century Revival*, The Banner of Truth Trust, Vol. 1, 1970, Vol. 2, 1980.

17 Brown-Lawson, *John Wesley and the Anglican Evangelicals of the Eighteenth Century*, p. 153.

18 See Dallimore, *George Whitefield*, p. 23.

19 See Brown-Lawson, *John Wesley and the Anglican Evangelicals of the Eighteenth Century*, p. 155.

20 Rack, *Reasonable Enthusiast*, p. 97.

way Wesley used his authorities to confirm his views and the source from which those views came. That is perhaps nowhere more obvious than in the controversies with the Calvinists and the arguments over predestination. It is also clear that Whitfield thought that his Calvinistic views were biblically based and Anglican, although the interpretation of scripture was far removed from that of Wesley.

Brown-Lawson refers to various letters that Whitefield wrote to Wesley in 1739-40, with the comment 'Certainly on 25 June 1740 there was a request of Whitefield that Wesley should never speak against Election in his sermons.'[21] Matters had been brought to a head by the publication of Wesley's sermon *Free Grace*.[22] The text was Romans 8:32. This sermon was published with a hymn on *Universal Redemption* attached. The hymn is probably by Charles Wesley although some have thought it to be by John. The sermon is another example of Wesley provoking controversy, although he would have probably said that he was arguing for what he saw to be the truth of the matter. Albert Outler made the point that 'This sermon is noteworthy as the signal of a major schism in the ranks of English evangelicals, the consequences of which have outlasted the lives of the antagonists.'[23]

On April 30 1739 Wesley had written to James Hutton and the Fetter Lane Society.[24] In this letter, Wesley expressed his considerable agitation about whether to publish the sermon and finally decided to do so after drawing lots on the subject where the outcome was 'Print and Preach.'[25] Dallimore makes the point that, whether uncertain to preach or not, Wesley had already partly prepared the sermon and the drawing of lots was only to obtain divine direction in the matter.[26]

Dallimore, referring to the sermon, quotes Julia Wedgwood's comment

> In this sermon he [Wesley] does not once confront the difficulties which must be accepted by any one who, from his point of view, should reject predestination. He does not see that, if the design of Christ was to save all and the result is that He only saves some, His work was a failure.[27]

This quotation gives a view on the event from the Calvinist side. It may be noted that Wesley did not argue his case entirely from the Bible but by using the logical skills that he had acquired at Oxford, and, as with his

---

21   Brown-Lawson, *John Wesley and the Anglican Evangelicals of the Eighteenth Century*, p. 166.
22   *BE* Vol. 3, pp. 542-563.
23   *BE* Vol. 3, p. 542.
24   *BE* Vol. 25, pp. 637-641.
25   *BE* Vol. 25, p. 640.
26   See Dallimore, *Life and Times*, Vol. 1, p. 309.
27   Dallimore, *Life and Times,* Vol. 1, p. 313.

quotations from other authors, he argued selectively. He did not dispassionately present both sides of the case, perhaps not even seeing that there was another side. Following his quotation from Wedgwood, Dallimore makes the point that:

> The sermon 'Against Predestination' marked the actual beginning of Wesley's own movement.' Some Wesley scholars may question that conclusion but it is true that the sermon did mark the split between Wesley and Whitefield. Whether it was Wesley's intention or not, it is a fair comment to write: 'Thus in circulating the sermon Wesley widened the breach he had begun by preaching it.'[28]

Here again Wesley showed that the earlier influences that fashioned his beliefs were justified in his eyes by what he saw as the biblical evidence in their favour. The sermon was a direct attack on the doctrine of predestination. In it Wesley used reason to argue against the doctrine, claiming that the doctrine: 'hath also a direct and manifest tendency to overthrow the whole Christian revelation.[29] He presented what he saw as the Calvinist position with clarity and then attacked it, showing what he felt to be its absurdity. Wesley wrote, defining predestination in the words:

> The sense of all this is plainly this: 'by virtue of an eternal, unchangeable, irresistible decree of God: One part of mankind are infallibly saved, and the rest infallibly damned; it being impossible that any of the former should be damned, or that any of the latter should be saved.'[30]

From this Wesley argued that the view implied that all preaching is in vain. The style of the sermon was one of straight speaking in which his opposition to the doctrines of Whitefield and others was clear; in Wesley's understanding they were thoroughly flawed. He wrote 'Manifestly does this doctrine tend to overthrow the whole Christian revelation, by making it contradict itself; by giving such an interpretation of some texts as flatly contradicts all the other texts, and indeed the whole scope and tenor of Scripture.'[31]

Arnold Dallimore comments on the sermon:

> We do Wesley no wrong in assessing his motives in separating from the Moravians and from Whitefield. He definitely believed the Moravians were at fault in their failing to use the sacrament of the Church of England, and even though he had not correctly understood Calvinism, in his misconception of it he was certain that it was erroneous. But he also possessed a sense of his own

---

28   Dallimore, *Life and Times*, Vol. 2, p. 28.
29   *BE* Vol. 3, p. 551.
30   *BE* Vol. 3, p. 547.
31   *BE* Vol. 3, p. 554.

superiority together with a mighty ambition, and these tendencies were basic to his actions.[32]

This quotation presents a view of the events that differs somewhat from that of traditional Wesley scholarship, but it does illustrate the way in which conclusions about the arguments of those engaged in a dispute are differently assessed by those who comment on the debate. Dallimore also comments: 'Wesley now began to declare a still more divisive doctrine which he termed 'Christian Perfection.'[33] This refers also to Wesley's work *A Plain Account of Christian Perfection*. It is of note that Dallimore writes: 'Though Wesley could be a master of clarity on most subjects, in *Christian Perfection* he was the very opposite.[34]

In 1741 Whitefield returned to England from America and encountered divisions within those who supported the evangelical revival. Dallimore makes the point that 'The real truth of this matter is largely unknown, for although reports of it have been frequently published, almost all are so strongly biased in Wesley's favour that both his action and Whitefield's are presented very falsely.'[35] This refers to the differences between Wesley and Whitefield over predestination and Christian Perfection. Commenting on Whitefield's return from America in 1741, Dallimore asserts that Calvinism gained more strength for Whitefield: 'This had resulted from his study of the scripture and his reading of reformed and puritan authors, and also from the influence of the many men of Calvinistic beliefs he had met in America.'[36] Wesley and Whitefield certainly both appealed to scripture but interpreted it according to other influences and other authors that they had read and whose arguments they accepted.

Whitefield's answer in 1741 to Wesley was contained in a published pamphlet, *A Letter to the Rev. Mr. John Wesley in Answer to his Sermon Entitled 'Free Grace.'*[37] In it he criticised Wesley's practice of casting lots, referring to an earlier situation when Wesley was returning from America and Whitefield setting out for America. On that occasion Wesley had drawn lots, ordered Whitefield not to continue with his journey and, in Whitefield's view, had been proved wrong. However, although Whitefield argued his case forcefully, the tone of the letter was, in the main, irenical. Whitefield wrote 'Honoured Sir, how could it enter into your heart to chuse(sic) a text to disprove the doctrine of election, out of the 8th of Romans, where the doctrine is so plainly asserted.' He also wrote: 'This is

---

32   Dallimore, *George Whitefield*, pp. 67-8.
33   Dallimore, *George Whitefield*, p. 68.
34   Dallimore, *Life and Times*, Vol. 1, p. 318.
35   Dallimore, *George Whitefield*, p. 103.
36   Dallimore, *Life and Times*, Vol. 2, p. 43.
37   This letter is quoted in full in Dallimore, *Life and Times,* Vol. 2, pp. 552-69.

the established doctrine of Scripture, and acknowledged as such in the 17th Article of the Church of England, as Bishop Benson himself confesses; yet dear Mr Wesley absolutely denies it.'[38]

Whitefield and Wesley both saw clearly the arguments in favour of the positions that they held but discounted the biblical interpretation and doctrinal position of the other. The disputants both appealed to scripture. They both used reason. They both were ministers in the Church of England who subscribed to the Thirty-nine Articles. Nevertheless, they had earlier been influenced to come to different understandings of Anglican teaching and biblical interpretation.

The first of Wesley's Conferences took place in 1744 during the heat of the dispute. Maximin Piette comments: 'This first annual conference decided doctrinal standards, fixing them inalterably, in opposition to faith without works and the teaching of Calvin.'[39] Piette, referring to his own studies of Wesley, stated 'From these writings, to be found in the eighth volume of his *Works*, it is abundantly clear that Wesley was heartily attached to the doctrines of the Church of England.'[40] The point that this comment misses is that many of Wesley's opponents were also claiming allegiance to the Church of England, and that his theology was rooted in the understanding of the teaching of that Church gained in his earlier days.

Piette then immediately refers to the Thirty-nine Articles and comments 'Everyone interpreted them, as they do today, in the sense in which they feel inclined. John substituted Arminianism for the Calvinism which others wished to read into them.' The fact is that Wesley selectively interpreted Articles in a way that supported his Arminian Anglican position.

It is clear that, despite the friendship between Wesley and Whitefield being broken for a period of time, there were real efforts on both sides to continue in a fellowship that would allow some degree of working together. Brown-Lawson's observation is 'The argument, as will be seen, rested on the interpretation of Scripture.'[41] He states that Wesley took election to mean vocation which was not the Calvinist understanding of the meaning of the word. At this point Wesley argued his case by a ruthless logic that pushed the Calvinist case to its extreme conclusion - the election of some to eternal salvation and others to eternal damnation - and then further argued that this denied the concept of God's attribute of perfect love and offended against basic morality. Again Whitefield and Wesley alike appealed to scripture but interpreted it differently. Wesley was preconditioned from his

38 Dallimore, *Life and Times*, Vol. 2, p. 556.
39 Maxim Piette, *John Wesley and the Evolution of Protestantism*, Sheed and Ward, 1937, p. 423.
40 Piette, *John Wesley and the Evolution of Protestantism*, p. 433.
41 Browne-Lawson, *John Wesley and the Anglican Evangelicals of the Eighteenth Century*, p. 191.

earliest years to believe the way he did and therefore he was forced to understand scripture in a way that did not include predestination as taught by Whitefield.

In 1752 Wesley published *Predestination Calmly Considered*.[42] This, however, was argued by logic and not by reference to scripture. Wesley maintained that in the Bible election was normally to a task, or calling, not to an eternal destiny. Where it referred to eternal happiness it was conditional on belief. The pamphlet begins with a summary of the history of the doctrine of predestination. Wesley distinguished between the doctrine of election and that of reprobation but argued strongly that the former inevitably had as its consequence the latter 'For election cannot stand without reprobation.'[43] This was a major point in Wesley's argument over predestination. He quoted extensively verses that contradicted election to reprobation, commenting 'But if the Case be thus, you leave not Room either for Reward or punishment.'[44] Again there is reference to scripture but the argument is mainly by logic and the impression given is very much that the Bible is used here as a secondary line in Wesley's defence. He faced the argument that the verses which seemed to oppose election should be read in the light of those that appeared to espouse election to reprobation and commented 'I must answer very plain; if this were true, we must give up all the Scriptures altogether.'[45] However, he went on to state that this was not the case but it is a major point in understanding his method of using the Bible.

Wesley also discussed human freewill, arguing that there was at least limited human freedom of choice. He discussed the final perseverance of the elect, but argued that a person could be genuinely saved and subsequently fall. This contradicted Calvinist teaching 'It remains, that those who live by Faith may yet fall from God, and perish everlastingly.'[46] Thus God was not irresistible and this was argued with reference to scripture. From this it is clear that Wesley tried to argue by reference to the Bible but he was frequently establishing a position that he already held by the exercise of logic or reason. He refused to allow that those who differed from him were scriptural.

---

42   John Wesley, *Predestination Calmly Considered*, printed by W.B. and sold at the Foundery; by T. Trye; and by R. Akenhead, 1752. This little work was frequently reprinted in the eighteenth century.

43   Wesley, *Predestination Calmly Considered*, p. 7, paragraph IX.

44   Wesley, *Predestination Calmly Considered*, p. 31, paragraph XXXVII. In this and other quotations, the original capital letters are retained.

45   Wesley, *Predestination Calmly Considered*, p. 32, paragraph XXXIX.

46   Wesley, *Predestination Calmly Considered*, p. 71, paragraph LXXVII.

In 1754 Wesley spent time in Hot Wells, near Bristol, writing his *Explanatory Notes upon the New Testament*.[47] Of note are the comments he made on Romans chapters 8 and 9. One passage that would have caused him problems is 8:28-30. Of special concern would be Romans 8.29, 'whom he foreknew, he also predestinated conformable to the image of his son.' Here, however, Wesley emphasised God's foreknowledge, ignoring the obvious reference to predestination. He simply did not take the verse at its face value. On verse 30, he emphasised that God called, but allowed for human response. He tried to escape the predestination implications of the verse in his comment 'St. Paul does not affirm, either here or in any other part of his writings, that precisely the same number of men are called, justified and glorified. He does not deny that many are called who are not justified.'[48]

Another example of Wesley's biblical interpretation of a passage apparently supporting predestination is found in a comment at the beginning of his notes on Romans 9. He wrote of Paul 'That he had not the least thought of personal election or reprobation is manifest.'[49] He went on to give some reasons for the statement but it is clear that at this point Wesley came to the text with the presupposition that it could not mean what his opponents believed and the passage had to be given an alternative interpretation. It was an Anglican Arminian theology that prevailed over the most straightforward and obvious understanding of the meaning of the text. In this chapter of Romans there is reference to the election of Israel. Therefore Wesley commented on Romans 9:31 'Israel [...] hath not attained the law of righteousness,' and answering the question 'why?' 'Is it because God eternally decreed they should not? There is nothing like this to be met with.'[50] Wesley put the blame on Israel, not God: '*Because they sought it not by faith.*' In this way he turned the meaning of a passage that appeared to support a Calvinist interpretation into something that conformed to his own theological position.

Whitefield died and was buried in America in 1770. At Whitefield's earlier request, Wesley preached at a service in London which many regarded as the official memorial to Whitefield.[51] Outler prefaced the sermon with a brief résumé of the history of the relationship that existed between Wesley and Whitefield. The sermon was divided into three sections. The first dealt with Whitefield's life and death, the second with his

---

47 John Wesley, *Explanatory Notes upon the New Testament*, 1754, reprinted in 1976 by Epworth Press.
48 Wesley, *Explanatory Notes upon the New Testament*, p. 551.
49 Wesley, *Explanatory Notes upon the New Testament*, p. 554.
50 Wesley, *Explanatory Notes upon the New Testament*, p. 561.
51 The Sermon, *On the Death of the Rev. Mr George Whitefield,* is No. 53 in *BE* Vol. 2, pp. 324-353, with notes by Albert Outler.

character, and the third with the heading 'How shall we improve on this awful providence?'

Wesley recorded that Whitefield was influenced by the Methodists (so called) in the Holy Club in Oxford. 'By them he was convinced that we 'must be born again', or outward religion will profit us nothing.'[52] Wesley made no reference to the differences between them and none explicitly to the doctrines that divided them. He wrote 'Let us keep close to the grand scriptural doctrines which he everywhere delivered. There are many doctrines of a less essential nature, with regard to which even the sincere children of God are and have been divided for many ages.'[53] Calvinists would no doubt have been offended by the implication that predestination and other Calvinist doctrines were of lesser importance.

Perhaps this was not the appropriate occasion to explain how two Bible-based evangelical Anglicans came to different interpretation of scripture. Nevertheless, the sermon did create further tension with many of the followers of Whitefield. Both Wesley and Whitefield were evangelical Anglicans with a scriptural basis to their theology but Wesley was still strongly influenced by the Arminian High-Church Anglicanism of his earlier days in which he never ceased to believe. Wesley stressed their common acceptance of the authority of scripture but, on this occasion, did not make reference to their different approaches to understanding the text. The omission of any reference to the differences between them is glaring evidence for the fact that the Bible alone was not as clear and plain in its meaning to them as they would have liked to argue.

Wesley and James Hervey

The Second Calvinistic Controversy, as described by Brown-Lawson, was the dispute between Wesley and James Hervey. There are no modern biographies of Hervey but some details of his relationship with Wesley are given in scholarly works on Wesley. Brown-Lawson in *John Wesley and the Anglican Evangelicals of the Eighteenth Century* gives a number of details at various places in his work. An older work is to be found in the Religious Tract Society series, a copy of which is in the John Rylands Library, *Life of the Rev James Hervey M.A. Rector of Weston Flavell.* This is described as being abridged from a work by Rev John Brown. The library catalogue date is given as 1835, but the book itself is undated. Primary documents include letters between Wesley and Hervey to which reference is made.

Hervey was born in 1713 and died in 1758, having experienced periods of ill-health. He was a pupil of John Wesley at Oxford and joined the Holy

52   *BE* Vol. 2, p. 331.
53   *BE* Vol. 2, p. 341.

Club in 1733. He was ordained deacon in 1736 but came to evangelical faith in 1741 having read Jenks on Submission to Christ's Righteousness, Rawlin on Divine Providence, Marshall on Sanctification, Mr Thomas Hall on Divine Providence, and others.[54]

The point to be noted in this correspondence is that Wesley wrote out of his already clearly held understanding of the meaning of the Bible and did not engage in an open debate. The main dispute arose over Hervey's use of the phrase, beloved of Calvinists, 'the imputed righteousness of Christ.' In particular it related to the publication in 1755 of Hervey's work, *Theron and Aspasio, Or a Series of Dialogues and Letters upon the Most Important and Interesting Subjects.*[55] It was largely a dispute conducted in correspondence and published works. Hervey's work was critically reviewed by Wesley at the request of Hervey in a letter dated October 15 1756.[56] However, Hervey took objection to elements within the criticisms offered by Wesley. William Hervey, the brother of James, edited an edition of the work *Theron and Aspasio* in which is included *Aspasio Vindicated* and *Eleven Letters from Mr Hervey to the Rev John Wesley.* The edition of 1837 is in the John Rylands Library.

William Hervey quoted from James's letter to a friend, dated October 24 1758, '[Wesley] is so unfair in his quotations, and so magisterial in his manner, that I find it no small difficulty to preserve the decency of the gentleman, and the meekness of the Christian in my intended answer.'[57] In his letter, Wesley had agreed that parts of *Theron and Aspasio* were of value but he took exception to many sections within the work. Hervey had been Wesley's student at Oxford many years earlier and that may have influenced the way in which Wesley wrote. The style was to quote a phrase or two from Hervey's work and then to make brief comments on them. It reads very much like the work of a tutor marking a student's paper and frequently includes phrases such as 'This I cannot allow.' Wesley did not so much debate with Hervey as write from his own established position, criticising Hervey where he deviated from it. Although there is some interpretation of scripture in the letter, Wesley was not so much appealing to biblical authority in an attempt to find truth in conjunction with Hervey as to correct him from an already established position. It is clear that they

---

54 See Brown, *Life of the Rev James Hervey*, pp. 6-7.
55 James Hervey, *Theron and Aspasio, Or a Series of Dialogues and Letters upon the Most Important and Interesting Subjects*, ed. William Hervey, Thomas Egg and Sons, 1837 (first ed. 1765.)
56 Wesley's letter to Hervey runs to a considerable length and is quoted in full as Appendix One in Brown-Lawson, *John Wesley and the Anglican Evangelicals of the Eighteenth Century.*
57 Hervey, *Theron*, p. 406.

both claimed to appeal to the same sources for their belief but came to widely different conclusions.

Hervey was supported by a number of friends including William Cudworth. Brown-Lawson tends to take Wesley's sincerity for granted and, although critical of some aspects of Wesley's part in the dispute, he is more critical of his opponents. A quotation from Wesley's letter illustrates the nature of the way he criticised Hervey and illustrates the style of the letter itself:

> Then for Christ's sake, and for the sake of the immortal souls which He has purchased with His blood, do not dispute for that phrase, 'the imputed righteousness of Christ'. It is not scriptural; it is not necessary. Men who scruple to use, men who have never heard, the expression, may yet 'be humbled, as repenting criminals at His feet, and rely as devoted pensioners on His merits'. But it has done immense hurt. I have abundant proof that the frequent use of this unnecessary phrase, instead of 'furthering men's progress in vital holiness', has made them satisfied without any holiness at all - yea, and encouraged them to work all uncleanness with greediness.[58]

From this it is clear that Wesley was criticising Hervey for the use of the disputed phrase. He was concerned because, in his view, it was unscriptural and undermined what he saw as the essential moral consequence of justification, leading to sanctification and his doctrine of Christian Perfection.

Nevertheless, *Letter III* of Hervey included the passage:

> I would ask Mr Wesley, in what other way sinners can be justified or accepted, save only through imputed righteousness? - Through their own good deeds, and holy tempers? This supposes the fruit to be good, while the tree is corrupt; and would make salvation to be of works, not of grace.[59]

With Hervey's death in 1758 the dispute might possibly have come to an end. However, Hervey's brother William entered further into the controversy. The subsequent course of events is not of immediate concern at this point. The fact is that again both Wesley and James Hervey claimed to be Bible-based. The abridgement of John Brown's work quoted Hervey, without giving the reference for the source of the quotation, 'My reason in her sedatest moments assures me that Scripture cannot deceive, though I be unable to comprehend.'[60] Wesley and Hervey were Anglican clergymen professing belief in the Articles and Homilies. Both were evangelical in

---

58   Brown-Lawson, *John Wesley and the Anglican Evangelicals of the Eighteenth Century*, p. 356. This letter is also included by William Hervey in the edition of *Theron*, pp. 467-79. The quotation cited is to be found on p. 467.
59   Hervey, *Theron*, p. 496.
60   Brown, *Life of the Rev James Hervey MA*, p. 31.

theology, but one was Arminian and the other Calvinist. Wesley's biblical interpretation was thus seen to be Anglican and Arminian. Indeed, it was Anglican Arminianism just as Hervey's was Calvinistic Anglicanism. The influence of parents, upbringing and the Oxford years was inescapable as far as Wesley was concerned.

Brown-Lawson writes:

> Hervey, under the guise of Aspasio was putting his own interpretation on the Articles as the Calvinistic Evangelicals generally were doing on the Scriptures, especially Romans, Chapter Five. The Homily concerning *Salvation of Mankind* was cited for further support, whilst Clement, Justin Martyr and Chrysostom were the Fathers quoted.[61]

Although this is fair comment, it has to be stated that Wesley, too, was putting his own interpretation on scripture, the Articles and the Fathers. The dispute illustrates the manner in which Wesley interpreted scripture and used it, as well as the way Hervey understood and used it. Brown also made the comment:

> I am sorry to hear that Mr -------- should think my doctrine tends to the introduction of licentiousness; far, very far from it; it is the genuine doctrine of the scriptures, and the only doctrine to reclaim mankind, as it encourages them not to continue in their sins, but to turn to their injured Lord and receive salvation at his beneficent hands.[62]

Brown argued that Hervey taught holiness but not as the ground of salvation, only as its consequence. He also wrote his book without making any reference to Wesley or the dispute over Calvinism.

Brown's point is particularly obvious in Wesley's letter of October 15 1756 to which reference has already been made. His comments on the latter part of the Thirteenth Dialogue give clear examples.[63] He states 'There are many other expressions in this Dialogue to which I have the same objection - namely (1) that they are unscriptural; (2) that they directly lead to Antinomianism.' Wesley and Hervey disagreed over the interpretation of scripture but Wesley apparently could not see that any argument other than the one he approved was valid.

Thus it was that Wesley and Hervey both appealed to the Bible as the source of their doctrines but they came to opposing views of the truth

---

61 Brown-Lawson, *John Wesley and the Anglican Evangelicals of the Eighteenth Century*, p. 212.
62 Brown, *The Life of the Rev James Hervey MA*, p. 35.
63 See the text on pp. 365-6 in Brown-Lawson, *John Wesley and the Anglican Evangelicals of the Eighteenth Century*.

concerning important matters of faith and both did this while remaining within the established Church.

The Controversy Aroused by the Publication of the Minutes of the 1770 Conference

Wesley's strongly anti-Calvinist views are further illustrated in the third phase in the dispute. This Brown-Lawson calls 'The Minute Controversy.'[64] The minutes of Wesley's 1770 Conference included reference to Calvinism and the doctrine of justification by faith. Question 28 asked 'What can be done, to revive the Work of God where it is decayed?' The answer given was 'Take heed to our doctrine. We said in 1744 "We have leaned too much to Calvinism."' Expanding on the point, the minutes used phrases such as: 'man's faithfulness' and 'working for life.' The answer continued 'We have received it as a Maxim, "that a Man is to do nothing, *in order to receive Justification.*" Nothing can be more false. Whoever desires to find favour with God, should *cease from evil and learn to do well.*' A further question asked: 'Is not this "salvation by works?"' The reply given was: 'Not by the *merit* of Works, but by Works as *condition.*'

The minutes stirred up a furore among those of even moderate Calvinistic leanings. John Shirley, Richard and Rowland Hill and Augustus Montague Toplady, among others, were involved. It was perhaps also unfortunate that the death of Whitefield and Wesley's funeral sermon in London, referred to above, happened in the same year as the publication of the Minutes. Wesley made few written comments during the dispute, relying on his loyal assistants to answer the criticisms. For various reasons the dispute did not die down quickly and tracts continued to be written for a long period. It is possibly indicative of the consequences of the extent of the debate that the 1771 Conference noted that 17 of the 46 circuits reported decreases in membership. By the 1776 Conference, in response to question 26, it was commented: 'Calvinism has been the grand hindrance of the work of God.'

One of the chief protagonists on Wesley's behalf was Rev John Fletcher, Vicar of Madely.[65] Born 1729, died 1785, Fletcher grew up and

---

64 This is dealt with in *John Wesley and the Anglican Evangelicals of the Eighteenth Century*, Chapter 11. Wesley kept minutes of the Conferences from 1744 onwards. They are published as *Minutes of Several Conversations Between the Reverend Mr John and Charles Wesley, and Others.* A copy is to be found in the John Rylands Library although neither date of publication nor name of publisher is to be found in the work. The *Minutes* were largely written in the form of questions with answers.

65 A booklet giving an outline of Fletcher's life is: Peter S. Forsaith, *John Fletcher*, Foundery Press, 1994. Note may also be taken of George Lawton, *A Shropshire Saint,* Epworth Press, 1966, The Wesley Historical Lecture No. 26. A more recent work is Patrick Streiff, *Reluctant Saint? A Theological Biography of Fletcher of*

was educated in Switzerland, where he had hoped to enter the ministry. Education in Geneva made him well acquainted with the teachings of Calvinism and, because of his objections to aspects of certain of its doctrines, as well as the sense of unworthiness and the pressure of others, he turned elsewhere. Eventually he came to England and became an Anglican priest. Wesley had wanted Fletcher to succeed him as leader of the Methodist people but Fletcher was unwilling and, in the event, Wesley outlived Fletcher. Fletcher was a loyal and determined protagonist in the dispute. Defending the fact that he embraced the doctrine of justification by faith alone, in *An Answer to Mr. Rowland Hill's Tract, entitled, Imposture Detected*, Wesley commented I never renounced it yet, and I trust, never shall. The '*horrid* Minutes' Mr. Fletcher has so effectively vindicated that I wonder Mr. Hill should mention them any more.'[66]

Under the heading 'Criteria for Theological Debate,' Patrick Streiff comments:

> Without question, Scripture had supreme authority in theological debate, in his arguments within the Church. However, Fletcher referred also to tradition, to show that his interpretation of Scripture was in harmony with the reformed tradition of the Church of England. However, this tradition provided no common ground with Baptists and Quakers, and in their case, therefore, Fletcher based his arguments on Scripture and reason.[67]

In this Fletcher was using authorities recognised by Wesley. Streiff also comments:

> In the 1760's, Fletcher used four categories of argument: Scripture, tradition, reason and experience. He took this fourfold basis from John Wesley, and in doing so revealed the extent to which he had been influenced by the Dutch-English early Enlightenment.[68]

On the same page Streiff writes 'Scripture and reason became the main categories, with experience and tradition following on behind them.' On the following page 'Reason is absolutely necessary for the right understanding of Scripture. However, reason cannot make statements on faith independently, without reference to Scripture.' Without making reference to the Wesley Quadrilateral, Streiff offers arguments that suggest that Fletcher echoed an appeal to authority from Wesley along these lines.

Madely, Epworth Press, 2001. This is an English version, abbreviated and revised, of a dissertation published in German in 1984.

66   *BE* Vol. 9, pp. 406-7.
67   Strieff, *Reluctant Saint?*, p. 97.
68   Strieff, *Reluctant Saint?*, p. 193.

In 1768 the Countess of Huntingdon founded a College in Trevecca, Brecon. Fletcher became its first president but resigned in 1771 to side with Wesley in the Minute dispute. Peter Forsaith comments: 'Fletcher had encountered Calvinism in Geneva, and was well read in its tenets, as he was familiar with much biblical, classical and other learning.'[69] Forsaith further comments that: 'Fletcher produced his *Checks to Antinomianism* which were to become classics of Methodist doctrine.' Although regarded as a Methodist saint, Fletcher was a formidable disputant on behalf of Wesley and the Arminian Methodists.

On this subject Lawton makes the point: 'In the controversial warfare Fletcher is extremely assiduous. He fights to win on every line; he fights in depth on all fronts. [...] Notably, this is true of his employment of scripture.[70] Writing further about the controversy, Lawton makes the further observation:

> The Calvinists turned the question into a dilemma and said that to make salvation a matter of merit is to denude faith, and to dishonour Christ, and to dethrone God. The Arminians maintained that Christ is Christ, and God is God, even though man as a free-willing being can only be saved in the formation of character.[71]

Referring to the 1771 Conference and Fletcher's *First Check to Antinomianism*, Streiff makes the point:

> While not passing over the differences from the Calvinistic Methodists, Fletcher demonstrated that John Wesley totally assented to and preached the basic doctrines of Christianity; the Fall, justification through the merits of Christ, sanctification through the operation of the Holy Sprit, and the worship of one true God, mysteriously differentiated as Father, Son and Holy Spirit.[72]

It is not necessary to follow the argument through all the events of the period. It is clear that both sides appealed to scripture as authoritative but interpreted it differently from each other. Although there was considerable allegiance to Calvinism in Dissenting Churches, the debate largely involved parties who regarded themselves as fundamentally Anglican, but either Arminian Anglicans or Calvinistic Anglicans. The line of division was drawn between Arminianism and Calvinism. The Arminian influences of Epworth, Wesley's reading at Oxford, and, to a much lesser extent, his Aldersgate experience predominated with him.

The publication of the minutes of the 1770 Conference of Wesley's preachers had caused a considerable furore but the dispute was predictable.

---

69   Forsaith, *John Fletcher*, p. 28.
70   Lawton, *Shropshire Saint*, pp. 67-8.
71   Lawton, *Shropshire Saint*, p. 38.
72   Strieff, *Reluctant Saint?*, p. 175.

It was also a fierce argument between members of the Church of England who claimed to be loyal to that Church and to the teaching of the Bible.

John Newton

John Newton (1725-1807) was a younger contemporary of Wesley.[73] Wesley supported Newton's desire to be ordained within the Church of England. They were not engaged in controversy. Newton embraced a milder form of Calvinism but he tried to remain in a good relationship with contemporary evangelicals of other persuasions. Most scholars do not deal with the relationship between Wesley and Newton to the same extent as they deal with disputes with Whitfield and Hervey. Nevertheless it is useful to give it some attention as it further illustrate the way Wesley read and interpreted the Bible, holding to his Arminian position.

There were some close comparisons that could be drawn between Wesley and Newton in respect of their style of writing and the authorities that they recognised. Thus Bruce Hindmarsh refers to Newton's *Authentic Narrative of Some Remarkable and Interesting Particulars in the Life of xxxxxx*, 1764 and devotes a section to *'Use of Scripture.'*[74] Newton regarded the Bible as the supreme authority and, like Wesley, used biblical language in his written works. Discussing Newton's understanding of the spiritual life, Hindmarsh refers to the authorities that Newton recognised and observed 'This was consistent with the theological method he displayed elsewhere, which sought to co-ordinate Scripture, reason, and experience.'[75] Thus Newton would appear to have drawn on the same sources as Wesley but came to different conclusions.

Referring to a disagreement with Nicholas Manners, a Methodist preacher whom Newton had known in his Liverpool days, Hindmarsh comments '[Newton] was increasingly convinced that a person became a Calvinist through personal experience, not by argument.'[76] Newton's experiences at sea and in his earlier days leading up to his evangelical conversion convinced him that everything was of grace. Newton's well known and popular hymn, *Amazing Grace*, was undoubtedly based on what had happened to him as a person. The lines 'God's grace has brought me safe thus far, And he will lead me home' express Newton's own experience and a Calvinist interpretation of it. Thus he was not in the high Calvinist tradition that argued solely from scripture. He found in scripture support for

---

73   A recent biography is that of D. Bruce Hindmarsh, *John Newton and the English Evangelical Tradition*, William B. Eerdmans, 1996.

74   Hindmarsh, *John Newton*, pp. 23-7.

75   Hindmarsh, *John Newton*, p. 254.

76   Hindmarsh, *John Newton*, p. 162.

the views that came to him in his own experience, after his own evangelical conversion, and the experience of others.

Hindmarsh also has a section on 'John Newton, John Wesley and Perfectionism.'[77] He notes that 'The perfectionism controversy had occasioned Newton's estrangement from Wesley.'[78] He further comments 'Moreover, although Newton identified lofty possibilities for the spiritual life, his teaching differed from Wesley on both assurance and perfection.'[79]

Newton and Wesley may have recognised the same authorities, but they brought to them their own prior experience and already formed theological conclusions. These led them to very different ways of interpreting the Bible. It is clear that the ex-slave-runner and the onetime Oxford don brought to their study of scripture vastly different experiences. Thus, once again, there was the common appeal to the Bible and membership of the Church of England, although the interpretation of both differed strongly. The earlier experiences of Wesley and Newton left one in the Arminian Anglican camp whereas the other was strongly influenced by at least a mild form of Calvinism.

John Wesley's Teaching on Christian Perfection in *A Plain Account of Christian Perfection*

Wesley's teaching on Christian Perfection stood in contrast to the position held by many of his Calvinistic Anglican contemporaries. Calvinists tended to see in Wesley's teaching on Christian Perfection a reversion into the doctrine of salvation by works, or human merit. Wesley was concerned, in his teaching, to deal with the consequences of justification resulting in sanctification or growth following new birth. He saw the doctrine as a corrective to the dangers of antinomianism which he felt was inherent in the Calvinist position.

Gunter makes the point:

> The distinctive doctrines of the early Methodist societies were two: justification by faith alone and Christian perfection. Ultimately Wesley and Whitefield parted ways over these two doctrines, Whitefield taking the path labelled by the anti-Methodists as "fideism" and Wesley the road of "perfectionism."[80]

Wesley summarised his teaching in *A Plain Account of Christian Perfection* in which he outlined what he asserted that he had believed and

---

77   Hindmarsh, *John Newton*, pp. 126-42.
78   Hindmarsh, *John Newton*, p. 135.
79   Hindmarsh, *John Newton*, pp. 255-6.
80   Gunter, *'The Limits of Love Divine,'* p. 42.

taught over the period 1725-65.[81] In it he recalled the way in which he came to an understanding of the doctrine. This was through the works of Bishop Taylor, *Rules and Exercises of Holy Living and Dying*, Thomas à Kempis, *Christian's Pattern*, and William Law, *Christian Perfection* and *Serious Call*. This was followed by reference to the sermon he preached on January 1 1733 before the University in St Mary's Church Oxford, from which he gave substantial extracts. He then traced the way in which he consistently presented the doctrine, with some slight changes over subsequent years, which Wesley would have regarded as not being of major consequence. It is of note that there is no reference to the Aldersgate experience of May 24 1738. Wesley recorded his feelings at the beginning of 1738 as 'the language not only of every believer, but of everyone that is truly awakened.'[82] The next paragraph referred to his conversation in August in Germany with Arvid Gradin. What happened between January and August is passed over in silence.

Wesley referred at some length to the tract *The Character of a Methodist*, 1739, before describing the way he continued to preach and teach the doctrine of Christian Perfection over the course of his life time. Although Wesley's account showed that he came to the doctrine through the work of Bishop Taylor, Thomas à Kempis and William Law, he commented 'In the year 1729 I began not only to read but to study the Bible, as the one, the only standard of truth, and the only model of pure religion.'[83] He also stated that from 1730 'I began to be *homo unius libri*, 'a man of one book,' regarding none, comparatively, but the Bible.'[84] During the course of *Plain Account*, Wesley frequently asserted that the doctrine was biblically based. He made references to specific texts drawn from a range of books in the Old and New Testaments. There were a number of references to verses in 1 John which included 2:15, 1 John 3:8, 1 John 4:17, 1 John 4:18, and 1 John 5:19. Moreover, his general style was to use biblical language and there were many occasions in the work where Wesley consciously or unconsciously used the text of 1 John and other Old and New Testament passages without directly ascribing them to their sources. As will be noted in both this and the next chapter, 1 John was a particularly favourite New Testament book with Wesley.

W.E. Sangster made a study of Wesley's doctrine of Christian Perfection in his work *The Path to Perfection*.[85] Sangster examined,

---

81 Wesley, *A Plain Account of Christian Perfection*, Epworth Press, 1952 edition, p.109, final sentence in section 27.
82 Wesley, *Plain Account*, p. 9.
83 Wesley, *Plain Account*, p.6.
84 Wesley, *Plain Account*, p.15.
85 W.E. Sangster, *The Path to Perfection*, Hodder and Stoughton, 1943. This was approved as a PhD thesis by the University of London in 1942. A large part of the

sympathetically but not uncritically, Wesley's understanding of the doctrine. The third chapter is headed 'The Doctrine Stated.' In this chapter Sangster made the point that Wesley lived in an age before the modern critical approach to the Bible:

> Wesley believed that this perfection was plainly taught in the Bible. It need hardly be stated that his citation of texts did not anticipate the findings of the higher critics, and he is happy to make his point with a word of national significance from Ezekiel as with a word of deep, personal religion from Paul.[86]

Sangster noted key Biblical quotations made by Wesley in *A Plain Account of Christian Perfection* including 1 John 4:17, 1 John 1:7, and 1 John 1:9. He also commented 'Ignoring the fact that most of his texts were garnered from one epistle (the First Epistle of John), Wesley contended that no close student of the New Testament could deny that the doctrine had emphatic scriptural warrant.'[87]

Commenting on Wesley's placing the Bible as his prime authority, Sangster quoted the Preface to Wesley's *Sermons* in 1746 'Nowhere is this more plainly set out than in the famous passage in which he proclaims himself *homo unius libri*.'[88] In the fourth chapter, headed 'Wesley's Approach to the Bible,' Sangster quoted from Wesley 'In conformity, therefore, both to the doctrine of St. John, and the whole tenor of the New Testament, we fix this conclusion: A Christian is so far perfect as not to commit sin.'[89] Sangster also noted 'The most quoted book is the First Epistle of John, from which he culled twenty texts, some of which he repeats frequently.'[90] The fifth chapter is entitled 'The Texts on Which He Built.' Pages 46-51 deal with the Johannine writings including the comment: 'A third of the texts on which Wesley chiefly relies for his doctrine of Christian Perfection are taken from the First Epistle of John.'[91] Here Sangster noted that Wesley quoted, among others, the verses from 1 John 1:5&7, 1 John 1:8-9, 1 John 2:6, 1 John 3:8-10, and 1 John 5:13. Sangster also noted that Wesley's opponents could quote from 1 John 1:8 and 1 John 1:10 to the effect that sin remained. Wesley's response was that these verses referred to the time preceding God's work in the believer.

Referring to Wesley and the doctrine of Christian Perfection, Sangster then commented:

---

   research involved a detailed study of Wesley's *Plain Account of Christian Perfection*.

86   Sangster, *The Path to Perfection*, p .28.
87   Sangster, *The Path to Perfection*, p. 29.
88   Sangster, *The Path to Perfection*, p. 33.
89   Sangster, *The Path to Perfection*, p. 35, quoting *Plain Account*, p. 22.
90   Sangster, *The Path to Perfection*, p. 36.
91   Sangster, *The Path to Perfection*, p. 48.

From that position he did not move through the years. When his opponents, stressing the utter pollution of human nature, insisted that there was sin in everything that everybody did, he usually left the controversy to his lieutenants but bent his own strength to raising up a spiritual community of people who would authenticate, in their own lives, the promise of God and the teaching of the Apostle. He believed that the argument could best be rebutted in that way.

Whether Wesley made changes in the way he presented his doctrine of Christian perfection or not over the years may be disputed but undoubtedly Sangster makes a valid point in drawing attention to the influence of 1 John on Wesley's thinking and his use of it in arguing the case for it.

It is thus clear that when scripture appeared to contradict Wesley's teaching, it had to be interpreted in some other way. Experience and reason were used to authenticate the views that Wesley held. Sangster recognised these questions in the comment:

> Did he [Wesley] find the doctrine in the Bible, or carry preconceived ideas to it? Would any mature and thoughtful reader studying the New Testament for the first time recognise this teaching on perfection as an integral part of the message - or learn of it later with no little surprise.[92]

At that point in his work, Sangster does not give an answer to the question he raises, but it is a question which has to be faced. In the following chapter Sangster comments 'We cannot say, on the ground of grammar that Scripture teaches that perfection is unattainable on earth' and 'On the other hand, it is important that those who maintain this doctrine should give due weight to the fact that no New Testament writer announces in plain words: "I am perfect."'[93]

Therefore, in the course of this work Sangster noted the use Wesley made of the Bible, in particular the amount of usage of 1 John. He showed that Wesley claimed to use the Bible as the source of his teaching and, that, for him, all the Bible was equally inspired, but that certain books, such as 1 John, were of greater influence on him than others. Although Sangster admitted that Wesley got his ideas from Taylor, à Kempis and Law, he did not sufficiently acknowledge that they confirmed him in seeing in the Bible a doctrine that he already held. Wesley came to the Bible as an Arminian Anglican. His beliefs go back to a period long before 1738 and were rooted in his life in Epworth and Oxford. This point is further emphasised if account is taken of the fact that other eighteenth-century evangelicals, including Calvinists, based their beliefs on scripture, but came to different conclusions and strongly disagreed with Wesley.

Thus Rack argues that:

---

92   Sangster, *The Path to Perfection*, p. 51.
93   Sangster, *The Path to Perfection*, pp. 54 and 55.

Wesley's perfectionism - the real heart of his message - could only have emerged from his peculiar background and experiences in Oxford, even though it was partly remoulded by what he learnt from the Moravians. Wesley was never quite a typical 'evangelical' for this reason.[94]

Gunter summarises Wesley's teaching in the late 1730's and the 1740's as:

First, the penitent can be saved (in an instant) from his sins and know, by the "witness of the Spirit," that it is so. Secondly, the sinner can only be saved by *faith alone* in Christ. Thirdly, this saving faith will produce active righteousness leading to holiness. Finally, this active righteousness will not be thwarted by educational deficiencies, social class barriers or even ecclesiastical conventionalities.[95]

To take one of these points by itself is to distort Wesley's view and it is liable to lead to misunderstanding. Nevertheless, in argument, Wesley was not able to hold all his teaching in balance and controversy developed with other evangelical Anglicans and, in particular, the Calvinists. Gunter further examines Wesley's doctrine of Christian Perfection in the chapter 'The Danger of Perfectionism.'[96] This is of particular note because it includes comment on Wesley's 1741 sermon, No. 40, on Christian Perfection and his use in that sermon of verses from 1 John. The sermon was written shortly after Wesley's meeting with Bishop Edmund Gibson in late 1740 and is intended to outline the doctrine of Christian perfection as Wesley understood it at that time. Gunter's arguments are supported by an examination of the sermon which was biblically based.

The text of the sermon is Philippians 3:12 but reference was made to the writings of Peter, James and John as well as Paul. In paragraphs II, 5 and 6, Wesley considered 1 John 3:8 and the subsequent verses which, he maintained, must be taken at their full face value. He would not accept any softening of them. However, in paragraphs II, 18-20, Wesley looked at the verses in 1 John that assert strongly that everyone has sinned. Wesley's argument was that everyone had sinned but that God in Christ offered forgiveness and that the call to holiness or righteousness followed from the new birth or the forgiveness of sins. Thus, according to Wesley, John was entirely consistent with himself. No doubt those with whom Wesley differed would read the scriptures differently.

Wesley's views may have been fashioned by scripture but they had their roots in the relationships and experiences that date from his earlier, pre-

---

94 Rack, *Reasonable Enthusiast*, p. 104.
95 Gunter, *The Limits of 'Love Divine,'* p. 118. On these points Gunter refers to Wesley's *The Principles of a Methodist* (1740), *Works VIII*, pp. 361-74.
96 Gunter, *The Limits of 'Love Divine,'* pp. 202-226.

1738, years in Epworth and Oxford. On the other hand, writing about Christian Perfection and the disputes of the 1760s, and referring to the *Plain Account of Christian Perfection* (1767), Rack makes the point 'Experience here was certainly fortifying, clarifying and even modifying the rather theoretical opinions he had earlier deduced from the Bible.'[97] The point about experience is certainly a true comment. How far it is correct to suggest that Wesley had derived the doctrine entirely in the first instance from scripture is open to question.

Additional Note on Wesley and Arminianism

Bernard Semmel's main purpose in writing his work *The Methodist Revolution* was to explore how that early Methodism prepared the way for the more liberal movements in the nineteenth century.[98] He was therefore not directly concerned with the source of Wesley's beliefs and teaching. Nevertheless he does trace the spread of the influence of Arminianism from the Netherlands to England through Archbishop Laud and others. Semmel makes the point: 'John Wesley was heir to this High Church Arminianism but for a considerable time he avoided the name 'Arminianism' with its invidious association for "true Protestants," of Laudianism or Anglo-Catholicism.'[99] Semmel then points out that Wesley was happy to describe himself as an Arminian in the 1770's.

Wesley strongly defended Arminius against any charge of heresy. He had some sympathy for the work of Pelagius who is usually regarded as heretical. Thus Wesley may have claimed that his opposition to Calvinism was rooted in scripture but he came to this element within his teaching through his High-Church Anglican background. However, as Semmel makes the point, '[Wesley's] High Church Arminianism was already becoming, from his sermon on Free Grace onward, an evangelical Arminianism, stressing, along with his appeals to justification by faith, Christ's offer of salvation to all.'[100]

Conclusion

This chapter has explored certain aspects of the controversy between Arminians and Calvinists. It has by no means given a critical examination of all the works of all the protagonists involved in the debate. Such would be impossible given the limitations of space and the purposes of this work.

---

97 Rack, *Reasonable Enthusiast*, p. 336.
98 Bernard Semmel, *The Methodist Revolution*, Basic Books, Inc. 1973, Heinemann, 1974.
99 Semmel, *The Methodist Revolution*, p. 82.
100 Semmel, *The Methodist Revolution*, p. 82.

Nevertheless, it has established conclusively that there were many on both sides who appealed to the authority of scripture as confirmed by experience and who claimed loyalty to the teaching and practice of the Church of England. Wesley's assertion that he was a man of one book and a loyal Anglican must be understood in that context. He was an Arminian Anglican, not just an Arminian or an Anglican. Consequently, as has been seen, Wesley selectively used the text of the Bible and Anglican documents to establish his position. Sometimes, as can be seen in the case of Romans 8.29, he simply ignored the plain meaning of the words. Other times he explains away any Calvinist interpretation that might be seen in them. The point has been made repeatedly in this and previous chapters that Wesley came to his views influenced by his family upbringing in Epworth Rectory and by his reading at Oxford, not just the Aldersgate experience of 1738. His biblical interpretation was that of an eighteenth-century High-Church Arminian Anglican.

The introduction to this work began with a reference to Rupert Davies's comment that the source of Wesley's doctrine of salvation was to be found solely in the Bible and nowhere else. It has now been made abundantly clear that this is far too simplistic. The dispute between Calvinists and Arminians both claiming that their teaching was rooted in scripture alone has vividly illustrated this point.

It is now to a study of Wesley's biblical interpretation that attention will be given in the next chapter.

Chapter 7

Wesley and his One Book

The Main Contention of this Book

Throughout this book it has been contended that Wesley brought to his interpretation of the Bible the presuppositions of an eighteenth-century High-Church Arminian Anglican and subsequently found confirmation of his theological position there. It has also been argued that this theological presupposition was not something Wesley discovered later in life, but that it had its roots in the influence of Samuel and Susanna Wesley in Epworth as well as the reading he undertook in Oxford, particularly in the period from 1725 and subsequent years. He did not go to scripture with a blank or even an open mind. In chapter 5 it was established that Wesley consciously remained a Church of England man throughout the whole of his life. Furthermore, in controversy, he used the biblical text, sometimes selectively, to prove the points that he wanted to make. It has been shown that this is something that many earlier Wesley scholars did not appreciate or acknowledge, although the insights afforded by Reader-Response criticism in biblical studies should have made this apparent in more recent years.

In the Introduction to this work there is a fuller discussion on Reader-Response criticism as used by many biblical scholars. Before giving further critical consideration to Wesley's claim to be a man of one book and an appraisal of certain primary documents, note has to be taken of the fact that writers, preachers and scholars use the biblical text in various ways, their interpretations differing from one another. As pointed out in the Introduction and earlier chapters, the results of scholarly research into biblical interpretation do not appear to have been applied by Wesley scholars to their work. Although it would be wrong to judge Wesley's beliefs and teaching against the criteria of scholarly work of which he could have no knowledge, it is argued here that the more modern approach of Reader-Response Criticism is helpful. It offers a useful tool to enable the scholar researching Wesley better to examine critically the way in which he came to his theological conclusions and the way in which he used the Bible. It may not affect whether or not his interpretation of the Bible was correct but it does help the reader understand the way he came to that particular interpretation.

In this chapter a closer critical examination of Wesley's use of the biblical text is conducted in order to test the contentions already made. This chapter also illustrates the manner in which Wesley's claim to be a man of one book may be understood. First, however, it is to be noted that at the level of critical biblical scholarship Wesley was, not surprisingly, a child of his own age. He tried to get closer to the original than the King James Version, using his own knowledge of the Greek and Hebrew texts but, nevertheless, he accepted most contemporary views regarding the authorship of the canonical books. Thus it is contended that it was within this context that he brought to his interpretation of the Bible an Arminian High-Church Anglican theology which he claimed to find rooted in the scriptures. It is his method of coming to an understanding of the meaning of the text that is of greater interest in this chapter.

It has been noted above that Wesley claimed to take the Bible as his supreme authority. A typical statement by Wesley on this point is his *Journal* entry for 5 June 1766 'I am a member of the Church of England, but I love good men of every church. My ground is the Bible. Yea, I am a Bible-bigot. I follow it in all those things, both great and small.'[1] It must, however, be noted that Wesley made that entry in the context of being a member of the Church of England. Although modern insights throw light on the way the Bible is read or understood, Wesley, with the scholarship of his day, simply claimed to be a man of one book. Donald Thorsen speaks for many scholars when he makes the point that:

> The important thing is the primacy that Wesley placed in Scripture; other sources of authority supplemented but never surpassed the Word. Wesley could believe this because he never expected tradition, reason, or experience to confute Scripture in any substantial way.[2]

Kenneth Collins makes the further point that Wesley's understanding of the importance of scripture can be traced back as early as 1729 and the early days of the Holy Club, writing 'In his *Plain Account of Christian Perfection*, for example, he [Wesley] states, "In the year 1729, I began not only to read, but to study, the Bible, as the one, the only standard of truth, and the only model of pure religion."'[3] It should, however, be noted that Wesley's belief in the authority of the Bible can be traced back even further to the lessons he learned in the Rectory at Epworth.

---

1   *BE* Vol. 22, p. 42.
2   Thorsen, *The Wesleyan Quadrilateral*, p. 72.
3   Collins, *A Real Christian*, p. 31, quoting from Jackson's *Works*, 11:367.

Mabel Richmond Brailsford is, perhaps, over simplistic when she writes 'John's genius was not original, and his strength drawn, as he believed, straight from God and the scriptures.'[4] Nevertheless this reflects the view of most earlier and many recent Wesley scholars. More recently, Donald Thorsen has commented 'Wesley did not reflect on a doctrine for long without considering how it related to tradition, reason, and experience as well as Scripture.'[5] Although true, it remains to be asked what were the influences that led Wesley to bring his evangelical theology to scripture for verification in the first place? Thorsen also states that:

> By faith Wesley affirmed the primary religious authority of Scripture. He brought the interpretation of Scripture into relation with tradition, reason, and experience in a way that relieved him of the dangers of a static and mechanical literalism in biblical interpretation. [6]

In an attempt to explain Wesley's interpretation of scripture, W. Stephen Gunter draws a distinction between Anglican and Puritan attitudes:

> If the Anglican conflict with Roman Catholicism was over the interplay between Scripture and tradition, the differences between Puritan and Anglican were between Scripture and scripture. Both would have capitalized the word, but I use this device to point out that the Anglicans and the Puritans were far apart on how to interpret the authority of Scripture.[7]

This was a reference to the differences in approach evidenced in late seventeenth-century thought and Gunter continued:

> In retrospect we can nuance these differences a bit more carefully by saying that the Anglicans utilized from tradition that which was not explicitly ruled out by Scripture, whereas the Puritans required a positive reference from Scripture. Wesley, although having both Anglican and Puritan roots, on this issue was in the Anglican tradition.

This point is relevant to this study but, of course, does not indicate how Wesley came to interpret scripture. Richard Heitzenrater makes a similar point to that of Gunter, referring to Wesley's statement on being a man one book in the sermon *On God's Vineyard*, when he comments:

---

4   Brailsford, *A Tale of Two Brothers*, p. 212.
5   Thorsen, *The Wesleyan Quadrilateral*, p. 75.
6   Thorsen, *The Wesleyan Quadrilateral*, p. 99.
7   W. Stephen Gunter, 'The Quadrilateral and the "Middle Way"' in *Wesley and the Quadrilateral - Renewing the Conversation*, ed. W. Stephen Gunter, Abingdon Press, 1997, p. 33.

In view of the wide-ranging bibliography read by Wesley and his companions, this statement should be understood as corresponding to the definition of a Methodist provided by Wesley's *Complete English Dictionary* of 1753 "one that lives according to the method laid down in the Bible."[8]

The Sermon *On God's Vineyard* was written in Witney in October 1787 and was based on the text in Isaiah 5:4. In the introductory paragraph to the sermon, Wesley acknowledged that the reference in the text to God's Vineyard could have been taken in various ways but for the purpose of this sermon he used it to refer to 'that Society only, which began at Oxford in the year 1729, and remain united at this day.' This was not strict exegesis but through it Wesley argued that he and the people who were called Methodist were from the outset a people whose supreme and only authority was based firmly in scripture. In fact, the whole of the first section of the sermon *On God's Vineyard* dealt with the doctrine that was both believed and taught by the Methodist people and the argument was sustained that the authority for all Christian doctrine was to be found in the Bible.

Wesley maintained the supreme authority of scripture in every attempt to determine Christian doctrine and to set out Christian practice. Any other influence or authority that he acknowledged was seen as subordinate to the Bible. This set up in his mind a tension out of which emerged his own refined theological position and he sought to prove it from scripture.

This may be further illustrated by Raymond George's reference to the conclusion of the Preface to the 1784 edition of *The Sunday Service of the Methodists in North America, with Other Occasional Services*,[9] where he quotes the words 'Many psalms left out, and many parts of the others, as being highly improper for the mouths of a Christian congregation.'[10] George also comments 'Wesley did not use those methods of exegesis now current among those who defend the use of the whole Psalter, and this throws some light on his view of the inspiration of Scripture.'[11] Clearly this reference to use of part of the Old Testament shows that Wesley could be selective in his use of the Bible.

Thorsen also notes that in Wesley's *Explanatory Notes on the New Testament*, he 'spoke of the ongoing need for inspiration or illumination from the Holy Spirit who serves as a guide for those who approach the reading of Scripture in the context of prayer.'[12] He adds 'Some theologians

---

8   Heitzenrater, *Mirror and Memory*, 1989, p.92.
9   John Wesley, *The Sunday Service of the Methodists in North America, with Other Occasional Services*, published by the author in 1784.
10   A. Raymond George, 'The People Called Methodists: 4. The Means of Grace' in *A History of the Methodist Church in Great Britain* Vol. 1, ed. Rupert Davies and Gordon Rupp, Epworth Press, 1965, p. 269.
11   George, 'The People Called Methodist: 4. The Means of Grace,' pp. 269-70.
12   Thorsen, *The Wesleyan Quadrilateral*, p. 129.

might refer to this theological understanding as the double-inspiration theory, when divine inspiration occurs in both the author and reader of Scripture.'

It is not part of Thorsen's argument but these points clearly illustrate the fact that the interpretation of scripture is a process in which the reader may bring to it ideas which were not in the mind of the original writer. That Wesley came to scripture with certain doctrinal presumptions which he believed to be inspired by the Holy Sprit is now clear but will be further illustrated below. It is also clear that he found confirmation of that theology in the way in which he read the biblical texts. Wesley read the Bible in the light of eighteenth-century scholarship but brought to it his own theological assumptions.

The Primary Sources to be Examined

In this chapter attention is given to Wesley's *Explanatory Notes upon the New Testament*, his *Explanatory Notes upon the Old Testament*, and some of his published sermons. The *Deed of Union of the Methodist Church* signed and sealed on September 20 1932 contains the statement: 'These evangelical doctrines to which the preachers of the Methodist Church are pledged are contained in Wesley's Notes on the New Testament and the first four volumes of his sermons.'[13] These words are reprinted annually in *The Constitutional Practice and Discipline of the Methodist Church* (*CPD*) together with the comment:

> The Notes on the New Testament and the 44 Sermons are not intended to impose a system of formal or speculative theology on Methodist preachers, but to set up standards of preaching and belief which would secure loyalty to the fundamental truths of the gospel of redemption and ensure the continued witness of the Church to the realities of the Christian experience of salvation.

The sermons quoted in this chapter are not exclusively drawn from the forty-four to which reference is made in *CPD*. However it must be noted that these doctrinal standards still have authority and this is made clear in the comments in *An Anglican-Methodist Covenant*, paragraph 107, p. 35. This is the document containing the proposals for a covenant relationship that was to be established between the Church of England and the Methodist Church and which was formally approved by the Methodist Conference of 2003 and the General Synod of the Church of England in

---

13   See p. 213 of the 2002 Volume 2 of *The Constitutional Practice and Discipline of the Methodist Church*, Methodist Publishing House.

July 2003.[14] For these reasons these works are both of note for understanding Wesley's interpretation of scripture and modern British Methodism's doctrinal standards.

Particular note is made here of references to the Johannine Epistles in the *Explanatory Notes* and of those sermons for which Wesley took as text verses from I John. This selection of material for study is justified because of the high esteem in which Wesley held the Johannine literature. Gregory Clapper draws attention to this point by quoting from Wesley's Preface to *Sermons on Several Occasions*:

> "If any man speak," in the name of God, "let him speak as the oracles of God;" and if he would imitate any part of these above the rest, let it be the First Epistle of St. John. This is the style, the most excellent style, for every gospel preacher. And let him aim at no more ornament than he finds in that sentence, which is the sum of the whole gospel, "We love Him, because He first loved us."[15]

This quotation is found at the beginning of a chapter dealing with Wesley's sermons. It is of significance in that it illustrates how that, in introducing his sermons, Wesley saw fit to draw attention to 1 John as of importance both in relation to style and content.

Scott Jones notes that Wesley 'advocates speaking "as the oracles of God."'[16] He comments that:

> In his *Journal* for July 18, 1765, he [Wesley] makes the [...] point, referring to 1 John as "the deepest part of the Holy Scripture," "by which, above all other even inspired writings, I advise every young preacher to form his style. Here are sublimity and simplicity together, the strongest sense and the plainest language! How can any one that would 'speak as the oracles of God' use harder words than are found here?"[17]

Wesley had the highest regard for both the style and content of 1 John. Although Wesley regarded the whole Bible, Old and New Testaments, as the Word of God, this further justifies the study of the use Wesley made of the Johannine epistles as a way to test his understanding of the primacy of the Bible as an authority and to examine the influences that affected his understanding of the epistles.

---

14 *An Anglican-Methodist Covenant*, Methodist Publishing House and Church House Publishing, 2001. The extract from the *Deed of Union* quoted above is also to be found on p. 66 of this document.

15 Quoted in Gregory S. Clapper, *John Wesley on Religious Affections: his Views on Experience and their Role in the Christian Life and Theology*, Pietist and Wesleyan Studies No 1, The Scarecrow Press, Inc. 1989, p. 98.

16 Jones, *John Wesley's Conception and Use of Scripture*, p.111.

17 Jones, *John Wesley's Conception and Use of Scripture*, pp. 112-3, quoting Wesley's *Works*, 22:13.

Although the main focus in this chapter is Wesley's interpretation and use of the Johannine Epistles, there is a section on Wesley's comments on certain other Old and New Testament texts that appear to contradict Wesley's Arminianism and the way in which he interpreted such passages. Wesley may have claimed to be a man of one book but when that book appeared to contradict his strongly held views, he had to adopt the ploy of arguing that the text meant something other than what many argued to be the plain and simple meaning of the passages in question.

Wesley's *Explanatory Notes upon the New Testament*[18]

In 1754 Wesley had a period of enforced rest in Hot Wells, near Bristol, due to illness and he used part of that time to work on his book, *Explanatory Notes on the New Testament*, which he had planned for use by the Methodist preachers. It was written to enable the preachers to understand the Bible without excessive notes. It should be noted that in the Preface to Wesley's *Explanatory Notes*, he made the point that it was not designed for scholars but simply for 'plain un-lettered men, who understand only their mother-tongue and yet reverence the Word of God, and have a desire to save their souls.'[19] Wesley believed that the reader needed to have some explanatory notes in order to understand the meaning of scripture. He was hence not a man of one book in the extreme literalist sense of saying that the Bible spoke for itself without any comment.

Wesley was aware that the books that made up the Bible had their own history, while claiming still to interpret the scriptures as his supreme authority. Wesley acknowledged that the *Explanatory Notes* were not original. He made extensive use of Bengel's *Gnomen Novi Testamenti* together with some use of the works of Dr Heylen, *Theological Lectures,* Dr Guyse and Dr Doddridge, *The Family Expositor.*[20] However, Wesley did not give detailed acknowledgement in the text of which notes were based on these works. It is sufficient for the present purpose to note that Wesley was content to use, certainly selectively, the work of these writers and to make their comments his own. Hans Frei comments on Bengel:

> As a literal reader and a purely textual or "lower" critic he avoided questions of historical or "higher" criticism, particularly those of the genuineness of texts. He took the authenticity of a text for granted, once he had got beyond the verbal

---

18   John Wesley, *Explanatory Notes upon the New Testament*, 1754. Reference here is made to the 1976 edition published by Epworth Press.

19   Wesley, *Explanatory Notes,* p.6.

20   See Wesley, *Explanatory Notes*, pp. 7-8.

variations in its documentary tradition. In his own day even his lower criticism was controversial enough.[21]

By writing the *Explanatory Notes* Wesley recognised that the Bible needed to be interpreted in order to be properly understood. In giving the English text of the New Testament, Wesley used the King James Version but he made many textual alterations. He wrote 'Neither will I affirm that the Greek copies from which this translation was made are always the most correct, and therefore I shall take the liberty as occasion may require, to make here and there a small alteration.'[22] It is clear that Wesley had the highest regard for the New Testament as Holy Scripture but that he acknowledged the need for what, at a later day, would be called textual criticism to recover the original words of the authors. Therefore he acknowledged the need for scholarly work to establish the authoritative text. The sources of the notes were selectively culled from various theological and ecclesiastical traditions.

James T. MacCorrie made a study of Wesley's *Explanatory Notes upon the New Testament*, and the influence of the Bible on Wesley. He comments that:

> Wesley used other people's understanding of the scriptures. This opens the door to differences of interpretation and application - Doddridge and Guyse - and even from his fellow Arminian, Bengel. Nevertheless, he respected them and learnt from them.[23]

In common with most eighteenth-century Bible students, Wesley believed that the Fourth Gospel, the three Epistles and Revelation were all written by John the disciple of Jesus whereas modern scholarship would acknowledge the influence of the apostle but argue that the author was possibly another John, possible a disciple of the apostle. This was not argued, except for the comment, 'The great similitude, or rather sameness, both of spirit and expression, which runs through St. John's Gospel and all his epistles is clear evidence of their being written by the same person.'[24] Commentaries by modern scholars contain considerable discussion about the original recipients of 1 John. Many would regard the author to have written out of a church that had experienced a major secession of a body of its members and that the letter was intended to deal with that situation. Although Wesley recognised that the work was written for a body of believers in the first Christian century, he further commented: 'In this

---

21   Hans W. Frei, *The Eclipse of Biblical Narrative, A Study in Eighteenth and Nineteenth Century Hermeneutics*, Yale University Press, 1974, pp. 176-7.
22   Wesley, *Explanatory Notes*, p. 6.
23   James T. MacCorrie, *Thoughts from a Warmed Heart*, Colourpoint, 2002, p. 172.
24   Wesley, *Explanatory Notes*, p. 902.

epistle he speaks, not to any particular church, but to all the Christians of that age; and in them to the whole Christian Church in all succeeding ages.'[25]

Wesley's comments on the Epistles help the reader to understand Wesley's biblical interpretation and to appreciate what he believed the author to have been writing. For him, the Epistles do not relate exclusively, perhaps not even mainly, to the situation in which they were set. He interpreted them as though they were written for every age including his own and brought to them the theology in which he had come to believe. His comments on the context of the epistles presuppose the eighteenth-century understanding of the circumstances in which the letters were written. With reference to 2 John, Wesley recognised the local setting of the work in the first century but did so in terms of the eighteenth-century biblical scholarship. Modern scholars usually regard this as having been written to a church described under the title of an 'elect lady,' the church members being described as children of that lady. Wesley, however, wrote 'this epistle, written to some Christian matron and her religious children.'[26] and he translates the opening words of the letter as 'The elder unto the elect Kuria and her children.' On verse 4, he made comment that the children were probably known to the Elder in their aunt's house. Wesley assumed that 3 John was written to Caius (Gaius) and links him with the person of the same name from Corinth mentioned by Paul in Romans 16.23.[27] However, there is no evidence, apart from the coincidence of name, to make that link.

Attention is given now to Wesley's treatment of three short passages in 1 John. The first is 1 John 1:1-4, The Prologue. 1 John does not begin in the same way as 2 and 3 John which are set much more in the style of first-century letters. Wesley noted that although 1 John is a letter, it is more in the nature of a tract.[28] Raymond Brown in his magisterial work on the Johannine Epistles discusses the literary genre of 1 John and notes that it is appropriate to question whether 'tradition has done justice to 1 John in calling it an epistle or letter, a question that I have seen traced back as far as Heideggar in 1681 (and Bengel in the 1750s).'[29] It is thus possible that Wesley's comment here was influenced by his use of Bengel. This reliance on the work of Bengel is obvious, and indeed acknowledged, elsewhere in the *Explanatory Notes*.

Wesley regarded the opening verses as a statement by the apostle John and therefore the references to seeing, handling and hearing were to be

---

25 Wesley, *Explanatory Notes*, p. 902.
26 Wesley, *Explanatory Notes*, p. 921.
27 Wesley, *Explanatory Notes*, p. 924.
28 See Wesley, *Explanatory Notes*, p. 902.
29 Raymond E. Brown, *The Epistles of John*, The Anchor Bible, Doubleday, p. 87.

understood as the testimony of an eyewitness to the life of Jesus. 'That which was from the beginning' (1 John 1:1) was taken to be the Word of God and the parallel with the opening verses of the Gospel was taken to mean that 1 John was referring to the incarnate Logos. Using the scholarly tools available to him, Wesley was arguing here for an interpretation of scripture which included an orthodox Christology as opposed to those who, in his day, were lapsing into deism and Unitarianism.

Modern scholars, without accepting that the words were written by an eyewitness, would discuss incipient docetism or early traces of gnosticism and argue that the author was arguing for the humanity of Jesus and the reality of a full incarnation. Most would see a clear distinction between the idea of the Logos in the Gospel and the message in 1 John. However, Wesley wrote in the light of the scholarship available to him. He used the text to affirm the traditional and orthodox Christology of a High-Church Anglican of his day.

Second, note is taken of 1 John 2:7-11, The New Commandment and the Old Commandment. The author of 1 John was at pains to make clear that the commandment to love one another was fundamental for Christian living. It was, in one sense, an old commandment, but it was also a new commandment. Wesley regarded the commandment as rooted in the distant past in the Old Testament. Nevertheless it was new in Christ. He wrote 'A commandment *which*, though it was given long ago, yet *is* truly new *in him and in you.*'[30] On the same page Wesley also wrote, 'there is no comparison between the state of the Old Testament believers and that which ye now enjoy: the *darkness* of that dispensation *is passed away; and* Christ *the true light now shineth* in your hearts.'

Modern scholarship would usually regard the contrast between the old and new commandments as being the contrast between what the believers had received from the beginning (from apostolic times) and what was related to the time in which the letter was set. This then related to the secession that had recently taken place. Consequently Kenneth Grayston writes 'The insistence that it was old rather than new suggests opposition to novelties introduced by the dissidents, for which impression support may be found in the tense of the verb translated **had**.'[31]

For Wesley, this commandment was reflected in his teaching on perfect love. He apparently did not notice the author's inconsistency in emphasising the commandment to love one another directed to the internal relationships within the continuing believing community, and the vehement, unloving, attitude he expressed towards those who had separated from it. Wesley also could engage in fierce controversy with his opponents and yet

---

30   Wesley, *Explanatory Notes,* p. 906.
31   Kenneth Grayston *The New Century Commentary The Johannine Epistles,* Wm B. Eerdmans Publ. Co., 1984, p. 67.

maintain his teaching of perfect love. It is clear that he came to this text with his doctrine of Christian Perfection in mind and used it to support his Arminian stance in which he emphasised the need to grow in personal holiness after the experience of the new birth. He used the passage to support his arguments about Christian perfection although, as was noted in earlier chapters, he came to it through his studies of à Kempis, Taylor and Law in the first instance.

The third comment on Wesley's use of 1 John is made on his note on 5:6-8 in which there is reference to water, blood and the Trinity. He took the reference to the water and the blood to be a reference to the baptism of Christ and to his death on the cross. He also noted the incident, at the death of Jesus, when water and blood came out of his side.[32] In every generation these words have caused considerable debate. More recently there has been a tendency to see a reference to the dissidents who may have denied the efficacy of the suffering and death of Jesus but Wesley's words as they stand are not dissimilar to much modern scholarly comment.

It should be noted that Wesley, in common with most of his contemporaries, accepted the reading in verse 8 as original 'And there are three that testify in heaven, The Father, the Word, and the Holy Ghost.' He saw in this the Christian doctrine of the Trinity. It is of note that Wesley was aware that some scholars had raised the question of whether the text was written by the original author of 1 John but he accepted it as such. A more modern comment is that of the New International Version of the Bible which has a footnote to verses 7 and 8 'Late manuscripts of the Vulgate *testify in heaven: the Father, the Word and the Holy Spirit, and these three are one. And there are three that testify on earth: the* (not found in any Greek manuscript before the sixteenth century).' His awareness of the textual issues surrounding this verse is clear in his sermon on the verse which is considered below. He also read the passage in the light of the developed doctrine of the Trinity as taught within the Church in his own day. Wesley wrote in accordance with the biblical knowledge and theological beliefs of the eighteenth century, but any reference to a developed doctrine of the Trinity is highly unlikely in a letter of the date of 1 John.

It will be necessary to return to this point when consideration is given to Wesley's sermon on The Trinity which was based on this text. Although he concluded that the text and the doctrine of the Trinity are in the original text of 1 John, it is of note that Wesley was prepared to discuss this critical point. His sermon on the Trinity is discussed below and this further illustrates the way that he used a text such as this. Wesley's interpretation of the text was that of an Anglican Trinitarian of his day. In his interpretation of the text he opposed deist and Unitarian views.

---

32 See Wesley, *Explanatory Notes*, p. 917.

It will be sufficient to examine just one passage from 3 John. 3 John 9-10 is about Diotrephes. Wesley believed that the epistle was written by the apostle John and, consequently, if there was criticism by the author of another church leader, he believed that the other person must have been at fault. However, the letter does not make any criticism of the belief or teaching of Diotrephes and so Wesley inferred that Diotrephes was the pastor of a church and that he 'wanted to govern all things according to his own will.'[33] Therefore iniquity was at work. It is possible that there was already a power struggle in the local church which would lead later to an emerging monarchial episcopate. Another New Testament scholar, William Loader, comments 'A more satisfactory explanation is that the refusal of hospitality relates not to doctrine at all, but to an emerging assertion of local leadership authority against leadership from outside.'[34] Wesley was aware that there were those within the Methodist body who were ready to assert their supposed authority and he may have had a blind spot with regard to his own, which he regarded as entirely for the benefit of the whole. Wesley's comments were appropriate in the light of contemporary scholarly understanding of 3 John, although they were influenced by the circumstances in which he found himself. This again is an example of the Bible being interpreted in terms of the eighteenth rather than the first century.

Before turning to certain of Wesley's sermons on texts drawn from the Johannine letters, it is helpful to take note of the way in which Wesley commented on certain texts from other parts of the Bible that do not support an obvious Arminian interpretation. Throughout this book it has been noted that Wesley quoted his sources selectively. This is true even of his use of the Bible. In the last chapter attention was given to his interpretation of verses in Romans chapters 8 and 9 that would appear to support the doctrine of predestination. This was also true of, for example, Ephesians 1:5 which reads 'Having predestinated us by Jesus Christ to the adoption of sons unto himself, according to the good pleasure of his will.'[35] Wesley accepted the Pauline authorship of this letter without question. He went on to avoid the much more obvious Calvinist interpretation of the words by what is almost linguistic contortion, writing 'Having foreordained that all who afterwards believed should enjoy the dignity of being sons of God, and joint-heirs with Christ.'[36] Verse 11 contains the words 'being predestined according to the purpose of him that worketh all things after the counsel of

---

33   Wesley, *Explanatory Notes*, p. 925.
34   William Loader, *The Johannine Epistles,* Epworth Commentaries, Epworth Press, 1992, p. 106.
35   The biblical quotations in this section are Wesley's translation in *Explanatory Notes*.
36   Wesley, *Explanatory Notes*, p. 703.

his own will.' Wesley commented that the 'unalterable decree' is 'He that believeth shall be delivered.' Thus he quietly and without comment read this passage in an Arminian way and subtly presented an interpretation that avoided the Calvinist view of predestination. Wesley's Arminian theology prevailed over what is surely a more obvious reading of the biblical text.

This way of dealing with, for Wesley, difficult texts is found in his comments on the word 'elect' in 1 Peter 1:2. He is forced into making a comment on the meaning of 'true predestination.'[37] This he describes as the 'fore-appointment of God' but he then described this in terms of God's 'free gift' with the corollary that it all depended on the person believing in the Gospel. Again this is an example of the manner in which a text apparently meaning one thing is interpreted in a way that conforms to his Arminian Anglicanism.

In conclusion then it is clear from Wesley's *Explanatory Notes Upon the New Testament* that he wrote as a scholar of his own day, in terms of scholarly understanding of the New Testament. His interpretation and use of the Johannine Epistles did not arise entirely and solely from his study of those books. He brought to that study a package of theological beliefs that he would justify from the text. The brief examination of Wesley's notes on some verses that do not support his position demonstrates that he accepted the authority of the Bible but that it had to be interpreted in a way that was acceptable to his views. These he would argue were in harmony with the whole teaching of the Bible.

What is true of Wesley's comments on the New Testament is also found again in his *Explanatory Notes on the Old Testament* (1765).[38] He could not accept a Calvinist interpretation of the text, even where it is the more obvious and simple way of reading it. In the Preface to the *Explanatory Notes* he stated that he used and abridged the works of Matthew Henry and Matthew Poole as the basis for the work. However, he made it clear that he was being deliberately selective 'What he [Henry] wrote in favour of *Particular Redemption*, is totally left out.'[39] This in itself is a glaring example of the way in which he dealt with views that he did not accept because they did not match his theological beliefs.

It is not necessary to go in detail through the three volumes, but note may be taken of one example: his comments on Isaiah 44:28. As would be usual in his time, in the introductory note to the whole book, Wesley assumed that it was the work of one person, Isaiah, son of Amoz, writing in the eight-century before Christ. Nevertheless, Wesley believed that the

---

37 See Wesley, *Explanatory Notes*, p. 872.
38 John Wesley, *Explanatory Notes upon the Old Testament*. Published first in instalments, then in 3 volumes. These were reprinted with an introduction by Schmul Publishers in 1975.
39 Wesley, *Explanatory Notes on the Old Testament*, Vol. 1, p. v.

prophet foretold accurately and in detail the person and work of Jesus Christ who was to come in the distant future.

Modern scholarship would find difficulty on this view of authorship with Isaiah 44:28 where there is reference to Cyrus, a major figure in the events of a future generation. For Wesley, as a man of his own generation, there was no difficulty in believing that God could put words into a book through Isaiah concerning people or events yet to come. However, it might be thought that this raised questions concerning predestination. If God foreknew, did he not also cause the events to happen? On this Wesley commented 'Whom God mentions by his proper name, two hundred years before he was born, that this might be an undeniable evidence of the exactness of God's foreknowledge.'[40] Wesley frequently referred to God's foreknowledge but neither saw nor believed that this meant fore-ordination or predestination. This illustrates the way he accepted the eighteenth century approach to biblical scholarship and, at the same time, wriggled verbally to deny any possibility that God predestined things to happen. It makes a sharp distinction between foreknowledge and fore-ordination. It also shows that he believed there to be a real difference between vocation and salvation in the sense that God would call people into His service but did not thereby predetermine whether ultimately they would be individually saved or damned.

This exploration in some depth of Wesley's comments on one text in Isaiah shows clearly that he accepted the Old Testament scholarship of his day but came to the Old Testament as an Arminian and refused to read in its pages any Calvinist interpretation of the words. A similar exercise could be undertaken on other passages, but the one given is perhaps sufficient to illustrate the point.

Wesley's Use of 1 John in His Sermons

Although Wesley acknowledged the importance of the Johannine Epistles and quoted them frequently, there are only five sermons in the Bicentennial Edition of his Works based on texts from 1 John. These are the sermons numbered 19, 55, 62, 77 and 78.[41] This is not to overlook Wesley's extensive use of material from the Johannine epistles in other sermons. See, for example, the sermon on 'Salvation by Faith',[42] preached in June 1738, especially Section II and the extensive quotations therein. See also the sermon on 'The Marks of the New Birth',[43] dating from 1748, with

---

40   Wesley, *Explanatory Notes upon the Old Testament*, Vol. 3, p. 2064.
41   References to where these may be found in *BE* are given below when these sermons are considered in more detail.
42   *BE* Vol. 1, pp. 117-130.
43   *BE* Vol. 1, pp. 417-430.

numerous quotations from 1 John in Section III. In *BE* Vol. 2, Sermon 40 'Christian Perfection', which dates from 1741, Section II, paragraph 5 and elsewhere quotes extensively from 1 John. Many other sermons could also be noted to illustrate this point.

The small number of sermons directly based on the Johannine Epistles may be a proper proportion in view of the low number of chapters in the letters in comparison with the size of the whole Bible, but is a little surprising in view of his comments on the priority he attached to the work of John as their author. A critical note of them is made to illustrate the way in which Wesley used scripture.

The first is Sermon 19: 'The Great Privilege of Those That are Born of God' -1 John 3:9 - Whosoever is born of God doth not commit sin.' This sermon and Sermon 18,[44] 'The Marks of the New Birth' were published in 1748 to give an exposition of the doctrine of the new birth and the ongoing Christian life, leading to Wesley's teaching on Christian Perfection.[45] On a superficial reading, the sermon would appear to be straightforward biblical exposition. However, more detailed study reveals that it is not simply scriptural interpretation.

A modern English-speaking commentator would be likely to make comment on the context in which 1 John was written. Raymond Brown, for example, makes comment on 1 John 3:9 and relates it to the writer's arguments concerning those who had seceded from the Johannine Church. Brown thus makes the point:

> I have insisted throughout that the author is attacking a static understanding of divine begetting that is held by the secessionists, for whom divine childhood is a once-for-all gift and not a life that has to express itself in the behaviour of the Christian. [46]

Wesley, however, extracted the verse from its context and used it as a simple statement of Christian truth concerning regeneration. The way he used the Bible reflected Wesley's theological position in its eighteenth-century context and dealt with his doctrine of Christian Perfection.

Wesley began by discussing the relationship between the doctrines of justification by faith and the new birth. Justification is a term frequently used in Pauline vocabulary, especially in Galatians and Romans. The doctrine has prominence in Luther and the Reformed tradition. The new birth is a particularly Johannine phrase. Wesley commented 'But though it

---

44 Sermon 19 is to be found in *BE* Vol. 1, pp. 431-443 and Sermon 18 is to be found in *BE* Vol. 1, pp. 417-430.

45 See Albert Outler's comments in *BE* Vol. 1, pp. 417-8. Sermon 19 is found in pp. 421-43.

46 Brown, *The Epistles of John*, p. 431.

be allowed that justification and the new birth are in point of time inseparable from each other, yet are they easily distinguished as being not the same, but things of a widely different nature.'[47] Wesley saw justification as the description of a change in relationship between a person and God, whereas new birth related to an inward change in the human soul.

Wesley further referred to the Johannine teaching on the new birth in Sermon 18, 'The Marks of the New Birth,' and in Sermon 45, 'The New Birth.'[48] The text used in Sermon 18 was John 3:8, 'Born of the Spirit.' Sermon 45 was on John 3:7, 'Ye must be born again.' Wesley clearly considered the new birth to be a distinctive Christian experience described in the Johannine literature. Nevertheless he was coming to the texts in the Gospel and the Epistles to find evidence to argue his case in the dispute with the Calvinists of his own age.

Consequently, in the first main section of Sermon 19, Wesley dealt with the doctrine of the new birth, treating the subject as an Arminian, but not accepting that there was any link between the new birth and baptism in the context of 1 John 3:9. This is made clear in Paragraph I.1 in the sermon. Wesley was not entirely consistent in that he did believe that baptism of babies was a new birth and did have a real influence on the child. He thought that the effect of his own baptism did not wear off until he was about 10 years old.

His interpretation was in terms of the individual experiencing birth into a spiritual relationship with God. There is no reference here to birth into community or family. We may contrast with Wesley's exposition the modern commentary of J.L. Houlden on the *Johannine Epistles*. Houlden sets his comments on 1 John 3:9 in the context of 1 John 2:28-3:24 which he entitles 'The Two Families', and writes 'In *v.* 9 we have a variant on the formulation in *v.* 6, but this time in terms of parenthood.'[49] Thus Houlden understands the writer of 1 John to be concerned about communities as families. He writes 'The two families, God's and the devil's, are to be distinguished by a clear test - that of conduct.'[50]

The distinction between the new birth as an individual experience, which by definition it must be, and the family into which one is born is a fine one. However, Wesley brought to the text an understanding which related specifically to individual rather than the family or community experience. Thus he gave an extended analogy of the human physical birth, describing the way that a baby entered the world that had surrounded him in his mother's womb, but making the point that the newly born became aware

---

47   Sermon 19, Para. 2 of the Introduction.
48   Sermon 45 is to be found in *BE*, Vol. 2, pp. 187-201.
49   J.L. Houlden, *The Johannine Epistles*, A. & C. Black, 1973, revised ed. 1994, p. 96.
50   Houlden, *The Johannine Epistles*, p. 97.

of, or sensitive to, the surrounding world after birth had taken place. The comparison was then worked out; the person born of the Spirit by that act became aware of the spiritual world. In paragraph I.8. Wesley wrote 'But when he is born of God, born of the Spirit, how is the manner of his existence changed! His whole soul is now sensible of God.' This interpretation of 1 John was set in terms of personal experience and eighteenth-century Arminian theology. That is not to make a value judgement on Wesley, but to make the point that he brought to the biblical text certain preconceived perfectionist ideas as well as giving an exposition, from his own perspective, of what the biblical author had written.

In developing the theme that the person born of God does not sin, Wesley had to face the problem that clearly there was evidence of goodly and godly people who did. In trying to resolve this Wesley did not refer to the apparent contradictions within 1 John itself. For example, he could have quoted 1 John 1:8 'If we say that we have no sin, we deceive ourselves.' Wesley did not do so but proceeded first to define sin in the more limited terms of 'an actual, voluntary 'transgression of the law'; of the revealed written law of God, of any commandment of God acknowledged to be such at the time that it is transgressed.'[51] This is, of course a limited view of the extent of sin and has been criticised as being too narrow a definition. Wesley then considered the difficulty of the text with reference to the experience of people acknowledged to be born of God and their sinful actions. He noted the story of David and Bathsheba in the Old Testament, and New Testament passages concerning Barnabus and Peter. Wesley argued that the person born of God could keep himself free from sin, but could possibly lapse. He summarised the section with the words 'Thus it is unquestionably true that he who is born of God, keeping himself, does not, cannot commit sin; and yet if he keepeth not himself he may commit all manner of sin with greediness.'

Wesley did not accept that there was contradiction within the Bible. He clearly could not bring himself to contradict scripture, but, where texts existed that he could not accept at their face value, he carefully proceeded to interpret them in a way that satisfied him, and which accorded with the word of the Bible and the experience of the person who could be described as 'born of God.' This again reflects his anti-Calvinistic views about the possible lapses of the believer. Wesley concluded the sermon making three points. The first dealt with the way in which loss of faith and inward or outward sin may be connected. The second dealt with the life of God in the soul of a believer. The third was concerned with the need of the soul to respond continually to the divine life in order to maintain the life without sin.

---

51   See Para. II.2 of Sermon 19.

It has thus been shown that this sermon was not just a simple exposition of the text. Wesley believed that he had given a clear interpretation of the words of the writer whom he believed to be the apostle John. Nevertheless, Wesley wrote as a person of his own time. He brought to the text the faith and beliefs that were part of his own Arminian Anglican experience and then claimed to get them from the Bible.

A similar process is seen in Sermon 55: 'On the Trinity - 1 John 5:7 - There are three that bear record in heaven, the Father, the Word, and the Holy Ghost: and these three are one.' This sermon was preached in 1775 in Ireland. Wesley's 'Advertisement' states that he preached on the text and was then requested to write down what he had preached.[52] He asked for the reader to make allowance for the fact that he was not able to consult other books when so writing.[53] This may well be an explanation of instances where certain quotations are not accurately given, but also indicates that his exegesis of the text was fashioned by the beliefs he held.

Most of Wesley's sermons were concerned with experimental or practical theology. In this sermon, Wesley did not give a speculative or philosophical argument nor did he give a full exposition of the text. He gave some reasons for accepting, in faith, the doctrine of the Trinity while admitting that a rational argument leading to a full understanding of the ideas contained within it were perhaps beyond human comprehension. Outler pointed out that Wesley's 'trinitarian doctrine outlined in the sermon faithfully follows in the traditional Anglican line hewed out by Bishop John Pearson' and that this Wesley would have seen at Oxford.[54]

Wesley was aware of and admitted that there were questions as to whether the text was original to 1 John. Although many people had questioned it, Wesley advanced the reasons why he thought it to be part of the original author's text. Most modern scholarship would doubt this conclusion. The words in question are sometimes known as the 'Johannine Comma.' Raymond Brown has an extended appendix in his commentary with that heading. In it he writes:

> Today scholars are virtually unanimous that the Comma arose well after the first century as a trinitarian reflection upon the original text of I John and was added to the biblical MSS hundreds of years after I John was written.'[55] He also quotes Greeven: 'The Johannine Comma must be evaluated as a dogmatic expansion of

---

52   See the note by Outler in *BE* Vol. 2, p. 373. Sermon 55 is found on pp. 374-86.
53   *BE* Vol. 2, p. 374.
54   See *BE* Vol. 2, p. 373.
55   Brown, *The Epistles of John*, p. 776.

the scriptural text stemming from the third century at the earliest in North Africa or Spain.[56]

Wesley's arguments were based on the work of J.A. Bengel, who had, at one time, strongly doubted the genuineness of the text. Rather than follow the works of English critics, Wesley considered the arguments put forward by Bengel who had also been a considerable influence on him when he wrote his *Explanatory Notes Upon the New Testament*. Whereas modern scholars would see the words as having been added as a comment on 1 John, in paragraph 5 of the sermon, Wesley advanced the opinion that they could be understood best as having been in the text and later omitted, perhaps due to the influence of Arianism. Possibly of more importance than the conclusion to which Wesley came, is the fact that he entered into such a debate. He did not take the view that the received text was so sacred as not to be questioned. It could be considered, and defended, by the exercise of reason. Wesley himself was firmly convinced that the words were genuine and came from the hand of the apostle John and he was prepared to use such scholarly resources as were available to him to establish his point.

In the sermon, Wesley made specific reference to Dean Swift's tract on the Trinity and to the Athanasian Creed, but refused to insist that people should use the words 'Trinity' or 'Person,' although he himself was happy to do so.[57] Thus Wesley, in opposition to the deists, believed in the doctrine of the Trinity, but his main argument was that it was to be accepted, even as a mystery, rather than understood fully in a philosophical manner. He gave many examples of things that were generally accepted as true, but could not be proved, both in the natural world and in scientific research. These he used to illustrate the idea that the doctrine of the Trinity might be believed without necessarily being fully understood.

Wesley also drew a contrast between believing what he termed the *facts* and the *manner* in which the facts were to be interpreted. Wesley did not insist on belief in one particular interpretation of the doctrine of the Trinity, but insisted that the facts bound up in the words of a text such as 1 John 5:7 were to be accepted. It is therefore clear that his understanding of the doctrine of the Trinity is one that came to him not through biblical texts but through tradition and the Anglican Church's teaching. Referring to the tract of Dean Swift and the Athanasian Creed, he assumed that these gave a proper interpretation of 1 John 5:7. He did not start with the text and then show how its ideas were developed by later writers. He accepted both the text and the doctrine of the Trinity in the form in which he had received it.

---

56   Brown, *The Epistles of John*, p. 786, quoting Greeven, 'Comma Johanneum', *RGG 1*, 1854.
57   See Sermon 55, Paras. 3 and 4.

The source of his understanding of 1 John, in this instance, was rooted firmly in tradition and the teaching of the Church of England.

Having made that connection between text and doctrine, and having resisted any attempt to make a particular form of the creed obligatory on all believers, Wesley went on to argue that 1 John 5:7 and the facts contained within the doctrine of the Trinity were bound up in human experience and were to be accepted on those grounds. 'But the thing which I here particularly mean is this: the knowledge of the Three-One God is interwoven with all true Christian faith, with vital religion.'[58] In this Wesley illustrated the way in which, for him, Christian experience was to be regarded as authoritative alongside scripture, although it could not replace the authority of the Bible.

In this sermon Wesley's main concern was to deal with the doctrine of the Trinity. The text was convenient in the sense that it came the nearest to supporting the doctrine as Wesley understood it. In this sermon Wesley was, without making it too explicit, relying on the authority of tradition, the Church of England and experience. In his opinion they did not contradict the biblical passage, but it is possible to see that they were assumed and taken to the text rather than directly arising from it. For that reason it is obvious that Wesley's beliefs were those of an eighteenth-century High-Church Arminian Anglican. It may be doubted, however, whether it is possible to base so fundamental a doctrine on one disputed text in the New Testament but Wesley was bringing all his accumulated baggage of Anglican and, in this instance, Catholic, tradition to the interpretation of the meaning of the biblical text.

The third sermon of which note is taken is number 62: 'The End of Christ's Coming - 1 John 3:8 - For this purpose was the Son of God manifested, that he might destroy the works of the devil.'[59] It dates from 1781. Outler pointed out that Wesley preached on this text at least 27 times between 1742 and 1789 and that he had a preoccupation with the problem of moral evil.[60]

This sermon purports to be an exposition of the biblical text, but in reality it is Wesley's attempt to deal with the problem of evil. If God is believed to be the creator, to be all powerful and to be all loving, how then is it possible to account for evil, especially moral evil? There are two main questions. The first is to account for the presence of evil in the creation of a good, loving God. The second is to understand the way that God deals with the consequences of the presence of evil. These questions were addressed by Wesley in the body of the sermon.

---

58   Sermon 55, Section 17.
59   The sermon is to be found in *BE* Vol. 2, pp. 471-484.
60   *BE* Vol. 2, p. 471.

As was frequently the case in his use of texts from 1 John, Wesley did not go into any detail about the context of the verse or the issues being addressed by the author of the epistle. A modern scholar such as Kenneth Grayston sees 1 John 3:8 as being set in the context of a debate with the author's opponents. 'The writer introduces **the devil** partly to strengthen his polemic. [...] This was a familiar denunciation of religious opponents who seemed to threaten the safety of the community.'[61] Wesley's concerns were different from those of modern scholars. Wesley used the biblical text in order to lead into what he argued were answers to the questions arising from the problem of evil. Although the sermon was based on a Johannine text, the content was that of an eighteenth-century preacher and theologian facing the issues of his own day. It could be said that the text was a pretext in order to deal with the subject, although Wesley himself would not have accepted that comment.

The opening paragraphs of the sermon were not directly related to the text. They were a discussion of the way writers of his own and earlier ages, Christian and non-Christian, dealt with the themes of virtue and vice. The point made was that, however much virtue may have been applauded or vice condemned, the writers were not able to point to the way to achieve one or avoid the other. Then, in the first main section of the sermon, Wesley addressed the question 'What are 'the works of the devil' here mentioned?' In it he refers to the creation of the human race in that man was made in the '*natural*' and '*moral*' image of God. Wesley argued, as an Arminian, that man was endued with a *will* and was a *free agent*. He then argued that, for this reason, a power to choose good or evil was given. The key sentences read as follows.

Indeed it has been doubted whether man could then choose evil, knowing it to be such. But it cannot be doubted he might mistake evil for good. He was not infallible, therefore not impeccable. And this unravels the whole difficulty of the grand question, *unde malum*? 'How came evil into the world?' It came from 'Lucifer, son of the morning:' it was 'the work of the devil.'[62]

Wesley then proceeded to narrate the Genesis story of Adam and Eve with the serpent having the role of the devil. This, like most of his contemporaries, Wesley took to be an historical account of the origin of sin in the world. Sin could therefore be seen to be the work of the devil and not the responsibility of the good and loving powerful creator God. It is of note that in the International Critical Commentary, A. E. Brooke followed a similar line, although not quite with the literalism of Wesley. However, Brooke noted 'There is nothing in the passage to suggest that the writer

---

61   Grayston, *The Johannine Epistles*, p. 106.
62   Sermon 62, Para I.8.

held a "dualistic" view of the origin of evil, considering the Devil "an originally evil being"; but it is manifest that he believed in a personal Tempter.'[63] Probably the author of 1 John did not hold a dualistic view of the origin of evil and neither did Wesley. Wesley, however, thought the source of evil to be the devil, but he did not explain adequately how it was possible for what was morally bad to arise in the creation of a good and loving God. If the devil, as a real being, introduced evil into experience at a point early in human history, it has not been made clear how this is possible if dualistic views of the origin of evil are rejected.

It is perhaps of note that in paragraph I.8 of the sermon, Wesley used a quotation from Milton's *Paradise Lost*, and it may be that his exposition of 1 John 3:8 and 'the works of the devil' was considerably influenced by Milton's work. If so, Wesley brought to the text ideas from non-biblical sources.

Because Wesley was concerned to consider the way in which God dealt with evil, especially moral evil, he proceeded to discuss the Johannine phrase 'the Son of God was manifested.' Modern scholars may think that the author was countering the arguments of those who had docetic or Gnostic tendencies and was emphasising the incarnation. Jesus in his coming was the manifestation of the Son of Man (and the Christ). In the first three paragraphs of this section of the sermon, Wesley outlined the ways in which the Son of God was manifested in Old Testament times to Adam and Eve, to Enoch and to others. He wrote as a man of the eighteenth century, although he did express some reservations about the way in which Isaac Watts treated the subject. Nevertheless, Wesley made it clear that the principal way in which the Son of God was manifested was in the historical setting of the coming of Jesus and the incarnation, making reference to the New Testament Gospel story. The section concluded with two references to the Fourth Gospel and one to the letter to the Galatians. Wesley argued that the manifestation of the Son of God is completed in the heart of the believer by which the works of the devil are destroyed. In this way Wesley was preparing for the answer to the second question raised by the problem of evil: How does God deal with moral evil, given that it is to be found in creation and within human lives? In the third section of the sermon Wesley attempted to answer this question, asserting:

> We then see, not by a chain of *reasoning*, but by a kind of *intuition*, by a direct view, that 'God was in Christ, reconciling the world to himself, not imputing to them their former trespasses,' not imputing them to *me*.[64]

---

63   A.E. Brooke, *The Johannine Epistles*, T. & T. Clark, 1912, p. 88.
64   Sermon 62, Para. III.1, quoting 2 Cor. 5:19.

This statement was supported by a number of quotations, of which only one was from 1 John, and in no cases were the sources of the quotations given. This illustrates Wesley's presupposition that the whole Bible is equally inspired and that every section can be understood by reference to another and is a good example of the way that Wesley quoted, without acknowledgement, from all parts of the Bible to interpret particular passages and verses. Moreover, Wesley was pressing beyond the words of the text that he had chosen for the sermon. It is also an example of the way that Wesley quoted the Bible to support views that he already held. He was trying to answer how God dealt with evil and not just expounding the words of the author of 1 John at this point. In fact the author in 1 John 3:8 does not offer an explanation or a solution to the problem.

Wesley then discussed the way in which 'the Son of God strikes at the root of that grand work of the devil, pride.'[65] The sermon again contains quotations from the Bible, many from Pauline writings. However, he also noted that 'the Son of God does not destroy the whole work of the devil in man, as long as he remains in this life.'[66] He referred to bodily weakness and sickness together with other human imperfections that remain until death. The concluding paragraphs of the sermon were then addressed to the hearers to reinforce an evangelical appeal to respond to what Wesley terms the 'real religion of Jesus Christ.'[67]

It is clear from this sermon that Wesley claimed to be giving an exposition of a text in 1 John, but he was in reality addressing, in eighteenth-century terms, the problem of evil. In the way in which he used other, often Pauline, texts to help interpret 1 John 3:8, his writing was consistent with his own view that the Bible was equally inspired and thus the work of one writer could be used to illustrate the finer points of meaning of another. Wesley may have thought that he approached 1 John 3:8 to find the meaning of scripture but in reality he carried to that text ideas that were already formulated in his mind as a man of his day, influenced by an High-Church Arminian theology.

Fourth, note is taken of Sermon 77: 'Spiritual Worship - 1 John 5:20 - This is the true God, and eternal life.'[68] This sermon dates from 1780. Outler noted that this sermon and Sermon 78 were based on 1 John 5:20-21 and that 'Together, they add up to a single essay in a Christocentric doctrine of spirituality.'[69] The sermon is of note because the introduction deals with Wesley's understanding of the authorship and purpose of 1 John. Wesley regarded 1 John as the work of the apostle John but written in old age as a

---

65   Sermon 62, Para. III. 2.
66   Sermon 62, Para. III. 3.
67   Sermon 62, Para. III. 6.
68   The sermon is found in *BE* Vol. 3, pp. 88-102.
69   *BE* Vol. 3, p. 88.

tract rather than as a letter because he was no longer able to preach to the people. In this, Wesley accepted the generally held views of eighteenth-century biblical scholarship.

Wesley commented that the text did not directly concern faith (Paul had dealt with that) or inward and outward holiness (of which Paul, James, and Peter had written) but rather 'of the foundation of all, the happy and holy communion which the faithful have with God, the Father, Son and Holy Ghost.'[70] Thus, to this extent, Wesley did acknowledge that the different biblical writers had their own immediate purpose in writing. By implication, Wesley clearly regarded 1 John as dealing with a fundamental, if not the fundamental, teaching on the relationship between the Christian and God.

However, in accordance with his view of biblical inspiration and authority, Wesley made the further point in his opening paragraph that in writing to and through the Christians of his own age, John was writing to those of all succeeding ages. The remainder of the introduction to the sermon gave a résumé of the epistle and a summary of chapter 5, verses 1-12, leading up to the text, 1 John 5:20. In typical Wesley style, there were biblical quotations woven into his text. Wesley assumed without argument that 1 John 5:20 referred to Jesus Christ as the second person of the Trinity. This, however, does imply that the author of 1 John had a highly developed Christology, which would have created no problems for Wesley. This was the usual interpretation of the verse among earlier scholars and writers. It is also a view still held by many.[71] In paragraph I.1, Wesley gave his understanding of the meaning of this Christology using the language of Romans, the Fourth Gospel, and Philippians. He also referred to phrases from the Nicene and Athanasian creeds. Although purporting to be justifying the use of the creeds in the light of the text, Wesley's familiarity with the two creeds, as understood within Anglican theology and liturgy, influenced his interpretation of the verse from 1 John. In paragraph 3, Wesley went on to assert that Christ was thus the 'Creator of all things.' Again this was supported by reference to Paul and the Fourth Gospel.

In the following five paragraphs, Wesley referred to Jesus Christ as God in that he was the '*Supporter* of all things that he hath made.' He is 'the *Preserver* of all things.' He is 'the true '*Author* of all' the *motion* that is in the universe.' In this section Wesley showed himself aware of the work of Isaac Newton, although critical of it. Writing from a literalist standpoint with regard to the biblical books, Wesley brought to the New Testament his understanding of contemporary physics as well as dissenting in part from it.

Wesley then argued that Christ was 'the *Redeemer* of all the children of men.' He was 'the *Governor* of all things.' This included all people. He was

---

70   See Sermon 77, Para. 2 of the Introduction.
71   See Brooke, *The Johannine Epistles*, pp. 152-3, for a brief discussion on this point.

'the *End* of all things.' It is clear that, in this section of the sermon, Wesley went beyond what was in the mind of the author of 1 John and interpreted the text in terms of the theology of his own day, his own church, and the major creeds. He also wrote against the background of contemporary scientific knowledge.

Turning to that part of the text that stated that he [Christ] was eternal life, Wesley made three points arising directly from the words used and the tenses of the verbs employed by the author of 1 John. He pointed out that the tenses were present, not future.[72] Wesley believed in a future life but he saw this reference as being to a present experience. He also stated that the reference was to life, not resurrection, although Christ was that also.[73] Wesley then gave account of what he understood the author to mean. He stated that Christ was the life of vegetable, animal and rational life.[74] This, however, was not the real meaning of the text. He went on to discuss the spiritual life which is described in terms of the relationship of the believer with Christ. The use of scriptural material, in Wesley's usual style, includes references to 1 Corinthians, Galatians, Romans and 1 Thessalonians.[75] Once again Paul's writings are used to interpret 1 John.

In the sixth Para. II.6, Wesley continued in this style. Without directly referring to the doctrine of Christian Perfection, there is perhaps an allusion to it in the quotation from Colossians 2:10:

And when we are ἐν αὐτῷ πεπληρωμένοι, 'complete in him', as our translators render it - but more properly when we are 'filled with him'; when 'Christ in us, the hope of glory' is our God and our all ... then we are completely happy.[76]

Here again, it may be noted, Wesley was prepared to correct the King James Version. The whole paragraph contains allusions to other verses of Pauline letters. It also includes the phrase 'The Lord of every motion there,' which is a direct quotation from Wesley's hymn 'Divine Love.'[77] This section of the sermon also shows the way in which Wesley brought to the Johannine text ideas gained from other parts of the New Testament as well as Wesley's own work based on a German hymn writer.

In the final main section of the sermon, Wesley outlined the inferences that he drew from his exposition of the text. In it Wesley dealt with the subject of happiness, giving also his personal testimony on the subject. He

---

72 Sermon 77, Para. II.1.
73 Sermon 77, Para. II.2.
74 Sermon 77, Para. II.3.
75 Sermon 77, Paras. II.4 and II.5.
76 Sermon 77, Para. II.6.
77 From the German [of Gerhard Tersteegen], *Hymns and Sacred Poems*, 1739, p. 79, *Poet. Wks.* I.72.

equated happiness with the knowledge and love of God which was the way in which he had interpreted the author of 1 John's phrase 'eternal life.' Wesley made the points that this happiness was another name for Christian religion, that every Christian was, not just should have been, happy and that there was no happiness outside Christian experience. In the final paragraph of the sermon, Wesley enforced his conclusions, using language drawn from many parts of the Bible, although not from 1 John. In this paragraph, as indeed in the whole section, Wesley's words assumed, but not explicitly, a doctrine of Christian perfection. Clearly the choice of texts from which his words were drawn was such as to support his conclusions. They also included the argument that the Christian was to make moral and spiritual effort to achieve the desired ends. It is of note, but perhaps not surprising, that Wesley did not discuss any biblical phrases or arguments that might have supported an opposing view.

The sermon claimed to give Wesley's exposition of the text, 1 John 5:20, but it is illustrative of the way his understanding of the doctrine of Christian perfection under-girded much of his biblical interpretation. Wesley only used biblical material that supported his view, but attention needs to be given elsewhere to the way he explained texts that do not support his views, even if he did not accept that there were such verses.

Fifth, note may be taken of Sermon 78: 'Spiritual Idolatry - 1 John 5:21 - Little children, keep yourselves from idols.'[78] It dated from 1781. In the opening paragraphs of this sermon, Wesley referred to what he understood to be the context of 1 John and the author's use of certain words. Wesley accepted without discussion that the author was the apostle John and referred to the tradition that in the frailty of advanced age, he had to be carried into the congregation, no longer able to preach, simply saying 'Beloved children, love one another.' This goes back to Jerome. However, Wesley commented that the text, 1 John 5:21, was equally important advice given to the readers by John. Wesley also commented on the author's use of the Greek words παιδια and τεκνια, making the point that the former had the meaning of 'babes in Christ' whereas the latter would better be translated 'beloved children', indicating a relationship with the author. The distinction is not supported by most modern lexicons such as that of Bauer.[79] The lexicon notes that τεκνιον, in the New Testament, was only used in the vocative plural by Jesus to his disciples or a Christian apostle or teacher to his spiritual children. Παιδιον, however, is normally used to describe a very young child or infant, but not particularly to describe a 'babe in Christ.'

---

78   The sermon is found in *BE* Vol. 3, pp. 103-14.
79   See Walter Bauer, *A Greek-English Lexicon of the New Testament and other Early Christian Literature,* translated by William F. Arndt and F. Wilbur Gingrich from the 5th edition, University of Chicage Press, second ed. 1958.

Wesley's first main section of the sermon discussed what the author meant by idols. Noting that the epistle was directed to Christians who had either been Jews or were gentiles who had left pagan ways behind them, he did not think that the reference was to idols in the traditional, pagan, sense of the word. He also noted that they were not what Wesley thought were the idols worshipped by the Roman Catholic Church. In this, Wesley showed his own contemporary Anglican and Protestant attitude towards what he saw as the errors of Rome, the worship of 'angels, or the souls of departed saints, or images of gold, silver, wood, or stone.'[80] Wesley was a man of his own day but, recognising that the author of the Epistle predated such practices by many centuries, he argued that something other must have been meant by the term idols. Wesley referred to the preceding words in 1 John 5:20, 'This is the true God and eternal life.' Wesley commented 'Whatever takes our heart from him, or shares it with him, is an idol, or, in other words, whatever we seek happiness in, independent of God.'[81]

A.E. Brooke made a similar comment 'All the false images of God which men have made for themselves instead of accepting the true revelation of Him given in His Son.'[82] Brooke did not consider that the reference is primarily to pagan idols and not exclusively to the views of the Gnostic false teachers who were the author's adversaries.

Wesley devoted the remainder of this section to specific examples of what he saw as idols. The instances given were related to 'the desire of the flesh,' 'the desire of the eye,' '*diversions*, and *amusements*,' leading up to a discussion of the dangers of excessive interest in music, language, criticism, history, experimental and natural philosophy, love of money, and the idolizing any human creature, by which he was making reference to human relationships. In these paragraphs Wesley was drawing a fine line between what he saw as the legitimate enjoyment of aspects of life and that which took away from the placing of anything before the proper primacy of the place of God in the life of the Christian. In this it is arguable that Wesley was not so much drawing out the meaning of 1 John 5:21 as bringing to the text the ideas and conclusions of his own reflection on those who had written on holiness or Christian perfection over the centuries and in the more immediate past including the work of such writers as William Law, by whom he had been influenced. In this he was interpreting 1 John in terms relating to his own congregation and his own time.

Wesley, in his second and shorter main section, turned to the question 'how we may keep ourselves from them [idols].' It should be noted that the author of 1 John did not address this question. He gave the instruction without any guidance as to the way it might be kept. Thus Wesley's words

---

80   Sermon 78, Para. I.2.
81   Sermon 78, Para. I.3.
82   Brooke, *The Johannine Epistles*, p. 154.

at this point go beyond the text and give his own views on the subject. It is of note that Wesley took up the theme to which reference was also made in Sermon 77 that true happiness was not to be found in those things which detracted from true spirituality. He quoted Horace, Matthew Prior, Pope, Psalm 39, and Proverbs 14, but his words do not directly reflect any New Testament passage. Then Wesley concluded, in paragraphs II.3-6, by enforcing an appeal to the hearers and readers. These paragraphs included biblical references, although not to 1 John. They also included use of words from two of Charles Wesley's hymns. It is therefore clear that in drawing out the implications of the text, 1 John 5:21, Wesley used material from a number of sources, by no means all biblical. A contrast to note is to be found in paragraphs II.3 and II.4.

Wesley urged strenuous moral and spiritual effort in the attempt to obey the precepts of 1 John and then immediately added: 'But do not either resolve or attempt to execute your resolution trusting in your own strength.' Wesley, at the same time, was stressing both the need for effort to achieve the Christian goal and the need to rely on the grace of God in order to do so. Wesley steered a difficult course between the concept of the need to strive for Christian Perfection and the need to rely upon the grace of God to achieve that end.[83] The Arminian Wesley argued for the doctrine of Christian Perfection and the need for both dependence on the grace of God and human effort.

In this sermon Wesley purported to give an exposition of the text which was 1 John 5:21. At the same time it is possible to see that he brought to the sermon ideas gained from wider reading, the experiences both of himself and others and the controversies of the day. His preaching arose from his biblical interpretation but was, in part, an exposition of his firmly held doctrines such as that of Christian Perfection. Wesley interpreted the Bible as an eighteenth-century High-Church Arminian Anglican.

Conclusion

In this chapter attention has been given to Wesley's understanding and use of the biblical text. Unsurprisingly it has been seen that Wesley came to critical questions about the scriptures in the same way as did the scholars of his own time. It has been shown that he was aware of questions relating to establishing the best English text from the available Greek sources. Therefore the authoritative words for Wesley were those of the original writers translated into English. There do not appear to be any places where he dismissed the Authorised (King James) version as being completely in error but there were occasions when he offered his own translation of particular passages. This was to draw out what he saw as the full flavour of

---

83   See Sermon 78, Para. II.3.

the original text. He translated the Bible in a way that was typical of an eighteenth-century biblical student.

It was in the interpretation of the meaning of the Bible that Wesley showed his Arminian Anglicanism. The evidence of this chapter has confirmed the main arguments put forward throughout this book. As a reader of scripture Wesley brought to the text the ideas and beliefs that were consistent with his Arminian Anglican theology. Elsewhere in this work it has been argued that these were fashioned in his childhood in Epworth, developed through his reading in Oxford and focussed through his encounters with Moravianism and the experiences that centred round the Aldersgate event. The chapter has therefore illustrated from primary Wesley material the main points that have been argued in the earlier chapters. Wesley's own words were published for others to read. These documents provide the clues that enable the reader to form a judgement on the place the Bible played in his life. This chapter reviewing some of Wesley's words giving his biblical interpretation has therefore confirmed the main conclusions drawn from this study.

To say that Wesley was a man of one book is obviously a grave oversimplification of the facts. He was a man of many books, even if he read them selectively. He claimed that the Bible was his supreme authority. That is a slightly narrower claim than that of being a person of one book, but even in that assertion there is an oversimplification. It is true that he wanted to make scripture his, and other people's, authority and he appealed to it, albeit selectively, to support his arguments. At no point did he even hint that the sacred text was in error. If it appeared to mean something other than what he wanted it to say, he gave an explanation that brought the text into line with the basic Arminian Anglican position that he held. That is not to pass a judgement on the truth or falsehood of the teaching he offered but it is to set it in its proper perspective. All the influences that fashioned the man also affected the way in which he read the Bible and taught what he believed to be its meaning.

All that remains is to draw some conclusions from this study and they will be found in the following and final chapter.

Chapter 8

Some Conclusions

This book has been a study of the way in which John Wesley interpreted the Bible. Throughout the chief concern has been not so much with the conclusions that Wesley drew from his reading of the text, but rather with the presuppositions with which he approached the Bible in the first place. These presuppositions, it has been argued, largely determined what Wesley thought that the Bible 'really meant'. In short, the process with which he approached the Bible was one of *eis*egesis rather than *ex*egesis although he would not have seen it in that way.

In the context of biblical studies this argument may not seem to be radically new because those familiar with Reader-Response criticism as used by New Testament scholars are already aware of the argument that the interpretation of the Bible involves an encounter between the reader and the text. The original meaning of the authors is of interest to those involved in the process of reading and the reader frequently believes that what s/he is trying to understand is what the author actually intended. The experience of reading is, however, an encounter in which the reader takes to the text, consciously or unconsciously, a great deal of baggage. This influences fundamentally the way that the scripture is understood. As has been shown in the preceding chapters, this was certainly the case with Wesley. Even so, no one has yet explored this example of reader-text dynamics. Wesley as a reader of the Bible is not a subject that previously has been adequately explored.

Wesley's use of the Bible and his understanding of the meaning scripture has become increasingly clear in the course of this work. In giving attention to the response Wesley made to the biblical text, it has been argued that he came to the task as an eighteenth-century High-Church Arminian Anglican and what he thought the text 'really meant' was largely determined by the complex traditions through the lens of which he was reading. His reading of the text was not only that of a High-Church Arminian Anglican. He firmly believed that the conclusions he drew were true and he found it difficult to believe that others could be correct in the way in which they interpreted the same words.

In the context of specifically Wesley studies, the argument presented here is substantially new, or at least the degree and consistency with which it has been argued are. As has been demonstrated, many Wesley scholars, especially those working in a North-American context, have believed that the methodology Wesley employed in his interpretation of scripture was to be found in his balancing of tradition, reason, and experience. His work has also been seen to be based on his understanding of empiricism, influenced at least to some extent by John Locke. However, it has gone virtually without challenge that Wesley thought that when it came to religious knowledge the Bible was supreme – not just theoretically but actually. The evidence presented in this book has challenged that assumption and challenged it fundamentally.

The arguments advanced in this work, then, have taken the question of Wesley's empiricism further by contending that for Wesley (whether he appreciated it or not) his experience and reason was subsumed into the High-Church Arminian Anglicanism that he then took to the text of the Bible. It was this mixture of tradition, reason and experience which he subsequently found to be the key to understanding the meaning of scripture. There is a circular argument here: what he found in the text confirmed his beliefs, but it was those beliefs that determined the way he read scripture. The text acted as a mirror, providing him with the biblical 'evidence' which he would then argue confirmed his beliefs. Biblical scholars will not be surprised to learn this. Wesley scholars have been rather slower in the uptake.

This work has explored and evaluated the influences that fashioned the thought and ministry of John Wesley insofar as he understood and interpreted the Bible. It has been made clear that his claim to be a man of one book is a major oversimplification of what was a very complex personality. John Munsey Turner, for example, comments:

> We can briefly survey the sources of Wesley's teaching presupposing the Bible as the primary source. The Anglican Reformers and behind them Luther and Calvin gave him the necessary undergirding of justification by faith. The Articles and Homilies of the Church of England were 'patient' of an Arminian interpretation. [...] From the Moravians came his clear assertion of the necessity of new birth and the assurance of faith... From the Anglicanism of the Caroline tradition, especially Jeremy Taylor and William Law (and also earlier Thomas à Kempis), came the stress on the Christian life as utter devotion to Christ. The Cambridge Platonists must not be ignored.[1]

It has been shown that while Wesley may have claimed to be a man of one book and while he said that for him it was the Bible that was the source of theological knowledge, and the supreme authority for faith and conduct, there were other more fundamental influences at work. These include the

---

1 John Munsey Turner, *John Wesley, the Evangelical Revival and the Rise of Methodism in England*, Epworth Press, 2002, p. 124.

profound influence of Susanna and Samuel Wesley at Epworth. They include also what Wesley had imbibed during the time he spent at Oxford, and especially the influence of the books that he read while he was there. Such influences, it has been argued, gave Wesley the context in which his later work was to be set.

It has also been shown that many of Wesley's earlier biographers, sometimes unconsciously but sometimes quite deliberately, recounted the story of Wesley's life in such a way as to enhance his character, emphasise the biblical basis of his thinking and, of considerable importance to themselves, to vindicate the style of the kind of Methodism that they themselves had adopted. They did not give attention to the complexity of sources from which his theological conclusions were obtained. Many ignored or did not accept sufficiently the fact that Wesley was fundamentally influenced by the Church of England into which he had been born and within which he remained all his days. It remains now to draw some further clear conclusions.

The first relates to the style of the scholarship and the manner in which scholarly debate has been conducted as it has attempted to describe Wesley in his eighteenth-century context. Those who are familiar with biblical scholarship are aware of the cut and thrust of debate and the sometimes fierce argument used to establish points, making out the case for a particular understanding of the subject. See, for example, D.A. Bullen, *A New Perspective on Paul? A Critical Evaluation of the Work of E.P. Sanders*, 1999, an unpublished M. Phil. Thesis, Liverpool Hope University College. This gives an account of the debate over the work of E.P. Sanders. In the chapter on the scholarly reviews of his work there is shown to be a fierceness in the criticisms that is missing, by contrast, in the work on Wesley. The fact that the Wesley scholars are much fewer in number and form a fairly close-knit community may partly explain this phenomenon.

That is not to deny that some Wesley scholars within the Wesleyan body did argue strongly in opposition to biographies produced by other, usually Anglican, authors. That has been illustrated in Chapter 1. This, however, proves the point being made. Within the Methodist body there has been a lack of criticism and a resistance to those who have perhaps looked more objectively at Wesley than its own scholars have done. The fact that he was a major figure in eighteenth-century church history and that he had a profound influence on subsequent events is enhanced and not diminished when he is seen as he was. It is not necessary or helpful to produce a false picture of a figure who is the more interesting when seen as he really was. Nevertheless the nineteenth-century attitude that was reluctant to depict Wesley as anything other than a highly venerated, saintly, figure with little, if any, fault, seems to have survived in Wesley scholarship, at least until fairly recently.

In any situation it may be difficult to obtain a fully objective account of a historical figure and his/her work. Nevertheless this study does illustrate the point that it is possible to write about a person of an earlier generation with a hidden agenda. Such a work becomes a polemical rather than a scholarly exercise. Thus some work was coupled with a rewriting of history to the point where Wesley's life, work and writings were used to justify positions held within the Wesleyan Methodism of the authors' own days. This was achieved sometimes by a highly selective use of the materials available. In other instances it would appear that the primary documents were themselves edited to help sustain the desired conclusion. An instance of this is seen in the work of Thomas Jackson and the way he 'edited' journals and works of both John and Charles Wesley. This editing of the works of others is strangely reminiscent of the way that Wesley himself used written material in his own works.

Later scholarship has accepted all too readily the secondary documents without serious questions being asked. In order to understand Wesley as a person of his own day claiming to read the Bible as his ultimate source of authority, it is necessary to open up a debate using the primary documents that are now becoming available.

Secondly, although all biographers of Wesley have to some extent noted Wesley's Anglican context, the story of his life is often told as that of an enlightened, biblically-based figure who was working within the Established Church, but assuming that this was merely what can be best described as the framework of the story. This context is not seen as being of the essence of Wesley. He may have been an Anglican, so the argument sometimes runs, but he was a Bible-based Anglican and his doctrine and life were based solely upon the Bible. However, as has been shown, Wesley remained within the Church of England through conviction, not because it was just a convenient setting in which to do his work. The Established Church contained those who differed in churchmanship and theological conviction as much in the eighteenth century as in the twenty-first. It is therefore essential to see Wesley within the context of his own time. That has been part of the task tackled in this work.

It has been shown that Wesley was influenced by the Moravians and yet he discovered that all he had gained from them was to be found within the Bible and Anglican formularies. Everything he rejected from them was, in his opinion, unbiblical and not Anglican. His understanding of the gospel was Anglican in essence and that did not fundamentally change. Wesley was an eighteenth-century Arminian Christian who was in that particular tradition within the Church of England, by birth, by upbringing and by conviction. This is not to make a judgement on the nineteenth- or twentieth-century Wesleyan or Methodist Churches and the biblical interpretation of their scholars. It is merely to argue that it is necessary to separate their historical assessment of Wesley from their own biblical and theological work in their generation.

This has been a study of Wesley as a reader of the Bible. It need not, of necessity, affect the theology or practice of the contemporary British Methodist Church in relation to either the Church of England or the other Free Churches, nor Methodism's own understanding of the meaning of scripture. It does not affect the theological standards of the American United Methodist Church in its relationships with its ecumenical partners. It does, however, have the implication that references to Wesley in contemporary debates need to be historically accurate. Wesley's biblical scholarship was that of the eighteenth-century, not that of the twentieth- or twenty-first-century. It would, of course, be anachronistic to judge Wesley because he was not aware of later literary criticism. So also, his interpretation of the biblical passages was that of someone in his generation and with his inbuilt convictions. If Wesley's words or Wesley's activities are referred to within the context of contemporary debates, it is necessary that this is done with respect for historical fact and with understanding.

There is a further, more practical, point. In chapter 7 a note was taken of clause 4 of the Methodist Deed of Union and the fact that Wesley's *Notes Upon the New Testament* and certain of his sermons did not 'impose a system of formal or speculative theology on Methodist preachers.' They do, however, offer a means of interpreting the constitution of the Methodist Church without completely tying it to an eighteenth-century theology or method of biblical interpretation. Counsel's opinion determined which of Wesley's sermons were the forty-four referred to in the Deed of Union.[2] Clause 5 of the Deed of Union deals with the interpretation of doctrine: 'The Conference shall be the final authority within the Methodist Church with regard to all questions concerning the interpretation of its doctrines.'[3]

The arguments in this book are relevant here as well. It has been shown that coming to Wesley's words relating to biblical interpretation with the approach of Reader-Response criticism gives a much clearer understanding of his scriptural and theological teaching. It is simply not enough any more to say that Wesley believed the Bible. Contemporary biblical studies have shown that this is far too simplistic. The twenty-first-century reader needs to see Wesley, including what he had to say on the Bible, in Wesley's own context. Such authority that Wesley's *Explanatory Notes* and *Forty Four Sermons* have for modern British Methodism needs therefore to be reinterpreted in terms of present day thought. This does not undervalue the work of Wesley, but it does set it in its proper perspective.

Although it is sometimes disputed, the influence of a form of empiricism on Wesley, perhaps influenced by the work of John Locke, was

---

2   See John Wesley, *Forty-four Sermons*, Notes, p. ii. .
3   *CPD* Vol. 2, 1996, p. 213.

strong. The empirical approach with the emphasis on reason and experience has been seen to be evident in the disputes Wesley had with others. Reason was a tool and experience provided the data to help interpret scripture in the way that accorded with Wesley's theological beliefs. However, for Wesley, experience was that of an eighteenth-century Arminian Anglican and his use of reason was also Anglican. Both helped interpret the Bible and to some extent determined what he found within it.

In summary then, it is clear that Wesley has to be read in the context of his own age. His biblical interpretation cannot be lifted out of that context into another, and later, world without adaptation. If his words are to have any relevance for the present age they must first be understood in the context of the age in which he lived.

Most important, perhaps, in the conclusions to be drawn from this work is a fresh understanding of what it means to describe Wesley as a man of one book. By applying some of the insights of Reader-Response criticism it has been shown here that the claim that Wesley was such cannot be sustained in the strictest meaning of that term. This has been largely missed by Wesley scholars to date. The fact that the study of Reader-Response is relatively new does mean that it would be inappropriate to look for some awareness of it in the older works. More recent authors writing about Wesley should, however, have been aware of its implications for an understanding of his method of biblical interpretation. This new approach would by no means rule out the study of the words, works and actions of Wesley himself to see if there was not some way in which his use of biblical texts and his understanding of biblical truth was either distinctive to Wesley or was reflective of the context in which he found himself. This may have been either a conscious or an unconscious influence on the way that scripture was understood by him. Wesley was not an original or a systematic theologian. Nevertheless he did use his considerable intellectual skills to advance and defend his views in the many controversies in which he was involved, especially those with the Moravians and the Calvinists.

Throughout this book, then, it has been contended that Wesley came to scripture within an eighteenth-century High-Church Anglican and Arminian mindset. For Wesley, what the Bible plainly said was not necessarily what others, Calvinists for example, saw the Bible as plainly saying. Tradition, reason and experience all played their part in the way in which Wesley understood the Bible, but their authority, seen as subservient to that of scripture, was understood as being within the context of the Anglicanism that he embraced throughout his life. To say that Wesley was a complex personality and that the influences that fashioned him too were complex is perhaps to state the obvious. Unfortunately many of his biographers have completely missed that complexity and have thereby presented a one-sided, distorted and therefore inaccurate assessment of him. The consistent argument of this book has been that his whole life is best understood when he is seen as an Anglican from birth to death. That is the clue to the understanding of Wesley and his biblical interpretation that so many have missed, and yet which is the way into unravelling some of the complexities that made him what he was.

The research undertaken in the preparation of this book has shown up two areas at least in which further research is required in order to enable a fuller assessment to be made of John Wesley's place in history.

One of them relates to the life and person of Samuel Wesley. It has been strongly argued that Samuel was a greater influence on John Wesley than is sometimes allowed. It is also true that he was more than just the Rector of a Parish Church somewhat off the mainstream of English life. He was involved in the emergence of Anglican societies, the S.P.C.K., a Convocation proctor, and a writer of more works than just his commentary on Job. Some of Samuel Wesley's correspondence has more recently been added to the Methodist Archives Centre in the John Rylands Library. It would therefore be of value if someone would research the available material and produce an account of his life and a reassessment of his character. This would be of value in its own right and give some further insight into the life of the Church of England of his day. It would also give a better understanding of the family background within which John and Charles Wesley were raised. Such a study would not in any way replace the work already undertaken on Susanna Wesley but would supplement and balance it. It would be a reminder that Samuel as well as Susanna was an influence on John and Charles Wesley and through them on the Methodism that emerged in the years long after Samuel's death.

The second area needing further research is that of the history of the Methodist societies from 1784 to the opening years of the nineteenth century. 1784 has been seen as a major turning point in Methodist history as it was the time of the Deed of Declaration which set up the legal authority of the Conference, especially for the time that would follow the deaths of John and Charles Wesley. It was also the year of the first of Wesley's ordinations, at that time for the American societies. It has been argued that from that year onwards Charles Wesley was fighting a rearguard action in conjunction with a minority within Methodism against a growing majority who were looking for separation from the Church of England and that John Wesley's resolve, if not his words, were considerably weakened in that matter. Recent research has produced some evidence that the resistance to any separation from the established Church was very much stronger than earlier Wesleyan historians have allowed. A reappraisal of the way in which the separation ultimately took place and the way the continuing Wesleyan Methodist body emerged as a distinctive church would certainly clarify historical events. It would also show how Wesley's biographers recounted the story of his latter years in ways that suited their own case. Such a work would enable a more balanced view of the theological and ecclesiastical stance of Wesley to be made. Frank Baker makes comment about this period that 'Throughout this trying decade, however, for the most part dirty Methodist linen was not washed in public, and Methodism remained a strong evangelical force.'[4] It was in this period that the earliest Wesley biographies were published and they indicate an obvious reason why he was presented as a man of one book, and, in the mainstream Wesleyan tradition, without great emphasis on his Anglican context. The process was basically one in which an attempt was made to 'cut out the middle man'; if it could be argued (or at least stated often enough) that Wesley believed the Bible then there was no need for Anglicanism. The implied argument is simple. The biographers might have said 'Wesley believed the Bible, the Bible contains the truth, we follow Wesley so therefore we are Bible-based people too and as such have the truth.'

It is in this respect that yet further research should be undertaken with regard to Wesley's biblical interpretation inasmuch as it relates to the understanding of ordination and the nature of the church. There is more work to be done on the way in which the Methodist Societies and a Conference of itinerant preachers separated from the Church of England and became a church with a ministry, believing this to be a proper development of the work of Wesley. Clearly the Methodist Church believes that its form of presbyters is a ministry which is properly ordained. That view is not being challenged here but research needs to be undertaken into the origin of Methodist ministry in order to grasp the manner in which it emerged.

This work has not explored the influence of John on Charles Wesley or the possibility of the influence of Charles on John. The manner in which Charles interpreted the Bible was undoubtedly similar to that of John, although many assert that Charles was more firmly rooted in the Church of England than his older brother. The reasons that led to an estrangement between the brothers for a period, Charles virtually ceasing to itinerate, have usually been seen as relating to Charles settling into domestic happiness, accepting family responsibilities and remaining keenly loyal to the Established Church. Additional research may further illustrate the way in which their respective understanding of the Bible and both theological and non-theological factors influenced their actions. Charles has been seen as the hymn-writer of Methodism, with biblically based words, often severely monitored by John. Work based at Liverpool Hope University and elsewhere has helped in the production of a definitive edition of Charles's sermons and future publication of his letters and Journal. This primary material will provide opportunity to explore some of the questions here being raised.

---

4   Baker, *John Wesley and the Church of England*, p. 323.

The final comment on the influences that fashioned Wesley as a person in his beliefs and his life's work is perhaps best summed up in Wesley's words in 1790, noted in chapter 1, 'I live and die a member of the Church of England, and that *none who regard my judgement or advice* will ever separate from it.' At the age of 87 and within a year of his death, Wesley had no reason to make such a statement unless it was fundamental to his beliefs. It depicts the kind of reader of the biblical text and the eighteenth-century man that he was.

John Wesley - a man of one book? Wesley was a man of many books, believing just one, the Bible, to be supreme in its authority for faith and practice. Throughout this work there has been an investigation into the manner in which he came to that book, the presuppositions that he took to that task, and the method by which he interpreted it. As has been seen, it was more complex than Wesley, or many of his biographers, have previously allowed.

Bibliography

Primary Sources (John Wesley)

Benson, Joseph (ed.), *The Journal of the Rev. John Wesley*, 16 Vols, Conference Office, 1809-13

Curnock, Nehemiah (ed.), *The Journal of John Wesley, Standard Edition*, 6 Vols, Epworth Press, 1909-16

Jackson, Thomas (ed.), *The Works of John Wesley*, 14 Vols, John Mason, 1831

Sugden, E. H. (ed.), *The Standard Sermons of John Wesley*, 2 Vols, Epworth Press, 1931

Telford, John (ed.), *The Letters of John Wesley, Standard Edition*, 8 Vols, Epworth Press, 1931

Wesley, John, *A Christian Library*, Vol. *1 of 50* Vols, Felix Farley, 1748

Wesley, John, *A Plain Account of Christian Perfection*, Epworth Press, 1952 ed.

Wesley, John, *An Earnest Appeal to Men of Reason and Religion (with Farther Appeal to Men of Reason and Religion)*, London, eighth ed., 1796

Wesley, John, *Explanatory Notes upon the New Testament*, Epworth Press, 1976 (first ed. 1754)

Wesley, John, *Explanatory Notes upon the Old Testament*, Vols. 1-3, Schmul publishers, 1975 (first ed. 1765)

Wesley, John, *Predestination Calmly Considered*, printed by W.B. and sold at the Foundery; by T. Trye; and by R. Akenhead, 1752

Wesley, John, *Sermons on Several Occasions*, (John Wesley's Forty-four Sermons), Epworth Press, 1944

Wesley, John, *The Sunday Service of the Methodists in North America with Other Occasional Services*, Published by Wesley in London, 1784

The Bicentennial Edition of the Works of John Wesley, Clarendon Press and Abingdon Press, 1975 onwards, Editor-in-Chief Frank Baker

Vol. 1	*Sermons I, 1-33*, edited by Albert C. Outler, Abingdon Press, 1984
Vol. 2	*Sermons II, 34-70*, edited by Albert C. Outler, Abingdon Press, 1985
Vol. 3	*Sermons III, 71-114*, edited by Albert C. Outler, Abingdon Press, 1985
Vol. 4	*Sermons IV, 115-151*, edited by Albert C. Outler, Abingdon Press, 1987
Vol. 9	*The Methodist Societies*, History, Nature, and Design, edited by Rupert E. Davies, 1989
Vol. 11	*The Appeals to Men of Reason and Religion and Certain Related Open Letters*, edited by Gerald R. Cragg, Abingdon Press, 1875
Vol. 18	*Journals and Diaries 1 (1735-1738)*, edited by W. Reginald Ward and Richard P. Heitzenrater, Abingdon Press, 1988

Vol. 19   *Journals and Diaries 2 (1738-1743)*, edited by W. Reginald Ward
                 and Richard P. Heitzenrater, Abingdon Press, 1990
Vol. 20   *Journals and Diaries 3 (1743-1754)*, edited by W. Reginald Ward,
                 Abingdon Press, 1991
Vol. 21   *Journals and Diaries 4 (1755-1765)*, edited by W. Reginald Ward,
                 Abingdon Press, 1992
Vol. 22   *Journals and Diaries 5 (1765-1775)*, edited by W. Reginald Ward,
                 Abingdon Press, 1993
Vol. 25   *Letters I (1721-1739)*, edited by Frank Baker, Oxford University
                 Press, 1980
Vol. 26   *Letters II (1740-1755)*, edited by Frank Baker, Oxford University
                 Press, 1982

Primary Source (Susanna Wesley)

Wallace, Charles (Junior), *Susanna Wesley: The Complete Writings*, Oxford University
    Press, 1997

Works Relating to John Wesley and Others Published between 1791 and 1900

Anonymous (An Old Methodist), *John Wesley in Company with High Church Men*,
    Church Press Company, 1870
Anonymous, *The Life of John Wesley*, Seeley Jackson and Halliday, 1856, a volume in a
    series superintended by Robert Bickersteth
Benson, Joseph, *An Apology for the People Called Methodists Containing a Concise
    account of their Origin and Progress, Doctrine, Discipline and Designs Humbly
    Submitted to the Consideration of the Friends of True Christianity*, Conference
    Office, 1812
Brown, John, *The Life of Rev James Hervey M.A. Rector of Weston Flavell*, Religious
    Tract Society, 1835
Brown, Robert, *John Wesley's Theology - A Lecture*, Jackson, Walford and Hodder,
    1865
Christie, T.W, *Methodism - A Part of the Great Christian Apostasy - A review of the Life
    and Doctrines of John Wesley*, Simpkin, Marshall and Co., 1881
Clarke, Adam, *Memoirs of the Wesley Family*, R.J. Kershaw, 1823
Coke, Thomas and Henry Moore, *The Life of the Rev. John Wesley, A.M. Including an
    Account of the Great Revival of Religion in Europe and America, of which he was the
    Chief Instrument*, London, 1792
Cooke, Joseph, *Methodism Condemned by Methodist Preachers or a Vindication of the
    Doctrines Contained in Two Sermons on Justification by Faith and the Witness of the
    Spirit for which the Author was Expelled from the Methodist Connexion*, T. Wood,
    Rochdale, 1807
Coslet (Mrs), (Edith Waddy), *The Father of Methodism - A Sketch of the Lives and
    Labours of the Rev John Wesley M.A.,* Wesleyan Conference Office, second ed. 1879
Dobbin, O.T., *Wesley the Worthy and Wesley the Catholic*, Ward & Co., 1850
Ellis, James, *John Wesley*, James Nisbet & Co., 1891

Hampson, John, *Memoirs of the late John Wesley A.M. with a Review of his Life and Writings and a History of Methodism, from its Commencement in 1729, to the Present Time*, 3 Vols, Sunderland, 1791

Hervey, James, William Hervey ed., *Theron and Aspasio*, Thomas Tegs and Sons, 1837, first ed. 1765

Hobrow, W., *Sermon on the Death of Rev J Wesley A.M. Chaplain to the Countess Dowager of Bucan Delivered at the New Chapel Liverpool in Edmund Street Liverpool Sunday March 27th 1791*. No publisher is given so it was probably privately circulated but printed by H. Hodgson of Castle Street, Liverpool. A copy is in the Liverpool University Library.

Hockin, Frederick, *John Wesley and Modern Methodism*, Rivingtons, 1887

Knox, Alexander, *Considerations on a Separation of the Methodists from the Established Church*, Bristol, printed by Bulgin and Rosser, 1794

Moore, Henry, *The Life of the Rev John Wesley A.M. Fellow of Lincoln College Oxford*, London, John Kershaw, 2 Vols, 1824-5

Myles, William, *A Chronological History of the People Called Methodists of the Connexion of the late Rev. John Wesley, From their Rise in the Year 1729 to their Last Conference in 1802*, Conference Office, 1803, third ed. enlarged

Nightingale, Joseph, *A Portraiture of Methodism Being an Impartial View of the Rise, Progress, Doctrines and Manners of the Wesleyan Methodists in a Series of Letters, Addressed to a Lady*, Longman, Hurst, Rees and Orme, 1807

Overton, J.H., *John Wesley*, Methuen & Co., 1891

Rigg, James H., *The Churchmanship of John Wesley, and the Relations of Wesleyan Methodism to the Church of England*, Wesleyan Conference Office, Preface 1878

Sandwith, Humphrey, 'Methodism, and its Relation to Church and State,' series of articles in *Wesleyan Methodist Magazine*, May-December, 1829

Smith, George, *History of Methodism*, Vol. 1 *Wesley and his Times*, Longman Green, Longman and Roberts, fourth ed., 1863

Southey, Robert, *The Life of Wesley*, Bell and Dolby, 1864, first ed. 1820

Stevens, Abel, *The History of the Religious Movement of the Eighteenth Century Called Methodism Considered in its Different Denominational Forms, and in its General Relation to Protestantism*, John Willey and Co., 3 Vols., 1863-5, also published by Conference Office, 1878

Stevens, Abel, *The Illustrated History of Methodism Being an Account of the Wesleys, their Contemporaries and their Times and a Summary of the Events to the Conference at Leeds, July 1882 by Rev R. Green*, James Sangster & Co., 2 Vols, no date

Stevenson, George J., *Memoirs of the Wesley Family*, S. W. Partridge and Co., Preface January 1878

Taylor, Isaac, *Wesley and Methodism*, Brown, Green and Longmans, 1831

Tyerman, Rev. L., *The Life and Times of John Wesley*, 3 Vols, Hodder and Stoughton, sixth ed. 1890, first ed. 1871

Urlin, R. Denny, *John Wesley's Place in Church History*, Rivington, 1870

Urlin, R. Denny, *The Churchman's Life of Wesley*, SPCK, New Edition Revised and Corrected, undated, circa 1885

Watson, Richard, *Observations on Southey's "Life of Wesley"*, T. Blanchard, 1820

Watson, Richard, *The Life of Rev. John Wesley, A.M.*, John Mason, fourth ed. 1835, first ed. 1831

Watson, Richard, *The Works of Richard Watson*, Vol. V (Containing *The Life of John Wesley, A.M.* and *Observations on Southey's Life of Wesley*), seventh ed., John Mason, 1858

Wedgwood, Julia, *John Wesley and the Evangelical Reaction of the Eighteenth Century*, Macmillan and Co., 1870.

Whitehead, John, *The Life of the Rev. John Wesley, A.M.*, Stephen Couchman, Vol. 1 1793, Vol. 2 1796

Wesley Studies and Related Subjects from 1901 Onwards

A Lamp to my feet and a Light to My Path: The Nature of Authority and the Place of the Bible in the Methodist Church, The Methodist Publishing House, 1998.

Abraham, William J., 'The Wesleyan Quadrilateral' in *Wesleyan Theology Today* in *Wesleyan Theology Today*, ed. Theodore Runyon, Kingswood Books, 1985

Abraham, William J., *Wesley for Armchair Theologians*, Westminster John Knox Press, 2005.

Ayling, Stanley, *John Wesley*, Collins, 1979

Baker, Eric W., *A Herald of the Revival (A Critical Enquiry into the Relation of William Law to John Wesley and the Beginnings of Methodism)*, Epworth Press, 1948

Baker, Frank, *Charles Wesley's Verse*, Epworth Press, 1964

Baker, Frank, *John Wesley and the Church of England*, Epworth Press, 1970, second ed. 2000

Barber, Peter, 'Text or Pretext: An Historical Perspective on the Preacher's Use of Scripture' in *Beyond the Boundaries, Preaching in the Wesleyan Tradition*, Wesley Westminster Series, No. 8, ed. Richard Sykes, Applied Theology Press, 1998

Birch, Bruce C., 'Biblical Theology: Issues in Authority and Hermeneutics' in *Wesleyan Theology Today* Runyon, Theodore, (ed.), Kingswood Books, 1985

Bowmer, John C., *The Sacrament of the Lord's Supper in Early Methodism*, Dacre Press, 1951

Brailsford, Mabel Richmond, *A Tale of Two Brothers: John and Charles Wesley*, Rupert Hart-Davis, 1954

Brantley, Richard E, *Locke, Wesley, and the Method of English Romanticism*, University of Florida Press, 1984

Brown-Lawson, A., *John Wesley and the Anglican Evangelicals of the Eighteenth Century*, The Pentland Press, 1994.

Butler, David, *Methodists and Papists: John Wesley and the Catholic Church in the Eighteenth Century*, Darton Longman and Todd, 1995

Campbell, Ted A., *John Wesley and Christian Antiquity Religious Vision and Cultural Change*, Kingswood Books, 1991

Campbell, Ted A., 'The Interpretive Role of Tradition,' in *Wesley and the Quadrilateral - Renewing the Conversation*, ed. W. Stephen Gunter, Abingdon Press, 1997

Campbell, Ted A., 'The "Wesleyan Quadrilateral": The Story of a Modern Methodist Myth' in *Doctrine and Theology in the United Methodist Church*, ed. Thomas A. Langford, Kingswood Books, 1991

Cannon, William R., *The Theology of John Wesley*, Abingdon Press, 1948

Carter, David, *James H. Rigg*, Foundry Press, 1994

Casto, Robert Michael, *Exegetical Method in John Wesley's Explanatory Notes on the Old Testament*, (Thesis Duke University), 1977

Church, Leslie F., *More About the Early Methodist People*, Epworth Press, 1949

Church, Leslie F., *The Early Methodist People*, Epworth Press, 1948

Clapper, Gregory S., *John Wesley on Religious Affections: his Views on Experience and Emotion and their Role in the Christian Life and Theology*, The Scarecrow Press (Pietist and Wesleyan Studies No 1), 1987

Cobb, John B. Jr, *Grace and Responsibility: A Wesleyan Theology for Today*, Abingdon Press, 1994

Collins, Kenneth J., *A Faithful Witness: John Wesley's Homiletical Theology*, Wesley Heritage Press, 1993

Collins, Kenneth J., *A Real Christian: The Life of John Wesley*, Abingdon Press, 1999

Collins, Kenneth J., *The Scripture Way of Salvation: The Heart of Wesley's Theology*, Abingdon Press, 1997

Cragg, Gerald R., *The Church and the Age of Reason 1648-1789*, Penguin Books 1990, first published Pelican Books, 1960

Dallimore, Arnold A., *George Whitefield*, The Wakeman Trust, 1990

Dallimore, Arnold A., *George Whitefield: The Life and Times of the Great Evangelist of the Eighteenth Century Revival*, The Banner of Truth Trust, Vol. 1, 1970, Vol. 2, 1980

Dallimore, Arnold A., *Susanna, the Mother of John and Charles Wesley*, Evangelical Press, 1992

Davies, Rupert E., *Methodism*, Epworth Press, 1963, revised 1985

Davies, Rupert, 'The People Called Methodists "Our Doctrines"' in *A History of the Methodist Church in Great Britain,* Vol. 1, eds. Rupert Davies and Gordon Rupp, Epworth Press, 1965

Davies, Rupert E. and Gordon Rupp, Eds., *A History of the Methodist Church in Great Britain*, Epworth Press, Vol. 1, 1965, Vol. 2, 1978 (A. Raymond George was a joint editor with Davies and Rupp in Vol. 2)

Dawes, Stephen B., 'John Wesley and the Bible' in *Proceedings of the Wesley Historical Society*, Vol. 54, February 2003

Edwards, Maldwyn, *Family Circle: A Study of the Epworth Household in Relation to John and Charles Wesley*, Epworth Press, 1949

Edwards, Maldwyn, *John Wesley and the Eighteenth Century: A Study of his Social and Political Influence*, Epworth Press, 1933, revised 1955

English, Donald, 'John Wesley: A Preacher for Today' in *Beyond the Boundaries, Preaching in the Wesleyan Tradition*, ed. Richard Sykes, Applied Theology Press, 1998

Fitchett, W. H., *Wesley and His Century: A Study in Spiritual Forces*, Smith, Elder and Co., 1906

Flew, R. Newton, *The Idea of Christian Perfection in Christian Theology,* Clarendon Press, 1934

Forsaith, Peter S., *John Fletcher*, Foundry Press, 1994

Fowler, James W., 'John Wesley's Development in Faith' in *The Future of the Methodist Theological Traditions*, ed. M. Douglas Meeks, Abingdon Press, 1985

Frei, Hans W., *The Eclipse of Biblical Narrative, A Study in Eighteenth and Nineteenth Century Hermeneutics*, Yale University Press, 1974

George, A. Raymond, 'The People Called Methodists: 4. The Means of Grace' in *A History of the Methodist Church in Great Britain* Vol. 1, ed. Rupert Davies and Gordon Rupp, Epworth Press, 1965

Green, J. Brazier, *John Wesley and William Law*, Epworth Press 1945

Green, Richard, *John Wesley Evangelist*, Religious Tract Society, 1905

Green, Richard, *The Works of John and Charles Wesley: A Bibliography*, C. H. Kelly, 1896, second ed. revised and enlarged, 1902

Green, V.H.H., *John Wesley*, Nelson, 1964

Green, V.H.H., *The Young Mr Wesley*, Wyvern Books, 1963, originally published by Edward Arnold, 1961

Greetham, Mary and Peter, *Samuel Wesley*, Foundry Press, 1990

Gunter, W. Stephen, *The Limits of 'Love Divine,'* Kingswood Books, 1989

Gunter, W. Stephen, 'The Quadrilateral and the "Middle Way"' in *Wesley and the Quadrilateral - Renewing the Conversation*, ed. W. Stephen Gunter, Abingdon Press, 1997

Gunter, W. Stephen, ed., *Wesley and the Quadrilateral: Renewing the Conversation*, Abingdon Press, 1997

Harrison, G. Elsie, *Son to Susanna*, Ivor Nicholson and Watson, 1937

Hattersley, Roy, *A Brand Plucked from the Burning: The Life of John Wesley*, Little, Brown, 2002

Heitzenrater, Richard P., 'Great Expectations: Aldersgate and the Evidences of Genuine Christianity' in *Aldersgate Reconsidered*, ed. Randy L. Maddox, Kingswood Books, 1990

Heitzenrater, Richard P., 'In Search of Controversy and Consensus: The Road to the 1988 Doctrinal Statement' in *Doctrine and Theology in the United Methodist Church*, ed. Thomas A. Langford, Kingswood Books, 1991

Heitzenrater, Richard P., *Mirror and Memory: Reflections on Early Methodism*, Kingswood Books, 1989

Heitzenrater, Richard P., *The Elusive Mr Wesley*, Vols. 1 and 2, Abingdon Press, 1984

Heitzenrater, Richard P., *Wesley and the People Called Methodists*, Abingdon Press, 1995

Hempton, David, *Methodism Empire of the Spirit*, Yale University Press, 2005

Hindmarsh, D. Bruce, *John Newton and the English Evangelical Tradition*, William B. Eerdmans, 1996

Idle, Christopher, *The Journal of John Wesley (Abridged)*, Lion Paperback, 1986

Jeffrey, David Lyle, *English Spirituality in the Age of Wesley*, William B. Eerdmans, 1994

Jones, Scott J., 'The Rule of Scripture' in *Wesley and the Quadrilateral - Renewing the Conversation*, ed. W. Stephen Gunter., Abingdon Press, 1997

Jones, Scott J, *John Wesley's Concept and Use of Scripture*, Kingswood Books, 1995

Kent, John, *Wesley and the Wesleyans: Religion in Eighteenth-Century Britain*, Cambridge University Press, 2002

Kimbrough, ST Jr, *Charles Wesley: Poet and Theologian*, Kingswood Books, 1992

Knox, R. A, *Enthusiasm*, Clarendon Press, 1991

Langford, Thomas A. (ed.), *Doctrine and Theology in the United Methodist Church*, Kingswood Books, 1991

Langford, Thomas A., *Practical Divinity: Theology in the Wesleyan Tradition*, Abingdon Press, 1984

Langford, Thomas A., 'The United Methodist Quadrilateral: A Theological Task,' in *Doctrine and Theology in the United Methodist Church*, ed. Thomas A. Langford, Kingswood Books, 1991

Lawson, Albert Brown, *John Wesley and the Christian Ministry: The Sources and Development of his Opinions and Practice*, SPCK, 1963

Lawton, George, *Shropshire Saint*, Epworth Press, 1960

Lindström, Harald, *Wesley and Sanctification*, Epworth Press, 1950

Lloyd, Gareth, *Charles Wesley: a New Evaluation of his Life and Ministry*, Unpublished thesis in Liverpool Hope University Library, 2002

Long, D. Stephen, *John Wesley's Moral Theology: The Quest for God and Goodness*, Kingswood Books, 2005.

MacCorrie, James T., *Thoughts from a Warmed Heart*, Colourpoint, 2002

Maddox, Randy L., *Aldersgate Reconsidered*, Kingswood Books, 1990

Maddox, Randy L., 'Reclaiming an Inheritance: Wesley as Theologian in the History of Methodist Theology' in *Rethinking Wesley's Theology for Contemporary Methodism*, ed. Randy L. Maddox, Kingswood Books, Abingdon Press, 1998

Maddox, Randy L., *Responsible Grace: John Wesley's Practical Theology*, Kingswood Books, 1994

Maddox, Randy L., *Rethinking Wesley's Theology for Contemporary Methodism*, Kingswood Books, 1998

Maddox, Randy L., 'The Enriching Role of Experience,' in *Wesley and the Quadrilateral - Renewing the Conversation*, ed. W. Stephen Gunter, Abingdon Press, 1997

Maddox, Randy L., "Vital Orthodoxy: A Wesleyan Dynamic for 21st Century Christianity," A Lecture delivered at Liverpool Hope University College 12/09/2002

McGonigle, Herbert Boyd., *John Wesley and the Moravians*, Morley's Print and Publishing, 1993

McGonigle, Herbert Boyd, *Sufficient Saving Grace: John Wesley's Evangelical Arminianism*, Paternoster Press, 2001.

McMaster, Johnston, 'Hermeneutics in the Wesleyan Understanding,' supporting paper to *Finding New Life - John Wesley's 'Scriptural Holiness' for the Third Millennium*, a report of the European Methodist Theological Commission, 2002/3

Meeks, M. Douglas, ed., *The Future of the Methodist Theological Traditions*, Abingdon Press, 1985

Miles, Rebekah, 'The Instrumental Role of Reason' in *Wesley and the Quadrilateral - Renewing the Conversation*, ed. W. Stephen Gunter, Abingdon Press, 1997

Monk, Robert C., *John Wesley and his Puritan Heritage*, Scarecrow Press, second ed. 1999

Moore, Robert L., *John Wesley and Authority: A Psychological Perspective*, Scholars Press (American Academy of Religion), 1979

Naglee, David Ingersoll, *From Everlasting to Everlasting: John Wesley on Eternity and Time*, Peter Lang, 2 Vols, 1991

Newton, John A., *Susanna Wesley and the Puritan Tradition in Methodism*, Epworth Press, 1968, second ed. 2002

Newton, John A., *The Wesleys for Today*, Methodist Newspaper Company Ltd, 1989

Nockles, Peter S., *The Oxford Movement in Context: Anglican High Churchmanship 1760-1857*, Cambridge University Press, 1994

Oden, Thomas C., *John Wesley's Scriptural Christianity: A Plain Exposition of his Teaching on Christian Doctrine*, Zendervan Publishing House, 1994

Orcibal Jean, 'The Theological Originality of John Wesley and Continental Spirituality', translated by R.J.A. Sharp, in *A History of the Methodist Church in Great Britain*, Vol. 1, ed. Rupert Davies and Gordon Rupp, Epworth Press, 1965

Orcibal, Jean, 'The Theological Originality of John Wesley and Continental Spirituality', translated by R.J.A. Sharp, in *A History of the Methodist Church in Great Britain*, Vol. 1, ed. Rupert Davies and Gordon Rupp, Epworth Press, 1965

Outler, Albert C., 'A New Future for Wesley Studies: An Agenda for Phase III' in *The Future of the Methodist Theological Traditions*, ed. M. Douglas Meeks, Abingdon Press, 1985

Outler, Albert C., *John Wesley*, Oxford University Press, 1964

Outler, Albert C., 'The Wesleyan Quadrilateral in John Wesley' in *The Wesleyan Theological Journal*, 20, No. 1, 1985, pp. 7-18

Outler, Albert, 'The Wesleyan Quadrilateral in John Wesley' in *Doctrine and Theology in the United Methodist Church*, ed. Thomas A. Langford, Kingswood Books, 1991,

Piette, Maximin, *John Wesley and the Evolution of Protestantism*, Sheed and Ward, 1937

Podmore, Colin, *The Moravian Church in England, 1728-1760*, Clarendon Press, 1998

Pollock, John, *George Whitefield and the Great Awakening*, Lion Paperback, 1986, first ed. Hodder and Stoughton, 1973

Pollock, John, *Wesley the Preacher*, Kingsway Publications, 2000, first ed. Lion, 1989

Pollock, John, *Wilberforce*, Lion Publishing, 1977

Quiller-Couch, Sir Arthur, *Hetty Wesley*, J M Dent & Co., 1928 ed., first ed. 1903, new ed. 1908

Rack, Henry D., *Reasonable Enthusiast, John Wesley and the Rise of Methodism*, Abingdon Press, second ed. 1993, first ed. Epworth Press, 1989

Runyon, Theodore H., 'The Importance of Experience for Faith' in *Aldersgate Reconsidered*, ed. Randy L. Maddox, Kingswood Books, 1990

Runyon, Theodore, *The New Creation: John Wesley's Theology Today*, Abingdon, 1998.

Runyon, Theodore, (ed.), *Wesleyan Theology Today*, Kingswood Books, 1985

Rupp, Gordon, *Just Men*, Epworth Press, 1977

Sangster, W. E., *The Path to Perfection*, Hodder and Stoughton, 1943

Schmidt, Martin, *John Wesley: A Theological Biography*, Vol. 2, part one, Epworth Press, 1971, translation of the German edition, Zurich, 1966

Semmel, Bernard, *The Methodist Revolution*, Heinemann, 1974

Simon, John S., *John Wesley and the Religious Societies*, Epworth Press, 1921

Simon, John S., *John Wesley and the Methodist Societies*, Epworth Press, 1923

Simon, John S., *John Wesley and the Advance of Methodism*, Epworth Press, 1925

Simon, John S., *John Wesley the Master Builder*, Epworth Press, 1927

Simon, John S., *John Wesley, The Last Phase*, Epworth Press, 1934

Staples, Rob L., *Outward Sign and Inward Grace: The Place of Sacraments in Wesleyan Spirituality*, Beacon Hill Press, 1991

Stone, Ronald H., *John Wesley's Life and Ethics*, Abingdon Press, 2001.

Streiff, Patrick, *Reluctant Saint? A Theological Biography of Fletcher of Madely*, Epworth Press, 2001

Sykes, Richard (ed.), *Beyond the Boundaries: Preaching in the Wesleyan Tradition*, Applied Theology Press, 1998

Telford, John, *John Wesley into all the World*, Ambassador, 1999, reprint of first ed. 1902

Telford, John, *The Methodist Hymn Book Illustrated*, Epworth Press, 1934

Thorsen, Donald, A.D., *The Wesleyan Quadrilateral*, Light and Life, 1990

Tomkins, Stephen, *John Wesley: A Biography*, Lion Publishing, 2003

Towlson, Clifford, *Moravian and Methodist*, Epworth Press, 1957

Turner, John Munsey, *Conflict and Reconciliation: Studies in Methodism and Ecumenism in England 1740-1982,* Epworth Press, 1985

Turner, John Munsey, *John Wesley, the Evangelical Revival and the Rise of Methodism in England*, Epworth Press, 2002

Turner, John Munsey, "Wesley's Pragmatic Theology" in *Windows on Wesley: Wesleyan Theology in Today's World*, Applied Theology Press, 1997

Waller, Ralph, *John Wesley: A Personal Portrait*, SPCK, 2003

Watson, Philip S, *The Message of the Wesleys*, Francis Asbury Press, 1984

Williams, Colin W, *John Wesley's Theology Today*, Abingdon Press, 1960

Wood, A. Skevington, *Revelation and Reason: Wesleyan Responses to Eighteenth Century Rationalism*, The Wesley Fellowship, 1992

Wood, A. Skevington, *The Burning Heart*, The Paternoster Press, 1967

Works Relating to Biblical Studies and I John

Barton, John (ed.), *The Cambridge Companion to Biblical Interpretation*, Cambridge University Press, 1998

Brooke, A.E., *The Johannine Epistles*, T. & T. Clark, 1912

Dodd, C.H., *The Johannine Epistles*, Hodder and Stoughton, 1946

Grant, Robert M., with David Tracy, *A Short History of the Interpretation of the Bible*, SCM Press, second ed., revised and enlarged, 1984

Grayston, Kenneth, *The Johannine Epistles*, Eerdman, Marshall, Morgan Scott, 1984

Houlden, J.L., *The Johannine Epistles*, A. & C. Black, 1973, revised ed. 1994

Lieu, Judith, *The Second and Third Epistles of John*, T. & T. Clark, 1986

Loader, William, *The Johannine Epistles*, Epworth Press, 1992

Newport, Kenneth G.C., *Apocalypse and Millennium: Studies in Biblical Eisegesis*, Cambridge University Press, 2000

Powell, Mark Allan, with the assistance of Cecile G. Gray and Melissa C. Curtis, *The Bible and Modern Literary Criticism: A Critical Assessment and Annotated Bibliography*, Greenwood Press, 1992

Powell, Mark Allan, *What is Narrative Criticism? A New Approach to the Bible*, SPCK, 1993

Räisänen, Heikki, *Beyond New Testament Theology*, SCM Press, second ed., 2000

Räisänen, Heikki, 'The Effective History of the Bible: A Challenge to Biblical Scholarship' in *Scottish Journal of Theology 45*, 1992, pp. 303-24

Stacey, W. David, *Groundwork of Biblical Studies*, Epworth Press, 1979

Tompkins, Jane P. (ed.), *Reader-Response Criticism From Formalism To Post Structuralism*, The John Hopkins University Press, 1980

Other Works

à Kempis, Thomas, *The Imitation of Christ*, A fresh Translation and Introduction by
    Professor E.M. Blaiklock, Hodder and Stoughton, 1979

An Anglican-Methodist Covenant, The Methodist Publishing House and Church House
    Publishing, 2001

Encyclopaedia Britannica 2000 (CD ROM)

King, Peter, *An Inquiry into the Constitution, Discipline, Unity and Worship of the
    Primitive Church*, J. Robinson , 1691.

Stillingfleet, Edward, *Irenicum : a Weapon-salve for the Churches Wounds : or, the
    Divine Right of ParticularFforms of Church-government Discussed and Examined*,
    Henry Mortlock, 1661

The Constitutional Practice and Discipline of the Methodist Church, Vol. 2, Methodist
    Publishing House, 2002

Index

Studies in Evangelical History and Thought

(All titles uniform with this volume)
Dates in bold are of projected publication

Andrew Atherstone
Oxford's Protestant Spy
The Controversial Career of Charles Golightly

Charles Golightly (1807–85) was a notorious Protestant polemicist. His life was dedicated to resisting the spread of ritualism and liberalism within the Church of England and the University of Oxford. For half a century he led many memorable campaigns, such as building a martyr's memorial and attempting to close a theological college. John Henry Newman, Samuel Wilberforce and Benjamin Jowett were among his adversaries. This is the first study of Golightly's controversial career.

2006 / 1-84227-364-7 / approx. 324pp

Clyde Binfield
Victorian Nonconformity in Eastern England

Studies of Victorian religion and society often concentrate on cities, suburbs, and industrialisation. This study provides a contrast. Victorian Eastern England—Essex, Suffolk, Norfolk, Cambridgeshire, and Huntingdonshire—was rural, traditional, relatively unchanging. That is nonetheless a caricature which discounts the industry in Norwich and Ipswich (as well as in Haverhill, Stowmarket and Leiston) and ignores the impact of London on Essex, of railways throughout the region, and of an ancient but changing university (Cambridge) on the county town which housed it. It also entirely ignores the political implications of such changes in a region noted for the variety of its religious Dissent since the seventeenth century. This book explores Victorian Eastern England and its Nonconformity. It brings to a wider readership a pioneering thesis which has made a major contribution to a fresh evolution of English religion and society.

2006 / 1-84227-216-0 / approx. 274pp

John Brencher
Martyn Lloyd-Jones (1899–1981) and Twentieth-Century Evangelicalism

This study critically demonstrates the significance of the life and ministry of Martyn Lloyd-Jones for post-war British evangelicalism and demonstrates that his preaching was his greatest influence on twentieth-century Christianity. The factors which shaped his view of the church are examined, as is the way his reformed evangelicalism led to a separatist ecclesiology which divided evangelicals.

2002 / 1-84227-051-6 / xvi + 268pp

Jonathan D. Burnham
A Story of Conflict
The Controversial Relationship between Benjamin Wills Newton and
John Nelson Darby
Burnham explores the controversial relationship between the two principal
leaders of the early Brethren movement. In many ways Newton and Darby were
products of their times, and this study of their relationship provides insight not
only into the dynamics of early Brethrenism, but also into the progress of
nineteenth-century English and Irish evangelicalism.

2004 / 1-84227-191-1 / xxiv + 268pp

Grayson Carter
Anglican Evangelicals
Protestant Secessions from the Via Media, c.1800–1850
This study examines, within a chronological framework, the major themes and
personalities which influenced the outbreak of a number of Evangelical clerical
and lay secessions from the Church of England and Ireland during the first half
of the nineteenth century. Though the number of secessions was relatively
small—between a hundred and two hundred of the 'Gospel' clergy abandoned
the Church during this period—their influence was considerable, especially in
highlighting in embarrassing fashion the tensions between the evangelical
conversionist imperative and the principles of a national religious establishment.
Moreover, through much of this period there remained, just beneath the surface,
the potential threat of a large Evangelical disruption similar to that which
occurred in Scotland in 1843. Consequently, these secessions provoked great
consternation within the Church and within Evangelicalism itself, they
contributed to the outbreak of millennial speculation following the
'constitutional revolution' of 1828–32, they led to the formation of several new
denominations, and they sparked off a major Church–State crisis over the legal
right of a clergyman to secede and begin a new ministry within Protestant
Dissent.

2007 / 1-84227-401-5 / xvi + 470pp

J.N. Ian Dickson
Beyond Religious Discourse
Sermons, Preaching and Evangelical Protestants in Nineteenth-Century
Irish Society
Drawing extensively on primary sources, this pioneer work in modern religious history explores the training of preachers, the construction of sermons and how Irish evangelicalism and the wider movement in Great Britain and the United States shaped the preaching event. Evangelical preaching and politics, sectarianism, denominations, education, class, social reform, gender, and revival are examined to advance the argument that evangelical sermons and preaching went significantly beyond religious discourse. The result is a book for those with interests in Irish history, culture and belief, popular religion and society, evangelicalism, preaching and communication.
2005 / 1-84227-217-9 / approx. 324pp

Neil T.R. Dickson
Brethren in Scotland 1838–2000
A Social Study of an Evangelical Movement
The Brethren were remarkably pervasive throughout Scottish society. This study of the Open Brethren in Scotland places them in their social context and examines their growth, development and relationship to society.
2003 / 1-84227-113-X / xxviii + 510pp

Crawford Gribben and Timothy C.F. Stunt (eds)
Prisoners of Hope?
Aspects of Evangelical Millennialism in Britain and Ireland, 1800–1880
This volume of essays offers a comprehensive account of the impact of evangelical millennialism in nineteenth-century Britain and Ireland.
2004 / 1-84227-224-1 / xiv + 208pp

Khim Harris
Evangelicals and Education
Evangelical Anglicans and Middle-Class Education in
Nineteenth-Century England
This ground breaking study investigates the history of English public schools founded by nineteenth-century Evangelicals. It documents the rise of middle-class education and Evangelical societies such as the influential Church Association, and includes a useful biographical survey of prominent Evangelicals of the period.
2004 / 1-84227-250-0 / xviii + 422pp

Mark Hopkins
Nonconformity's Romantic Generation
Evangelical and Liberal Theologies in Victorian England
A study of the theological development of key leaders of the Baptist and
Congregational denominations at their period of greatest influence, including
C.H. Spurgeon and R.W. Dale, and of the controversies in which those among
them who embraced and rejected the liberal transformation of their evangelical
heritage opposed each other.
2004 / 1-84227-150-4 / xvi + 284pp

Don Horrocks
Laws of the Spiritual Order
*Innovation and Reconstruction in the Soteriology of Thomas Erskine
of Linlathen*
Don Horrocks argues that Thomas Erskine's unique historical and theological
significance as a soteriological innovator has been neglected. This timely
reassessment reveals Erskine as a creative, radical theologian of central and
enduring importance in Scottish nineteenth-century theology, perhaps equivalent
in significance to that of S.T. Coleridge in England.
2004 / 1-84227-192-X / xx + 362pp

Kenneth S. Jeffrey
When the Lord Walked the Land
The 1858–62 Revival in the North East of Scotland
Previous studies of revivals have tended to approach religious movements from
either a broad, national or a strictly local level. This study of the multifaceted
nature of the 1859 revival as it appeared in three distinct social contexts within a
single region reveals the heterogeneous nature of simultaneous religious
movements in the same vicinity.
2002 / 1-84227-057-5 / xxiv + 304pp

John Kenneth Lander
Itinerant Temples
Tent Methodism, 1814–1832
Tent preaching began in 1814 and the Tent Methodist sect resulted from
disputes with Bristol Wesleyan Methodists in 1820. The movement spread to
parts of Gloucestershire, Wiltshire, London and Liverpool, among other places.
Its demise started in 1826 after which one leader returned to the Wesleyans and
others became ministers in the Congregational and Baptist denominations.
2003 / 1-84227-151-2 / xx + 268pp

Donald M. Lewis
Lighten Their Darkness
The Evangelical Mission to Working-Class London, 1828–1860
This is a comprehensive and compelling study of the Church and the complexities of nineteenth-century London. Challenging our understanding of the culture in working London at this time, Lewis presents a well-structured and illustrated work that contributes substantially to the study of evangelicalism and mission in nineteenth-century Britain.

2001 / 1-84227-074-5 / xviii + 372pp

Herbert McGonigle
'Sufficient Saving Grace'
John Wesley's Evangelical Arminianism
A thorough investigation of the theological roots of John Wesley's evangelical Arminianism and how these convictions were hammered out in controversies on predestination, limited atonement and the perseverance of the saints.

2001 / 1-84227-045-1 / xvi + 350pp

Lisa S. Nolland
A Victorian Feminist Christian
Josephine Butler, the Prostitutes and God
Josephine Butler was an unlikely candidate for taking up the cause of prostitutes, as she did, with a fierce and self-disregarding passion. This book explores the particular mix of perspectives and experiences that came together to envision and empower her remarkable achievements. It highlights the vital role of her spirituality and the tragic loss of her daughter.

2004 / 1-84227-225-X / xxiv + 328pp

Don J. Payne
The Theology of the Christian Life in J.I. Packer's Thought
Theological Anthropology, Theological Method, and the Doctrine of Sanctification
J.I. Packer has wielded widespread influence on evangelicalism for more than three decades. This study pursues a nuanced understanding of Packer's theology of sanctification by tracing the development of his thought, showing how he reflects a particular version of Reformed theology, and examining the unique influence of theological anthropology and theological method on this area of his theology.

***2005** / 1-84227-397-3 / approx. 374pp*

Ian M. Randall
Evangelical Experiences
A Study in the Spirituality of English Evangelicalism 1918–1939
This book makes a detailed historical examination of evangelical spirituality between the First and Second World Wars. It shows how patterns of devotion led to tensions and divisions. In a wide-ranging study, Anglican, Wesleyan, Reformed and Pentecostal-charismatic spiritualities are analysed.
1999 / 0-85364-919-7 / xii + 310pp

Ian M. Randall
Spirituality and Social Change
The Contribution of F.B. Meyer (1847–1929)
This is a fresh appraisal of F.B. Meyer (1847–1929), a leading Free Church minister. Having been deeply affected by holiness spirituality, Meyer became the Keswick Convention's foremost international speaker. He combined spirituality with effective evangelism and socio-political activity. This study shows Meyer's significant contribution to spiritual renewal and social change.
2003 / 1-84227-195-4 / xx + 184pp

James Robinson
Pentecostal Origins
Early Pentecostalism in Ireland in the Context of the British Isles
Harvey Cox describes Pentecostalism as 'the fascinating spiritual child of our time' that has the potential, at the global scale, to contribute to the 'reshaping of religion in the twenty-first century'. This study grounds such sentiments by examining at the local scale the origin, development and nature of Pentecostalism in Ireland in its first twenty years. Illustrative, in a paradigmatic way, of how Pentecostalism became established within one region of the British Isles, it sets the story within the wider context of formative influences emanating from America, Europe and, in particular, other parts of the British Isles. As a synoptic regional study in Pentecostal history it is the first survey of its kind.
2005 / 1-84227-329-1 / xxviii + 378pp

Geoffrey Robson
Dark Satanic Mills?
Religion and Irreligion in Birmingham and the Black Country
This book analyses and interprets the nature and extent of popular Christian belief and practice in Birmingham and the Black Country during the first half of the nineteenth century, with particular reference to the impact of cholera epidemics and evangelism on church extension programmes.
2002 / 1-84227-102-4 / xiv + 294pp

Roger Shuff
Searching for the True Church
Brethren and Evangelicals in Mid-Twentieth-Century England
Roger Shuff holds that the influence of the Brethren movement on wider evangelical life in England in the twentieth century is often underrated. This book records and accounts for the fact that Brethren reached the peak of their strength at the time when evangelicalism was at it lowest ebb, immediately before World War II. However, the movement then moved into persistent decline as evangelicalism regained ground in the post war period. Accompanying this downward trend has been a sharp accentuation of the contrast between Brethren congregations who engage constructively with the non-Brethren scene and, at the other end of the spectrum, the isolationist group commonly referred to as 'Exclusive Brethren'.
2005 / 1-84227-254-3 / xviii+ 296pp

James H.S. Steven
Worship in the Spirit
Charismatic Worship in the Church of England
This book explores the nature and function of worship in six Church of England churches influenced by the Charismatic Movement, focusing on congregational singing and public prayer ministry. The theological adequacy of such ritual is discussed in relation to pneumatological and christological understandings in Christian worship.
2002 / 1-84227-103-2 / xvi + 238pp

Peter K. Stevenson
God in Our Nature
The Incarnational Theology of John McLeod Campbell
This radical reassessment of Campbell's thought arises from a comprehensive study of his preaching and theology. Previous accounts have overlooked both his sermons and his Christology. This study examines the distinctive Christology evident in his sermons and shows that it sheds new light on Campbell's much debated views about atonement.
2004 / 1-84227-218-7 / xxiv + 458pp

Kenneth J. Stewart
Restoring the Reformation
British Evangelicalism and the Réveil at Geneva 1816–1849
Restoring the Reformation traces British missionary initiative in post-Revolutionary Francophone Europe from the genesis of the London Missionary Society, the visits of Robert Haldane and Henry Drummond, and the founding of the Continental Society. While British Evangelicals aimed at the reviving of a foreign Protestant cause of momentous legend, they received unforeseen reciprocating emphases from the Continent which forced self-reflection on Evangelicalism's own relationship to the Reformation.
2006 / 1-84227-392-2 / approx. 190pp

Martin Wellings
Evangelicals Embattled
Responses of Evangelicals in the Church of England to Ritualism, Darwinism and Theological Liberalism 1890–1930
In the closing years of the nineteenth century and the first decades of the twentieth century Anglican Evangelicals faced a series of challenges. In responding to Anglo-Catholicism, liberal theology, Darwinism and biblical criticism, the unity and identity of the Evangelical school were severely tested.
2003 / 1-84227-049-4 / xviii + 352pp

James Whisenant
A Fragile Unity
Anti-Ritualism and the Division of Anglican Evangelicalism in the Nineteenth Century
This book deals with the ritualist controversy (approximately 1850–1900) from the perspective of its evangelical participants and considers the divisive effects it had on the party.
2003 / 1-84227-105-9 / xvi + 530pp

Haddon Willmer
Evangelicalism 1785–1835: An Essay (1962) and Reflections (2004)
Awarded the Hulsean Prize in the University of Cambridge in 1962, this interpretation of a classic period of English Evangelicalism, by a young church historian, is now supplemented by reflections on Evangelicalism from the vantage point of a retired Professor of Theology.
2006 / 1-84227-219-5 / approx. 350pp

Linda Wilson
Constrained by Zeal
Female Spirituality amongst Nonconformists 1825–1875
Constrained by Zeal investigates the neglected area of Nonconformist female spirituality. Against the background of separate spheres, it analyses the experience of women from four denominations, and argues that the churches provided a 'third sphere' in which they could find opportunities for participation.
2000 / 0-85364-972-3 / xvi + 294pp

Paternoster
9 Holdom Avenue,
Bletchley,
Milton Keynes MK1 1QR,
United Kingdom
Web: www.authenticmedia.co.uk/paternoster

July 2005